The Illustrated Treasury of
MODERN LITERATURE
for Children

First published in the USA 1985
Published by Exeter Books
Distributed by Bookthrift
Exeter is a trademark of Simon and Schuster, Inc.
Bookthrift is a registered trademark of Simon and Schuster, Inc.
NEW YORK, New York

This compilation copyright © The Hamlyn Publishing Group Ltd 1979, 1985

Illustrations copyright © The Hamlyn Publishing Group Ltd 1979, 1985

ISBN 0 671 07574 8

Printed in Italy

The Illustrated Treasury of
MODERN LITERATURE
for Children

Exeter Books

NEW YORK

Contents

The Authors

Today, there is such a bewildering choice of books to read that many children (and parents) find it hard to know where to begin. *The Illustrated Treasury of Modern Literature for Children* not only offers a large choice of exciting and appealing stories which are marvellous reading in themselves, but also opens up a whole world of interesting and imaginative ideas for further reading. This book is a splendid introduction to the work of twenty-six excellent authors, and the notes below give details of other books they have written.

Leon Garfield

Leon Garfield has written a number of award-winning novels and stories with vivid and lively historical backgrounds, including *Jack Holborn*, *Devil-in-the-Fog*, *Black Jack*, and *John Diamond*. With Edward Blishen he wrote *The God Beneath the Sea* and *The Golden Shadow*, two books which retell in modern terms, Greek myths. *Garfield's Apprentices* is a series of twelve short novels about London apprentices in the eighteenth century.

Thor Heyerdahl

Thor Heyerdahl is a very remarkable modern anthropologist and explorer who has also written *Aku-Aku* (about the mysterious Easter Island monuments), *The Ra Expeditions* (about his attempt to prove that the ancient Egyptians could have reached the Americas thousands of years before Columbus), and more recently *The Tigris Expedition*, which describes the voyage of a boat built of reeds down the Persian Gulf and into the Indian Ocean.

Margaret Mahy

Although Margaret Mahy is a New Zealander, her many short stories are set in a fantasy land where the Wild West and forests of lions and wolves meet. *The Dragon of an Ordinary Family*, *A Lion in the Meadow*, *The Great Piratical Rumbustification*, *The Birthday Burglar* and *A Very Wicked Headmistress* are eccentric tales which explore the relationship between fantasy and reality. *The Haunting* was awarded the Carnegie Medal in 1983. *The Changeover, A Supernatural Romance* is a novel for teenagers.

Nina Bawden

Nina Bawden was an evacuee herself in 1940, and was sent to the South Wales valley in which she has set the adventures of the evacuees in *Carrie's War*. *Rebel on a Rock* is a sequel in which the children become involved in a

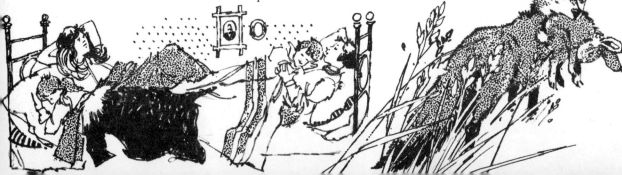

political coup in a Mediterranean country. Among her other books are *On the Run*, *The Peppermint Pig*, *The White Horse Gang*, *The Runaway Summer*, *A Handful of Thieves*, *Squib*, and *The Witch's Daughter*.

Cynthia Harnett

Cynthia Harnett loved history as a child and explored old houses looking for 'clues' about the lives of the people who lived in them centuries before. Her stories have sprung in part from this early love of history and are remarkable for their meticulous descriptions of everyday life centuries ago. Besides *The Wool-Pack*, which won the Carnegie Medal in 1951, they include *The Great House* (about an architect's life in 1700), *The Load of the Unicorn* (about Caxton and the introduction of printing), and *Ring Out Bow Bells!* (the story of the real Dick Whittington).

John Christopher

John Christopher is well known as a writer of fiction for adults as well as children. Much of his writing is science fiction and *The White Mountains* is the first in a series of three books for children set in a future when the Earth is controlled by strange and terrifying aliens. It is followed by *The City of Gold and Lead* and *The Pool of Fire*. Another exciting science fiction trilogy by John Christopher consists of *The Prince in Waiting*, *Beyond the Burning Lands*, and *The Sword of the Spirits*.

Betsy Byars

Many of Betsy Byars' books, like *The Eighteenth Emergency*, centre on a child who has some private fear or uncertainty which dominates his or her life. Just some of her many books are *The Night Swimmers*, *Goodbye, Chicken Little*, *The Pinballs*, *Cybil War*, *The T.V. Kid* and *Summer of the Swans*.

Roald Dahl

Roald Dahl has written a sequel to *Charlie and the Chocolate Factory* called *Charlie and the Great Glass Elevator* in which Willy Wonka again appears with Charlie and his family. He has also written *James and the Giant Peach*, *Danny, the Champion of the World*, *The Twits*, and *The B.F.G.*

Joy Adamson

Joy Adamson's story about Elsa the lioness entitled *Born Free* is an abridged version of her original book called *Elsa, the Story of a Lioness*. There is a sequel called *Living Free* which tells how Elsa returns to the Adamson's camp with her three cubs.

Alan Garner

The Owl Service was awarded the Carnegie medal in 1967 and the Guardian Award for Children's Fiction in 1968. Alan Garner's earlier

books *The Weirdstone of Brisingamen, The Moon of Gomrath* and *Elidor* are also concerned with the intrusion of strange and ungovernable forces into everyday life. These books are full of excitement and action but also demand a good deal from the reader who has to understand the significance of the fantasy happenings to those of everyday. *The Stone Book Quartet* (*The Stone Book, Granny Reardun, The Aimer Gate, Tom Fobble's Day*) tells the story of a family of craftsmen in Cheshire, England at four points in history: 1864, 1886, 1916, 1941.

Robert C. O'Brien

Mrs Frisby and the Rats of NIMH was awarded the John Newbery Medal in 1972 and has been made into a film called *The Secret of NIMH*. Robert C O'Brien wrote two other children's books. *The Silver Crown* is the highly imaginative story of a girl who receives a crown on her birthday, but is then forced to undertake a cross-country journey which leads her into extreme danger. Set in a valley which has miraculously escaped fall-out after a nuclear war, *Z for Zachariah* tells the story of two people who believe themselves to be the only survivors left alive on Earth.

Henry Treece

Henry Treece wrote many historical novels for children, most of them concerned with the confused and war-ridden times in Europe between the Roman invasion of Britain and the Norman Conquest. The Vikings in particular were one of his favourite subjects. Treece's aim was to show the harshness and ferocity of life at this time and not just to glory in the bravery of fighting men. *A Viking Saga* follows the life of Harald Sigurdson and is in three volumes: *Viking's Dawn, The Road to Miklagard* and *Viking's Sunset*. A second Viking trilogy is formed by *Hounds of the King, Man with a Sword* and *The Last of the Vikings*.

Laura Ingalls Wilder

Laura Ingalls Wilder's stories are about her own life when her family travelled as pioneers across America to the West. The first seven titles in reading order are, *Little House in the Big Woods, Little House on the Prairie, On the Banks of Plum Creek, By the Shores of Silver Lake, The Long Winter, Little Town on the Prairie* and *These Happy Golden Years*. Her eighth book, *Farmer Boy*, is about her husband's life on a farm in New York State.

K. M. Peyton

K. M. Peyton's *Flambards* trilogy is about the romance and adventures of Christine and Will, his passion for flying machines and her love of the country and horses. The three books are *Flambards* (which won the Guardian Award for Children's Fiction in 1970), *The Edge of the Cloud* and *Flambards in Summer*. K. M. Peyton has written many other novels including another trilogy: *Pennington's Seventeenth Summer*, *The Beethoven Medal*, and *Pennington's Heir*.

Katherine Paterson

Besides *The Great Gilly Hopkins* (which won the Children's Books Category of the American National Book Awards in 1979), Katherine Paterson has written two other children's books, both of which won the John Newbery Medal. *Bridge to Terabithia* is about two children who invent a secret kingdom, inspired by C. S. Lewis's *Chronicles of Narnia*, where they reign supreme. *Jacob Have I Loved* concerns the rivalry between twins on a lonely island in the Second World War.

Joan Aiken

Joan Aiken's stories are about fantastic characters having extraordinary adventures. Many of them are set in an historical England that never existed, with characters like Dido Twite and Simon (who becomes the Duke of Battersea) who reappear from book to book in the most extraordinary situations. Among her children's books are *The Wolves of Willoughby Chase*, *Black Hearts in Battersea*, *Night Birds on Nantucket*, *The Whispering Mountain*, *The Cuckoo Tree*, and *The Stolen Lake*.

John Rowe Townsend

John Rowe Townsend's *Gumble's Yard* was his first book and he has said that the idea for it came after reading in a newspaper about four children

who had been deserted. The sequel *Widdershins Crescent* takes the family to a new housing estate. In *Hell's Edge* a tough local boy in a north of England town clashes with a girl newly arrived from the south.

Mary O'Hara

Mary O'Hara's *My Friend Flicka* has been read all over the world, by children and adults, for many years. It is set in Wyoming, U.S.A., on a modern ranch and is a favourite because of the deep love the author shows for horses. Mary O'Hara has also written other stories about horses and Wyoming – *Green Grass of Wyoming* and *Thunderhead*.

Ruth Park

Playing Beatie Bow won the Australian Children's Book of the Year Award in 1981. An admired Australian writer, Ruth Park has written many books for younger children – the best-known is the Muddle-Headed Wombat series. *Come Danger, Come Darkness* is an historical adventure for older children about two brothers sent to live with their uncle, commandant of Norfolk Island's penal settlement, where they are to be trained as army officers.

Noel Streatfeild

Noel Streatfeild's first children's book *Ballet Shoes* was published as long ago as 1936, but it is still one of the best-loved stories about dancing. She followed *Ballet Shoes* with books which had the circus, tennis, the theatre, films and skating as their backgrounds. *The Painted Garden* and *White Boots* are two of her best-known books.

'BB'

'BB' has written that when he wrote *Wild Lone*, he felt himself becoming a fox. And his very close identification with the countryside and its inhabitants is a feature of all his books. *The Little Grey Men*, *Brendon Chase*, *Down the Bright Stream* and *The Pool of the Black Witch* are some of his other books.

Ronald Welch

Many of Ronald Welch's exciting historical novels centre around members of the Carey family. Philip Daubigny in *Knight Crusader* (winner of the 1954 Carnegie Medal) is a member of the Carey family and visits the family home in Wales at the end of the novel. In the subsequent stories his descendants serve their country in many wars. Harry Carey fights the Spaniards at the time of the Armada in *The Hawk*. Neil and Denzil Carey support the King against Cromwell in *For the King*. Charles Carey serves with Marlborough in France and the Low Countries in *Captain of Dragoons*. And the adventures of the Careys continue right up to the first World War with John Carey in *Tank Commander*.

C. S. Lewis

The best known of C. S. Lewis's 'Narnia' books is *The Lion, The Witch and The Wardrobe*, but there are six other books about Narnia of which *The Magician's Nephew* is the first in reading order, explaining how the wardrobe (which is the 'door' into Narnia) came to exist. Children will find all the books exciting fantasy stories, but part of their appeal is that they have an extra, allegorical, dimension. C. S. Lewis intended Aslan the lion, Lord of Narnia, to represent Christ. In *The Lion, The Witch and The Wardrobe* Aslan sacrifices his life to save the child who betrayed him.

Gene Kemp

The Turbulent Term of Tyke Tiler was awarded the Carnegie Medal in 1977. Gene Kemp, a former teacher, has written two other novels set at Cricklepit Combined School. Gowie Corby in *Gowie Corby Plays Chicken* is the terror of the school – his only friend is Boris Karloff the pet rat. However, his life is changed by the arrival of a black American girl called Rosie Angela Lee. *Charlie Lewis Plays for Time* is the third novel and centres on the Moffats, six of whom are at Cricklepit, and Charlie the narrator. When Mr Merchant (Sir) has an accident and is away for a term, he is replaced by Mr Carter who is as awful as Sir is wonderful.

Jim Corbett

Jim Corbett wrote several wonderful books about the people and animals of the Indian jungle, including two others about man-eaters: *The Temple Tiger* and *The Man-Eating Leopards of Rudraprayag*. Jim Corbett lived much of his life in the Kumaon hills, training British troops during the Second World War in jungle combat and during the First World War recruiting more than five thousand men from the hills to fight in France. So all his books are based on first hand experience.

Ian Serraillier

The Silver Sword is set in Europe at the time of the Second World War. War must be one of the most difficult subjects to write about, particularly when the story is intended for children to read. *The Silver Sword* is both realistic about the horrors of war and hopeful about the future. Ian Serraillier has written another story with a wartime setting called *There's No Escape*.

Smith

Leon Garfield

*In Leon Garfield's exciting novel we see what it was really like to live in
London in the late eighteenth century – a London which was only a tiny
fraction of its present size, but rough, dirty, smelly and full of life. It was
full of criminals too, whose fate if caught was usually harsh, and
frequently ended in transportation overseas or hanging!
Smith is a twelve year old orphan who lives by his wits in the dark alley-
ways of the city. His pick-pocketing activities lead to a terrifying encounter
with murderers and entangle him in a strange and dreadful mystery. Here
are the opening chapters of the story.*

H E was called Smith and was twelve years old. Which, in itself,
was a marvel; for it seemed as if the smallpox, the con-
sumption, brain-fever, gaol-fever and even the hangman's rope had
given him a wide berth for fear of catching something. Or else they
weren't quick enough.

Smith had a turn of speed that was remarkable, and a neatness in
nipping down an alley or vanishing in a court that had to be seen to
be believed. Not that it was often seen, for Smith was rather a sooty
spirit of the violent and ramshackle Town, and inhabited the
tumbledown mazes about fat St Paul's like the subtle air itself. A rat
was like a snail beside Smith, and the most his thousand victims
ever got of him was the powerful whiff of his passing and a cold
draught in their dexterously emptied pockets.

Only the sanctimonious birds that perched on the church's dome
ever saw Smith's progress entire, and as their beady eyes followed
him, they chattered savagely, '*Pick*-pocket! *Pick*-pocket! Jug him!
Jug-jug-jug him!' as if they'd been appointed by the Town to save it
from such as Smith.

His favourite spot was Ludgate Hill, where the world's coaches, chairs and curricles were met and locked, from morning to night, in a horrible, blasphemous confusion. And here, in one or other of the ancient doorways, he leaned and grinned while the shouting and cursing and scraping and raging went endlessly, hopelessly on – till, sooner or later, something prosperous would come his way.

At about half past ten of a cold December morning an old gentleman got furiously out of his carriage, in which he'd been trapped for an hour, shook his red fist at his helpless coachman and the roaring but motionless world, and began to stump up Ludgate Hill.

'*Pick*-pocket! *Pick*-pocket!' shrieked the cathedral birds in a fury.

A country gentleman – judging by his complexion, his clean old-fashioned coat and his broad-legged, lumbering walk which bumped out his pockets in a manner most provoking.
Smith twitched his nose and nipped neatly along like a shadow.

The old man's pace was variable: sometimes it was brisk for his years, then he'd slow down, hesitate, look about him – as if the Town had changed much since last he'd visited and he was now no longer confident of his way. He took one turning, then another; stopped, scratched the crisp edge of his wig, then eyed the sallow, seedy city gently as if to ask the way, till he spied another turn, nodded, briskly took it – and came straight back into Ludgate Hill . . .

A dingy fellow creaked out of a doorway, like he was hinged on it, and made to accost the old man: but did not. He'd glimpsed Smith. Looks had been exchanged, shoulders shrugged – and the old villain gave way to the young one.

On went the old gentleman, confident now in his bearings, deeper and deeper into the musty, tottering forest of the Town where Smith hunted fastest and best.

Now a sharpish wind sprang up, and the cathedral birds eyed the leaden sky (which looked too thick and heavy to admit them), screeched, and flew to the lower eminence of Old Bailey. Here, they set up a terrific commotion with their legal brethren, till both Church and Law became absorbed in watching the progress of Smith.

'*Pick*-pocket! *Pick*-pocket! Jug-jug-jug him!'

The old gentleman was very deep in Smith's country now, and paused many a time to peer down the shambling lanes and alleys. Then he'd shake his head vaguely and touch at his coat pocket – as if a queer, deep sense had warned him of a pair of sharp eyes fairly cutting into the cloth like scissors. At last he saw something familiar – some landmark he'd remembered – Godliman Street. Yes: he was in Godliman Street . . .

As suddenly as it had sprung up, the wind died – and the cathedral birds flew back to their dome.

'*Pick*-pocket! *Pick*-pocket!'

The old gentleman began to stump very particularly down Godliman Street, eyeing the old, crumbly houses that were lived in by God knew how many quiet, mysterious souls. And, as he went, he seemed to have two shadows – his own and another, a thin cautious shadow that was not so much seen as sensed . . .

This was the deepest heart of Smith's forest, hidden even from the cathedral birds. Here, the houses reared and clustered as if to shut out the sky, and so promoted the growth of the flat, pale and unhealthy moon-faces of the clerks and scriveners, glimpsed in their dark caves through dusty windows, silent and intent.

Now came a slit between two such properties, a quiet way roofed over at first-floor level: Curtis Alley, leading to Curtis Court.

Framed by the darkness of its alley, Curtis Court presented a grey and peaceful brightness – a neglected clearing in the forest of the Town, where nothing grew, and all save one of the enclosed houses had their eyes put out with bricks (on account of the tax).

As the old gentleman's steps echoed in the alley, a solitary, dusty raven flew up out of the court with a bitter croak.

Suddenly, the old gentleman gave an involuntary shudder, as if someone – something – had swiftly passed him by and made a draught.

'Someone's walked over me grave!' he muttered, shook his head and entered Curtis Court.

'Beg pardon, sir! Beg pardon –'

Out of a doorway on the left of the court came Smith. Which was the first time the old man had ever laid eyes on him; though all the way from Ludgate Hill there'd never been more than two yards between them.

He stopped, flustered, about six paces from the end of the alley. Which way was the damned urchin going? This way? That way? Angrily he shifted, and Smith, with a quaint clumsiness, brushed against him, and – it was done! In an instant! Smith had emptied the old gentleman's pocket of –

He halted. His eyes glittered sharply. Footsteps in the alley! It would be blocked! He changed direction as briefly as a speck in the wind – and vanished back into his doorway. But so quickly that, seconds after he'd disappeared, the old gentleman was still staggering and bewildered.

Out of the alley came two men in brown. Curious fellows of a very particular aspect – which Smith knew well. Uneasily, he scowled – and wished he might vanish through the crumbling bricks.

The old gentleman had recovered himself. He stared round angrily – till courtesy got the better of him.

'Good day to ye, gentlemen!' he said, with an apologetic smile.

The newcomers glanced quickly across the court towards the house that had kept one window, and grinned.

'And good day to *you*!'

They moved very neat, and with no commotion. They were proficient in their trade. The taller came at the old man from the front; the other took on his back – and slid a knife into it.

The old gentleman's face was fatefully towards a certain dark doorway. He seemed to peer very anxiously round the heavy shoulder of the man who was holding him – as if for a better view. His eyes flickered with pain at the knife's quick prick. Then he looked surprised – amazed, even – as he felt the cold blade slip into his warm heart.

'Oh! Oh! Oh my –' he murmured, gave a long sigh – and died.

His last sight on this earth had been of a small, wild and despairing face whose flooded eyes shone out of the shadows with all the dread and pity they were capable of.

(Smith was only twelve and, hangings apart, had seen no more than three men murdered in all his life.)

They say that murdered men's eyes keep the image of their last sight for – for how long? Do they take it, hereafter, up to the Seat of Judgement? Smith shivered. He'd no wish for his face to be shown in any place of judgement – in this world or the next!

In a terror as violent as his dislike, he watched the two men in brown. They were dragging the luckless old gentleman towards the darkness of the alley. (Why hadn't he stayed in the country where he'd belonged? What business had he to come stumping – so stupid and defenceless – into Smith's secret forest?)

Now Smith could hear the quick, fumbling sounds of searching; methodical gentry. Still no commotion. Oh, they knew what they were at! But the sounds grew harsh and hasty. Even irritable. Muttered one, 'God rot the old fool! He ain't got it!'

Came a new sound. A very queer one. A tapping, limping, scraping sound – as of a lame man's footsteps on the cobbles. Then a soft, gentlemanly voice.

'Well?'

'Nothing – nothing, yer honour!'

'Liars! Fools! Look again!'

Again the sounds of searching – accompanied by strained, indrawn breath.

'Told you so. Nothing.'

A groan: a very dreadful affair.

'Again! Again! It *must* be there!'

'Well it ain't, yer honour! And if we stays much longer, we'll be on our way to join 'im . . . on the end of a rope! Come – let's be off.'

'Again! Search once more!'

'With respect – do it yerself, sir.'

'No!'

'Then we're off! Quick! Quick! There's someone coming –'

There was a scuffling and scraping, then the alley and court were momentarily quiet. A shadow crossed the broken, moss-piped paving. It was the raven, making ready to return.

But Smith did not move yet. Voices and clustering footsteps could be heard coming from the far side of the alley. The pale-faced clerks and scriveners and thin-necked attorneys had caught the scent of spilt blood. They'd come out of their rooms and chambers to congregate solemnly and stare.

(But no one came out from the houses within the court; not even from the house with the single window.)

Now the crowd had grown and oozed into the court itself. The raven flapped sourly up to a gable and croaked with a sardonic air; Smith had invisibly joined the outskirts of the crowd, muttering away with the best of them; then he was through, like a needle through shoddy, to Godliman Street and beyond.

As he went, a door opened in the court, and someone came quietly out . . .

A quarter mile off, on the other side of St Paul's, Smith stopped running. He sat on some steps and fumbled in his ragged, ancient coat. What had he got this time? Something valuable. Something that had been worth the old gentleman's life.

He fished it out. A document. *A document?* Smith stood up, swore, spat and cursed. For, though he was quicker than a rat, sharper than a stoat, foxier than a fox, though he knew the Town's corners and alleys and courts and by-ways better than he knew his own heart, and though he could vanish into the thick air in the twinkling of an eye, he lacked one necessary quality for the circumstance in hand. He could not read. Not so much as a word!

Darkness came prematurely to the Town, owing to the sun's habit of vanishing into the tall chimney pots of Hanover Square – where, for all Smith knew, it blazed away in the rich parlours till the time came for it to be trundled off to Wapping and begin its course anew.

By four o'clock, the dome of St Paul's stood black and surly against the darkening sky, and its huge shadow was flung eastward over the narrow streets and lanes of that part of the Town.

At last Smith gave up his efforts to force the cramped and awkward ink-lines to yield up their secret. For the light was gone and his eyes, wits and soul were aching with strain. A hundred stratagems had presented themselves to him – and a hundred stratagems he'd rejected. He'd thought of applying to the various scholars of his acquaintance . . . but which one could he trust? He'd thought of cutting the document into its various lines – or even words – and giving each of them to a different reader. But what if he muddled the order, or lost something that proved to be vital?

He walked; he sat; he tramped as far as the churchyard in Old Street, where he leaned up against a headstone, puffed at his short clay pipe, and fished out the document yet again. He stared; he screwed up his eyes and face till he looked like an old walnut, but the dim air and his own dark ignorance made the document seem like the last will and testament of a very old, very lame, very inky spider – on its weary way home.

So Smith likewise, with a deep sigh, packed up his thoughts and went home.

Between Saffron Hill and Turnmill Street stood – or, rather slouched – the Red Lion Tavern. A very evil-looking, tumbledown structure, weatherboarded on three sides and bounded on the fourth by the great Fleet Ditch, which stank and gurgled and gurgled and stank by day and night, like the parlour of the Tavern itself.

This parlour was an ill-lit, noxious place, full of hoarse secrets and red-eyed morsels – not so much from all walks as from all falls of life. Thieves, pick-pockets, foot-pads, unlucky swindlers and ruined gamblers boozed and snoozed here, and were presided over by a greasy landlord who never sold a customer to the gallows for less than a guinea.

Here was Smith's home. Not in the dignity of the parlour itself, but in the cellar below it where he lodged with his sisters, Miss Bridget and Miss Fanny.

'Not nubbed yet?' remarked the landlord humorously, as Smith humped broodily in.

Smith, his head full of darker things than even the Red Lion Tavern, made no answer.

'I spoke to you, Smith.'

'Did you now! I thought it was a belch from the old Ditch!'

Two or three customers grinned, and Smith dodged deftly past the landlord to the cellar steps, but was not quite quick enough to miss a fist on his ear. He howled and vanished . . . and the landlord laughed fit to burst.

'Got him that time!'

'You asked for it! You brought it on yourself!' remarked Miss Bridget, looking up from stitching a brown velveteen coat.

'Poor little Smut!' murmured Miss Fanny, over a pair of grey breeches. 'One day he'll come down them steps stone dead!'

'*I'm* not complaining,' said Smith, rubbing his ear which, had it been clean, would have been red as a strawberry, but instead was now a warm black. 'Saw an old gent done in today.'

'Indeed? And what's that to do with abusing the landlord?'

'Me mind was on other things.'

''Tis no excuse! We brung you up to be genteel. Fanny and me feels the disgrace.'

'Put a dab of vinegar on your little lug, Smut,' said Miss Fanny. ''Twill take out the sting.'

She mentioned vinegar as there was a quantity of it in the cellar; for the sisters engaged in scouring and cleaning besides making genteel alterations to cast-off clothing from unfortunates who were hanged and so never had a chance to wear their last garments out. The velveteen coat and the grey breeches were bespoken by the hangman himself, for they'd come off a very high-stepping rogue indeed – and one everybody was sorry to see nubbed.

'But the law must take its course,' had said Miss Bridget, and, ''Tis an ill wind,' had said Miss Fanny, when Smith brought the garments in.

'Look what I got this time!' said Smith, after he'd wiped his ear with vinegar. He fished out the document and spread it on the table, full in the light of the tallows. 'Just before he was done in. Not a quarter of a minute!'

The Smith family stared at the document. None of them could read.

'What is it?' asked Miss Fanny.

''Twas what he was killed for,' said Smith, and went on to relate all the circumstances of the crime, not forgetting the unseen man with the limp, the thought of whom terrified him more than anything else.

'It's a deed to property,' declared Miss Bridget. 'For that queer thing' – she jabbed her needle at a piece of writing – 'that looks so like a horse and cart, is the word "property". Indeed it is. I'd know it anywhere!'

Smith was not convinced.

'Then why was he done in for it? And why was they so frantic when they couldn't find it? Poor old fool!'

'Reasons,' said Miss Bridget darkly and returned to the velveteen coat. 'Reasons.'

'*I* think,' said Miss Fanny, 'that it's a confession, or an accusation. For that's the sort of thing a murder's done for – excepting money; and it ain't money. Now – though I don't quarrel with Brid's "property", for I believe her to be right, there's a "whereas", most distinct; and that piece like a nest of maggots, there' – she pricked with her needle – 'I *know* to be "felonious". Oh yes indeed, Smut dear: you got a confession which will be very valuable if we can only find out what's been done. For, if they was willing and able to kill for it – well, they'll be equal willing to *pay* for it! Clever Smut!'

Smith frowned, still not convinced, but inclined more to a confession than a property deed. In his heart of hearts he thought the document might be something else altogether, but said nothing, having nothing to go on, nor any piece of knowledge to contradict his sisters with.

'So we must get it read out to us,' continued Miss Fanny, neglecting the breeches, 'so we can know where to apply.'

'And who, miss, would you ask?' queried Miss Bridget irritably.

'Lord Tom can read,' said Smith, thinking of his highwayman idol and friend.

'Lord Tom?' repeated Miss Fanny, blushing and smiling. 'The very scholar!'

Miss Bridget sneered. 'That high toby is so much in his cups, his mouth's grown like a spout! Mark my words, miss, I'd as soon trust him with anything worth money as I'd trust the landlord! Not that I think the paper's worth money at all: for it's neither more nor less than a deed to property.'

They went on arguing thus till the tallows burned low: with Miss Bridget inclining more and more to property, and Miss Fanny, who was softer and younger, being scarce nineteen, keeping to the romantic notion of a confession on whose value as blackmail they might all live happily ever after. But on one thing they were all agreed: the difficulty of finding anyone they could trust enough to read it to them.

At length, when the room was full of tallow smoke and shifting shadows, Miss Bridget and Miss Fanny retired to their curtained-off bedroom, and Smith to his corner in the workroom itself.

For some minutes one tallow remained alight, and afforded Smith a sombre view of the brown velveteen coat and the grey breeches bespoken by the hangman. They were upon a hook in a corner and presented a disagreeable resemblance to their aspect when their last owner had last worn them. Smith wondered if he was likely to come back for them, fearfully white and moaning about the cold. Well – they'd not fit him now!

He screwed up his face scornfully at the thought of ghosts; but continued to stare into dark corners till he fell asleep, and, when he awoke, did so with a startled air and looked about him with some relief to see the old brick and plaster walls and the dim grey daylight falling down the cellar steps . . . as if his dreams had given him cause to doubt his firm belief in no ghosts.

The document was still on the table. He folded it up and began to tiptoe towards the stairs.

'Where are you off to, Smut dear?'

Miss Fanny, much tousled and creased, had poked her head through the curtain.

'Newgate,' said Smith, briefly. 'Got business.'

'What are you going to do with our dockiment, Smut?'

'Don't know – yet.'

'Wouldn't it be safer here?'

'Why?'

'Well, dear – if them that wanted it did in an old man for it, they won't think twice about doing in a boy.'

'Don't know I got it! Never saw me! There's only you and Miss Bridget what knows.'

'Oh yes . . . that's true. But you never can tell, Smut. *Someone* may have seen you. Won't you leave it behind?'

'No.'

'Are you going to show it to Lord Tom?'

'Don't know. Maybe.'

'If he's going to Newgate,' came Miss Bridget's voice, still croaked with sleep, 'tell him to screw some money out of that Mr Jones – for there'll not be another stitch done till there's something on account! Hangmen is horrible customers! So degrading!'

Miss Fanny's head, which had vanished for the moment, reappeared.

'Mr Jones, Smut. Brid says, see Mr Jones.' Then she sighed. 'For the last time, dear – leave the dockiment behind. 'Twill be safe as houses. Oh, Smut! I've an 'orrible feeling you was seen and are in danger! Oh, Smut! I fear you'll be coming down them steps tonight stone dead!'

The Kon-Tiki Expedition

Thor Heyerdahl

In 1947 six men and a parrot set sail on a raft made of green balsa wood with the intention of crossing 4500 miles of the Pacific Ocean. Thor Heyerdahl wanted to prove that South American Indians could have made the trip centuries before in a similar craft. His book is the exciting account of how he and his Norwegian companions made their journey on the raft Kon-Tiki. In this extract we are given a description of some very unusual visitors to the craft.

THE very first day we were left alone on the sea we had noticed fish round the raft, but were too much occupied with the steering to think of fishing. The second day we went right into a thick shoal of sardines, and soon afterwards an eight-foot blue shark came along and rolled over with its white belly uppermost as it rubbed against the raft's stern, where Herman and Bengt stood barelegged in the seas, steering. It played round us for a while, but disappeared when we got the hand harpoon ready for action.

Next day we were visited by tunnies, bonitos and dolphins, and when a big flying fish thudded on board we used it as bait and at once pulled in two large dolphins (dorados) weighing from 20 to 35 lbs each. This was food for several days. On steering watch we could see many fish we did not even know, and one day we came into a school of porpoises which seemed quite endless. The black backs tumbled about, packed close together, right in to the side of the raft, and sprang up here and there all over the sea as far as we could see from the masthead. And the nearer we came to the equator, and the farther from the coast, the commoner flying fish became. When at last we came out into the blue water where the sea rolled by majestically, sunlit and sedate, ruffled by gusts of wind, we could see them glittering like a rain of projectiles, shooting from the water and flying in a straight line till their power of flight was exhausted and they vanished beneath the surface.

If we set the little paraffin lamp out at night flying fish were attracted by the light and, large and small, shot over the raft. They often struck the bamboo cabin or the sail and tumbled helpless on the deck. For, unable to get a take-off by swimming through the water, they just remained lying and kicking helplessly, like large-eyed herrings with long breast fins. It sometimes happened that we heard an outburst of strong language from a man on deck when a cold flying fish came unexpectedly at a good speed slap into his face. They always came at a good pace and snout first, and if they caught one full in the face they made it burn and tingle. But the unprovoked attack was quickly forgiven by the injured party, for this, with all its drawbacks, was a maritime land of enchantment where delicious fish dishes came hurtling through the air. We used to fry them for breakfast, and whether it was the fish, the cook, or our appetites, they reminded us of fried troutlings once we had scraped the scales off.

The cook's first duty when he got up in the morning was to go out on deck and collect all the flying fish that had landed on board in the course of the night. There were usually half a dozen or more, and one morning we found twenty-six fat flying fish on the raft. Knut was much upset one morning because, when he was standing operating with the frying pan, a flying fish struck him on the hand instead of landing right in the cooking fat.

Our neighbourly intimacy with the sea was not fully realised by Torstein till he woke one morning and found a sardine on his pillow. There was so little room in the cabin that Torstein was lying with his head in the doorway and, if anyone inadvertently trod on his face when going out at night, he bit him in the leg. He grasped the sardine by the tail and confided to it understandingly that all sardines had his entire sympathy. We conscientiously drew in our legs so that Torstein should have more room the next night, but then something happened which caused Torstein to find himself a sleeping-place on the top of all the kitchen utensils in the wireless corner.

It was a few nights later. It was overcast and pitch dark, and Torstein had placed the paraffin lamp just by his head, so that the night watches should see where they were treading when they crept in and out over his head. . . . About four o'clock Torstein was woken by the lamp tumbling over and something cold and wet flapping about his ears. 'Flying fish,' he thought, and felt for it in the darkness to throw it away. He caught hold of something long and wet that wriggled like a snake, and let go as if he had burned himself. The unseen visitor twisted itself away and over to Herman, while Torstein tried to get the lamp alight. Herman started up too, and this made me wake thinking of the octopus which came up at nights in these waters.

When we got the lamp alight, Herman was sitting in triumph with his hand gripping the neck of a long thin fish which wriggled in his hands like an eel. The fish was over three feet long, as slender as a snake, with dull black eyes and a long snout with a greedy jaw full of long sharp teeth. The teeth were as sharp as knives and could be folded back into the roof of the mouth to make way for what it swallowed. Under Herman's grip a large-eyed white fish, about eight inches long, was suddenly thrown up from the stomach and out of the mouth of the predatory fish, and soon after up came another like it. These were clearly two deep water fish, much torn by the snake-fish's teeth. The snake-fish's thin skin was bluish violet on the back and steel blue underneath, and it came loose in flakes when we took hold of it.

32

Bengt too was woken at last by all the noise, and we held the lamp and the long fish under his nose. He sat up drowsily in his sleeping bag and said solemnly:

'No, fish like that don't exist.'

With which he turned over quietly and fell asleep again.

Bengt was not far wrong. It appeared later that we six sitting round the lamp in the bamboo cabin were the first men to have seen this fish alive. Only the skeleton of a fish like this one had been found a few times on the coast of South America and the Galapagos Islands; ichthyologists called it *Gempylus*, or snake mackerel, and thought it lived at the bottom of the sea at a great depth, because no one had ever seen it alive. But if it lived at a great depth, this must at any rate be by day, when the sun blinded the big eyes. For on dark nights *Gempylus* was abroad high over the surface of the seas; we on the raft had experience of that.

A week after the rare fish had landed in Torstein's sleeping bag, we had another visit. Again it was four in the morning, and the new moon had set so that it was dark, but the stars were shining. The raft was steering easily, and when my watch was over I took a turn along the edge of the raft to see if everything was shipshape for the new watch. I had a rope round my waist, as the watch always had, and, with the paraffin lamp in my hand, I was walking carefully along the outermost log to get round the mast. The log was wet and slippery, and I was furious when someone quite unexpectedly caught hold of the rope behind me and jerked till I nearly lost my balance. I turned round wrathfully with the lantern, but not a soul was to be seen. There came a new tug at the rope, and I saw something shiny lying writhing on the deck. It was a fresh *Gemplyus*, and this time it had got its teeth so deep into the rope that several of them broke off before I got the rope loose. Presumably the light of the lantern had flashed along the curving white rope, and our visitor from the depths of the sea had caught hold in the hope of jumping up and snatching an extra long and tasty tit-bit. It ended its days in a jar of formalin.

The sea contains many surprises for him who has his floor on a level with the surface, and drifts along slowly and noiselessly. A sportsman who breaks his way through the woods may come back and say that no wild life is to be seen. Another may sit down on a stump and wait, and often rustlings and cracklings will begin, and curious eyes peer out. So it is on the sea too. We usually plough across it with roaring engines and piston strokes, with the water foaming round our bows. Then we come back and say that there is nothing to see far out on the ocean.

Not a day passed but we, as we sat floating on the surface of the sea, were visited by inquisitive guests which wriggled and waggled about us, and a few of them, such as dolphins and pilot fish, grew so familiar that they accompanied the raft across the sea and kept round us day and night.

When night had fallen, and the stars were twinkling in the dark tropical sky, the phosphorescence flashed around us in rivalry with the stars, and single glowing plankton resembled round live coals so vividly that we involuntarily drew in our bare legs when the glowing pellets were washed up round our feet at the raft's stern. When we caught them we saw that they were little brightly shining species of shrimp. On such nights we were sometimes scared when two round shining eyes suddenly rose out of the sea right alongside the raft and glared at us with an unblinking hypnotic stare – it might have been the Old Man of the Sea himself. These were often big squids which came up and floated on the surface with their devilish green eyes shining in the dark like phosphorus. But sometimes they were the shining eyes of deep water fish which only came up at night and lay staring, fascinated by the glimmer of light before them. Several times, when the sea was calm, the black water round the raft was suddenly full of round heads two or three feet in diameter, lying motionless and staring at us with great glowing eyes. On other nights balls of light three feet and more in diameter would be visible down in the water, flashing at irregular intervals like electric lights turned on for a moment.

We gradually grew accustomed to having these subterranean or submarine creatures under the floor, but nevertheless we were just as surprised every time a new version appeared. About two o'clock on a cloudy night, on which the man at the helm had difficulty in distinguishing black water from black sky, he caught sight of a faint illumination down in the water which slowly took the shape of a large animal. It was impossible to say whether it was plankton shining on its body, or if the animal itself had a phosphorescent surface, but the glimmer down in the black water gave the ghostly creature obscure, wavering outlines. Sometimes it was roundish, sometimes oval or triangular, and suddenly it split into two parts which swam to and fro under the raft independently of one another. Finally there were three of these large shining phantoms wandering round in slow circles under us. They were real monsters, for the visible parts alone were some five fathoms long, and we all quickly collected on deck and followed the ghost dance. It went on for hour after hour, following the course of the raft. Mysterious and noiseless, our shining companions kept a good way beneath the surface, mostly on the starboard side, where the light was, but often they were right under the raft or appeared on the port side. The glimmer of light on their backs revealed that the beasts were bigger than elephants, but they were not whales, for they never came up to breathe. Were they giant ray-fish which changed shape when they turned over on their sides? They took no notice at all if we held the light right down on the surface to lure them up, so that we might see what kind of creatures they were. And like all proper goblins and ghosts, they had sunk into the depths when the dawn began to break.

We never got a proper explanation of this nocturnal visit from the three shining monsters, unless the solution was afforded by another visit we received a day and a half later in the full midday sunshine. It was May 24, and we were lying drifting on a leisurely swell in exactly 95° west by 7° south. It was about noon, and we had thrown overboard the guts of two big dolphins we had caught early in the morning. I was having a refreshing plunge overboard at the bows, lying in the water, keeping a good look out and hanging on to a rope-end, when I caught sight of a thick brown fish, six feet long, which came swimming inquisitively towards me through the crystal-clear sea water. I hopped quickly up on to the edge of the raft and sat in the hot sun looking at the fish as it passed quietly, when I heard a wild war-whoop from Knut, who was sitting aft behind the bamboo cabin. He bellowed 'Shark!' till his voice cracked in a falsetto, and as we had sharks swimming alongside the raft almost daily without creating such excitement, we all realised that this must be something extra special, and flocked astern to Knut's assistance.

Knut had been squatting there, washing his pants in the swell, and when he looked up for a moment he was staring straight into the biggest and ugliest face any of us had ever seen in the whole of our lives. It was the head of a veritable sea monster, so huge and so hideous that if the Old Man of the Sea himself had come up he could not have made such an impression on us. The head was broad and flat like a frog's, with two small eyes right at the sides, and a toadlike jaw which was four or five feet wide and had long fringes hanging drooping from the corners of the mouth. Behind the head was an enormous body ending in a long thin tail with a pointed tail fin which stood straight up and showed that this sea monster was not any kind of whale. The body looked brownish under the water, but both head and body were thickly covered with small white spots. The monster came quietly, lazily swimming after us from astern. It grinned like a bulldog and lashed gently with its tail. The large round dorsal fin projected clear of the water and sometimes the tail fin as well, and when the creature was in the trough of the swell the water flowed about the broad back as though washing round a submerged reef. In front of the broad jaws swam a whole crowd of zebra-striped pilot fish in fan formation, and large remora fish and other parasites sat firmly attached to the huge body and travelled with it through the water, so that the whole thing looked like a curious zoological collection crowded round something that resembled a floating deep water reef.

A 25 lbs dolphin, attached to six of our largest fish-hooks, was hanging behind the raft as bait for sharks, and a swarm of pilot fish shot straight off, nosed the dolphin without touching it, and then hurried back to their lord and master, the sea king. Like a mechanical monster it set its machinery going and came gliding at leisure towards the dolphin which lay, a beggarly trifle, before its jaws. We tried to pull the dolphin in, and the sea monster followed slowly, right up to the side of the raft. It did not open its mouth, but just let the dolphin bump against it, as if to throw open the whole door for such an insignificant scrap was not worth while. When the giant came right up to the raft, it rubbed its back against the heavy steering oar, which was just lifted up out of the water, and now we had ample opportunity of studying the monster at the closest quarters – at such close quarters that I thought we had all gone mad, for we roared stupidly with laughter and shouted over-excitedly at the completely fantastic sight we saw. Walt Disney himself, with all his powers of imagination, could not have created a more hair-raising sea monster than that which thus suddenly lay with its terrific jaws along the raft's side.

The monster was a whale shark, the largest shark and the largest fish known in the world today. It is exceedingly rare, but scattered specimens are observed here and there in the tropical oceans. The whale shark has an average length of 50 feet, and according to zoologists it weighs 15 tons. It is said that large specimens can attain a length of 65 feet, and a harpooned baby had a liver weighing 600 lbs, and a collection of three thousand teeth in each of its broad jaws.

The monster was so large that when it began to swim in circles round us and under the raft its head was visible on one side while the whole of its tail stuck out on the other. And so incredibly grotesque, inert and stupid did it appear when seen full-face that we could not help shouting with laughter, although we realised that it had strength enough in its tail to smash both balsa logs and ropes to pieces if it attacked us. Again and again it described narrower and narrower circles just under the raft, while all we could do was to wait and see what might happen. When out on the other side it glided amiably under the steering oar and lifted it up in the air, while the oar-blade slid along the creature's back. We stood round the raft with hand harpoons ready for action, but they seemed to us like toothpicks in relation to the heavy beast we had to deal with. There was no indication that the whale shark ever thought of leaving us again; it circled round us and followed like a faithful dog, close to the raft. None of us had ever experienced or thought we should experience anything like it; the whole adventure, with the sea monster swimming behind and under the raft, seemed to us so completely unnatural that we could not really take it seriously.

In reality the whale shark went on encircling us for barely an hour, but to us the visit seemed to last a whole day. At last it became too exciting for Erik, who was standing at a corner of the raft with an eight-foot hand harpoon, and encouraged by ill-considered shouts, he raised the harpoon above his head. As the whale shark came gliding slowly towards him, and had got its broad head right under the corner of the raft, Erik thrust the harpoon with all his giant strength down between his legs and deep in the whale shark's gristly head. It was a second or two before the giant understood properly what was happening. Then in a flash the placid half-wit was transformed into a mountain of steel muscles. We heard a swishing noise as the harpoon line rushed over the edge of the raft, and saw a cascade of water as the giant stood on its head and plunged down into the depths. The three men who were standing nearest were flung about the place head over heels and two of them were flayed and burnt by the line as it rushed through the air. The thick line, strong enough to hold a boat, was caught up on the side of the raft but snapped at once like a piece of twine, and a few seconds later a broken-off harpoon shaft came up to the surface two hundred yards away. A shoal of frightened pilot fish shot off through the water in a desperate attempt to keep up with their old lord and master, and we waited a long time for the monster to come racing back like an infuriated submarine; but we never saw anything more of the whale shark.

We were now in the South Equatorial Current and moving in a westerly direction just 400 sea miles south of the Galapagos. There was no longer any danger of drifting into the Galapagos currents, and the only contacts we had with this group of islands were greetings from big sea turtles which no doubt had strayed far out to sea from the islands. One day we saw a thumping big sea turtle lying struggling with its head and one great fin above the surface of the water. As the swell rose we saw a shimmer of green and blue and gold in the water under the turtle, and we discovered that it was engaged in a life and death struggle with dolphins. The fight was apparently quite one-sided; it consisted in twelve to fifteen big-headed, brilliantly coloured dolphins attacking the turtle's neck and fins and apparently trying to tire it out, for the turtle could not lie for days on end with its head and paddles drawn inside its shell.

When the turtle caught sight of the raft, it dived and made straight for us, pursued by the glittering fish. It came close up to the side of the raft and was showing signs of wanting to climb up on to the timber when it caught sight of us already standing there. If we had been more practised we could have captured it with ropes without difficulty as the huge carapace paddled quietly along the side of the raft. But we spent the time that mattered in staring, and when we had the lasso ready the giant turtle had already passed our bows. We flung the little rubber dinghy into the water, and Herman, Bengt and Torstein went in pursuit of the sea turtle in the round nutshell, which was not a great deal bigger than what swam ahead of them. Bengt as steward saw in his mind's eye endless meat dishes and the most delicious turtle soup. But the faster they rowed, the faster the turtle slipped through the water just below the surface, and they were not more than a hundred yards from the raft when the turtle suddenly disappeared without trace. But they had done one good deed at any rate. For when the little yellow rubber dinghy came dancing back over the water, it had the whole glittering school of dolphins after it. They circled round the new turtle, and the boldest snapped at the oar-blades which dipped in the water like fins; meanwhile the peaceful turtle escaped successfully from all its ignoble persecutors.

The Haunting

Margaret Mahy

This compelling novel is no ordinary ghost story. It is not a house that is being haunted but a boy. The boy is Barney Palmer and the ghost is the ghost of his Great-Uncle Cole. Barney finds being haunted a terrifying experience which has repercussions on his whole family. Here are the opening pages of this fascinating story.

When, suddenly, on an ordinary Wednesday, it seemed to Barney that the world tilted and ran downhill in all directions, he knew he was about to be haunted again. It had happened when he was younger but he had thought that being haunted was a babyish thing that you grew out of, like crying when you fell over, or not having a bike.

'Remember Barney's imaginary friends, Mantis, Bigbuzz and Ghost?' Claire – his stepmother – sometimes said. 'The garden seems empty now that they've gone. I quite miss them.'

But she was really pleased perhaps because, being so very real to Barney, they had become too real for her to laugh over. Barney had been sorry to lose them, but he wanted Claire to feel comfortable living with him. He could not remember his own mother and Claire had come as a wonderful surprise, giving him a hug when he came home from school, asking him about his day, telling him about hers, arranging picnics and unexpected parties and helping him with hard homework. It seemed worth losing Mantis, Bigbuzz and Ghost and the other kind phantoms that had been his friends for so many days before Claire came.

Yet here it was beginning again...the faint dizzy twist in the world around him, the thin singing drone as if some tiny insect were

42

trapped in the curling mazes of his ear. Barney looked up at the sky searching for a ghost but there was only a great blueness like a weight pressing down on him. He looked away quickly, half expecting to be crushed into a sort of rolled-out gingerbread boy in an enormous stretched-out school uniform. Then he saw his ghost on the footpath beside him.

A figure was slowly forming out of the air: a child – quite a little one, only about four or five – struggling to be real. A curious pale face grew clearer against a halo of shining hair, silver gold hair that curled and crinkled, fading into the air like bright smoke. The child was smiling. It seemed to be having some difficulty in seeing Barney so that he felt that *he* might be the one who was not quite real. Well, he was used to feeling that. In the days before Claire he had often felt that he himself couldn't be properly heard or seen. But then Mantis had taken time to become solid and Ghost had always been dim and smoky. So Barney was not too surprised to see the ghost looking like a flat paper doll stuck against the air by some magician's glue. Then it became round and real, looking alive, but old-fashioned and strange, in its blue velvet suit and lace collar. A soft husky voice came out of it.

'Barnaby's dead!' it said. 'Barnaby's dead! I'm going to be very lonely.'

Barney stood absolutely still, feeling more tilted and dizzy than ever. His head rang as if it were strung like a bead on the thin humming that ran, like electricity, from ear to ear.

The ghost seemed to be announcing his death by his proper christened name of Barnaby – not just telling him he was going to die, but telling him that he was actually dead already. Now it spoke again.

'Barnaby's dead!' it said in exactly the same soft husky voice. 'Barnaby's dead! I'm going to be very lonely.' It wasn't just that it said the same words that it had said earlier. Its very tone – the lifts and falls and flutterings of its voice – was exactly the same. If it had added, 'This is a recorded message,' it would not have seemed very out of place. Barney wanted to say something back to it, but what can you say to a ghost? You can't joke with it. Perhaps you could ask it questions, but Barney was afraid of the answers this ghost might give him. He would have to believe what it told him, and it might tell him something terrible.

As it turned out this ghost was not one that would answer questions anyway. It had only one thing to say, and it had said it. It began to swing from side to side, like an absent-minded compass needle searching for some lost North. Its shape did not change but it swung widely and lay crossways in the air looking silly, but also very frightening.

'Barnaby's dead!' it said, 'Barnaby's dead! And I'm going to be very lonely.' Then it spun like a propeller, slowly at first then faster and faster until it was only a blur of silver-gold in the air. It spun faster still until even the colours vanished and there was nothing but a faint clear flicker. Then it stopped and the ordinary air closed over it. The humming in Barney's ears stopped, the world straightened out; time began again, the wind blew, trees moved, cars droned and tooted. Down through the air from the point where the ghost had disappeared fluttered a cloud of blue flakes. Barney caught a few of them in his hand. For a moment he held nothing but scraps of paper from a torn-up picture! He caught a glimpse of a blue velvet sleeve, a piece of lace cuff and a pink thumb and finger. Then the paper turned into quicksilver beads of colour that ran through his fingers and were lost before they fell on to the footpath.

Barney wanted to be at home at once. He did not want the in-between time of going down streets and around corners. There were no short cuts. He had to run all the way, fearing that at any moment he might be struck by lightning, or a truck, or by some terrible dissolving sickness that would eat him away as he ran. Little stumbles in his running made him think he might have been struck by bullets. His hair felt prickly and he wondered if it was turning white. He could imagine arriving at home and seeing his face in the hall mirror staring out under hair like cotton wool. He could imagine Claire saying, 'Barney, what on earth have you been up to? Look at the state of your hair.' How could he say, 'Well, there was this ghost telling me that I was dead.' Claire would just say sternly, 'Barney, have you been reading horror comics again?'

As it happened it was not Claire who met him when he got home but his two sisters, one on either side of the doorway – his thin knobbly sister Troy, stormy in her black cloud of hair, her black eyebrows almost meeting over her long nose, and brown, round Tabitha, ready to talk and talk as she always did.

'Where have you been?' she asked. 'You're late and have missed out on family news. But it's ok – the family novelist will now bring you up to date.' By 'the family novelist' Tabitha meant herself. She was writing the world's greatest novel, but no one was allowed to read it until she was twenty-one and it was published. However, she talked about it all the time and showed off by taking pages and pages of notes and talking about those, too.

'I stopped to . . .' Barney began. He felt his voice quaver and die out. He couldn't tell Tabitha about his ghost, particularly in front of

Troy who was five years older than he was and silent and scornful. But anyway – Tabitha was not interested in his explanations. She was too busy telling him the family news in her own way.

'We are a house of mourning,' she said in an important voice. 'One of our dear relations has died. It's really good material for my novel and I'm taking notes like anything. No one I know has ever died before.'

Barney stared at her in horror.

'Not Claire!' he began to say because he was always afraid that they would lose Claire in some way, particularly now that she was expecting a baby which Barney knew was dangerous work. But Tabitha was not upset enough for it to be Claire.

'Great-Uncle Barnaby . . . a Scholar relation,' she went on and then, as Barney's face stiffened and became blank she added, sarcastically, 'You do remember him don't you? You're named after him.'

'I'm going to be very lonely,' said a soft, husky voice in Barney's ear. He felt the world begin to slide away.

'Hey!' Troy's voice spoke on his other side. 'You don't have to be upset. He was old . . . and he'd been ill – very ill, for a while.'

'It's not that!' Barney stammered. 'I – I thought it might be me.'

'Lonely!' said the echo in his haunted ear.

'I thought it *was* me,' Barney said, and suddenly the world made up its mind and shrank away from him, grown to tennis ball size, then walnut size, then a pinhead of brightness in whirling darkness. On the steps of his own home Barney had fainted.

Barney's faint was only a very little one. Within a few minutes he was in his room having his forehead bathed by Troy and with Claire holding a glass of water to his lips. Tabitha watched with interest. Now she was over the fright of having her brother fall limp and pale at her feet she became very businesslike about it all.

'I might never get another chance like this,' she told anyone who could be bothered listening as she moved to study Barney from a different angle. 'We're such a healthy family, the chance of anyone fainting in the next ten years is absolutely nil. And my novel will be published by then.'

'You silly old thing!' said Claire gently to Barney. 'Just lie still for a bit, there's a good boy. You're looking better already.' She set out to make life enjoyable for him, put a fresh flowery pillowcase on his pillow, made Tabitha and her notebook go grumbling out of the room, and then went out herself to make him a lemon drink. Barney thought about pretending to be sicker than he was just for the pleasure of being looked after. It seemed a bit babyish, but after all, before Claire had come he had not had much kindness and fussing so surely he was allowed to make up for it now.

However, he looked and felt so much better by dinner time that, when Claire said he could get up if he wanted to, he did, and that was enjoyable too, for Claire sat him in the most comfortable chair, covered him over with a rug and gave him his dinner on a tray. Everyone else was having meat and vegetables but Barney had an egg especially poached to a beautiful yellow and white on a thick slice of hot, buttered toast. He was having all the fun of being an invalid without actually being sick. Sometimes his mind flicked back to the blue velvet ghost and then pulled away sharply. It was like no other haunting he could ever remember. Even now it seemed as if somewhere in just-past time some other Barney was still standing, staring at that smiling pale child and still hearing the husky voice repeating its odd message.

'Fancy our Barney fainting!' said Barney's father. 'You must have been thinking too hard at school, Barney.'

'If people fainted because of too much thinking I'd scarcely ever be conscious,' Tabitha began at once. 'I think and think all the time, and I've never fainted – not once.' She looked over at Barney enviously. 'Why do the best things always happen to other people and not to a promising writer?'

'If people fainted from too much talking . . .' began Troy and then fell silent. Seven words were a lot for Troy to say all at once like that.

'It could be the hot day – though it wasn't very hot,' Claire said, 'or shock of some sort, or just tiredness . . . The doctor didn't seem too worried.'

Tabitha smiled in a superior way as if she knew a great deal more about fainting than a mere doctor.

'People are supposed to faint if they get sudden bad news . . . if a girl friend is killed in front of their very eyes or they lose their money or something. Barney hasn't got a girl friend – not that we know of – and he hasn't got much money because I know where he keeps it and I counted it last week. There's not enough to be worth fainting over. And it can't be the great-uncle dying, can it? I mean Barney didn't know him much.'

'Barney's a sensitive boy,' Claire said thoughtfully.

'But he said that he thought it was *him* – he-himself-Barney – who was dead, didn't he, Troy?'

'Yes!' agreed Troy, staring at Barney as if he were a riddle and she might work out his answer.

'It was a pretty funny thing to say,' Tabitha went on. 'He said, 'I thought it was me,' twice, and then he just keeled over. I've got it written down in my notebook. I might get you to sign it later, Barn, just to prove it. You won't mind, will you?'

'Honestly, Tabitha, the sooner your novel is written and published the better,' Claire said crisply, seeing Barney was being made uncomfortable by these comments. 'No more talking about Barney's faint. He's better now – that's the main thing.'

'OK – let's talk about funerals,' Tabitha replied at once.

Settling back into the big chair Barney felt comfortable again. There was no way he could have explained about the ghost or its repeated message. No one would have believed him and he did not like remembering such strangeness. Partly to get over the memory of it he looked at his family, appreciating their usualness – his father, John, tall and rather bald, giving him an anxious glance and then grinning as their eyes met, Claire with her fair hair tied back from her face with a blue scarf, smiling around the table, Tabitha, fat and golden brown, and frowning Troy who seemed to move around in the heart of her own private storm, struggling against tempests no one else could see. They stayed still and were always themselves.

'Can we go to the great-uncle's funeral, Dad?' asked Tabitha. 'I've never been to a funeral before. We're allowed time off school for funerals and I'll tell you what – if I go I won't write any notes until I get home and no one's watching.'

'No!' her father said, very firmly. 'I might go but there's no need for the rest of you to be there. Though I think we should call in on your Grandfather and Grandmother Scholar, not to mention your great-grandmother sometime in the weekend ... tomorrow afternoon, say.'

'I say 'No' to that!' Tabitha cried at once. 'Visiting that great-grandmother is too much like visiting some witch who has lost her magic but kept her nastiness. Let's just stay at home and send them a card.'

'Tabby, that's not very nice,' Claire said reprovingly.

'Well, *she's* not very nice,' Tabitha argued. 'Visiting her is like having a long refreshing drink of vinegar.'

Barney, Tabitha and Troy had three sets of grandparents. There were their father's parents, the Palmers, whom they had always known and whom they visited every Christmas or New Year, and there were Claire's parents, the Martins, who were new grandparents and whom they saw nearly every week and certainly on birthdays. But in between these families was another set of relations, a spare set as it were. There were Grandpa and Grandma Scholar, the parents of Dove, the children's dead mother, and there were a few great-uncles: Great-Uncle Guy, Great-Uncle Alberic and Great-Uncle Barnaby, now dead. There was also a great-grand-mother – Great-Granny Scholar – a terrible old lady, a small, thin witch, frail but furious.

'She's probably very nice once you get to know her,' Claire said firmly.

'Not her!' Tabitha said cheerfully. 'I don't mind seeing Grandpa and Grandma Scholar – they're nice – but I can't stand Great-Granny with those little fierce eyes and all those wrinkles.'

'She can't help being wrinkled,' her father said. 'She's very old really, close on ninety.' But he did not sound as if he minded hearing Tabitha's criticism.

'I don't mind her being wrinkled,' Tabitha replied in surprise. 'It's just that all her wrinkles are so angry. She's like a wall with furious swear words scribbled all over it.'

This was exactly what Barney thought, but he stayed silent. In the years before Claire had married their father, silence had become a habit with Barney, particularly as Tabitha seemed determined to take up all the talking time. Perhaps that was why Troy was so silent, too.

'I don't think I've ever met her,' Claire said thoughtfully. 'Nor the great-uncles either for that matter – well, only very briefly – so I can't give an opinion.'

'I've got a picture,' Troy observed. 'A photograph! Of the uncles, that is.'

'That photograph!' Her father looked pleased. 'Have you got it handy, Troy? Run and fetch it.'

For a moment Troy looked as if she might argue. Then she pushed her chair back and went off down the hall to her room. When she came back she had the photograph with her.

Her father showed it to Claire.

'That's Grandpa!' he said. 'Ben! And that's Alberic, isn't it?'

'Guy,' Troy corrected him.

'Guy, then. He's the doctor. Well *that* must be Alberic, and that's Barnaby.'

'What about the little one!' Claire asked as her husband hesitated.

'I don't remember his name,' he said. 'He's dead! At least I think he's dead. He grew up to be rather a black sheep – ran away from home and was never heard of again. That sort of thing!'

Tabitha was delighted.

'What a day!' she exclaimed. 'Things have been going on, boring, boring, boring, and then all of a sudden a death and a faint and a lost great-uncle. I didn't know we had an extra one, did you, Troy? Perhaps he isn't dead and one day he'll turn up really rich and loaded with presents. He could be a millionaire by now. In a book he would be.'

'There *was* something funny about him,' mused her father. 'One of those – you know – not-to-be-talked-about-things, and no one *did* talk about it, so I've never found out what it was. I don't think Dove knew herself. Nothing disgraceful or catching: nothing you'd inherit ... just mysterious.'

'He may not have had anything disgraceful you'd inherit,' Claire studied the photograph carefully, 'but someone *did* inherit something, all the same. He looks just like our Barney. Or rather Barney looks just like him.'

'Barney can't see! Let Barney see,' Tabitha cried generously. 'Look Barn ... the four main great-uncles plus the lost, odd, mysterious, runaway, little, new great-uncle, with nothing disgraceful or catching, except that he looks like you.'

Barney only half wanted to see the photograph. He had to command his hand to reach out and take it gingerly.

Four tall young men and one boy! Like ghosts, the old faces of the present great-uncles could be seen haunting the faces of the young great-uncles in the photograph. Uncle Barnaby, whose name had been passed to Barney, looked out, smiling a fifty-five-year-old smile at him. Great-Uncles Guy and Alberic, and Grandpa Scholar too, all smiled the tired, patient smiles they still had. But the smallest great-uncle of all looked away at the side of the picture. He seemed to be standing a little apart from the others, added in carelessly at the last minute, the photographer not caring much whether he was looking at the camera or not. Barney was very relieved. He had been afraid that he might recognize this unknown great-uncle, but he did not. Perhaps the great-uncle did not look like him, he couldn't be sure of that, but he could be sure of one thing ... he wasn't wearing a velvet suit and he did not have a head of fair curls.

Carrie's War

Nina Bawden

*When Carrie is eleven and Nick, her brother, is nine, they become evacuees.
At the beginning of the Second World War, children were sent out of the
cities into country areas so that they would not be injured in air-raids. So
Carrie and Nick are sent to Wales, and have to stay with the bad-tempered
shopkeeper Mr Evans and his kind, but timid, sister 'Auntie Lou'. When
the children go to collect a goose for Christmas they meet Hepzibah, Mister
Johnny, and another evacuee – Albert Sandwich.
In Nina Bawden's marvellous story Carrie finds herself caught up in events
which are to haunt her for years and years.*

NICK had been born a week before Christmas. On his birthday
Auntie Lou gave him a pair of leather gloves with fur linings
and Mr Evans gave him a Holy Bible with a soft, red cover and
pictures inside.

Nick said, 'Thank you, Mr Evans,' very politely, but without
smiling. Then he put the Bible down and said, 'Auntie Lou, what
lovely gloves, they're the best gloves I've ever had in my whole life.
I'll keep them for ever and ever, even when I've grown too big for
them. My tenth birthday gloves!'

Carrie felt sorry for Mr Evans. She said, 'The Bible's lovely too,
you are lucky, Nick.' And later, when she and Nick were alone, 'It
was kind of him, really. I expect when he was a little boy he'd rather
have had a Bible for his birthday than anything else in the world,
even a bicycle. So it was kind of him to think you might feel like
that, too.'

'But I didn't want a Bible,' Nick said. 'I'd rather have had a
knife. He's got some smashing knives in the shop on a card by the
door. A Special Offer. I've been looking at them every day and
hoping I'd get one and he knew that's what I was hoping. I looked

at them and he saw me looking. It was just mean of him to give me a rotten old Bible instead.'

'Perhaps he'll give you a knife for Christmas,' Carrie said, though she doubted it, in her heart. If Mr Evans really knew Nick wanted a knife, he was unlikely to give him one. He thought it was bad for people to get what they wanted. 'Want must be your master,' was what he always said.

Carrie sighed. She didn't like Mr Evans, no one could, but Nick hating him so much made her dislike him less. 'He's getting us a goose for Christmas,' she said, 'that'll be nice, won't it? I've never had a goose.'

'I'd rather have a turkey!' Nick said.

The goose was to come from Mr Evans's older sister who lived outside the town and kept poultry. Nick and Carrie had never heard of her until now. 'She's a bit of an invalid,' Auntie Lou said. 'Bed-fast much of the time now. Poor soul, I think of her but I daren't go to see her. Mr Evans won't have it. Dilys has made her bed and turned her back on her own people, is what he says, and that's that. She married Mr Gotobed, the mine-owner, you see.'

The children didn't see but didn't like to ask. It made Auntie Lou nervous to be asked direct questions. So they said, 'Gotobed's a funny name, isn't it?'

'English, of course,' Auntie Lou said. 'That upset Mr Evans to start with! An Englishman *and* a mine-owner, too! She married him just after our dad was killed down the pit – dancing on our father's grave, was what Mr Evans called it. The Gotobeds were bad owners, you see; our dad was killed by a rock fall that would never have happened, Mr Evans says, if they'd taken proper safety precautions. Not that it was young Mr Gotobed's fault, *his* father was alive then, and in charge of the mine, but Mr Evans says all that family was tarred with the same brush, only thinking of profits. So it made him hard against Dilys. Even now her husband's dead, he's not willing to let bygones be bygones.'

Though he was willing to accept a goose at Christmas, apparently. 'They're always fine birds,' Auntie Lou said – as if this was sufficient reason. 'Hepzibah Green rears them. She's good with poultry. Fine, light hand with pastry, too. You should taste her mince pies! Hepzibah looks after Dilys *and* the place best as she can. Druid's Bottom was a fine house once, though it's run down since Mr Gotobed passed on and Dilys took bad. Needs a man's eye, Mr Evans says, though he's not willing to give it, and Dilys won't ask, of course.' She sighed gently. 'They're both proud people, see?'

'Druid's *Bottom*,' Nick said, and giggled.

'Bottom of Druid's Grove,' Auntie Lou said. 'That's the cwm where the yew trees grow. Do you remember where we picked those blackberries up by the railway line? The deep cwm, just before the tunnel?'

Nick's eyes widened. He said, '*That dark place!*'

'It's the yews make it dark,' Auntie Lou said. 'Though it's a queer place, too. Full of the old religion still, people say – not a place to go after dark. Not alone, anyway, I know I'd not care to, though I wouldn't let Mr Evans hear me say it. Wicked foolishness, he calls that sort of talk. There's nothing to be afraid of on this earth he says, not for those who trust in the Lord.'

Carrie was excited; she loved old, spooky tales. 'I wouldn't be afraid of the Grove,' she boasted. 'Nick might be, he's a *baby*, but I'm not scared of anything. Can I come with you, Auntie Lou, when you go to fetch the goose?'

But as it turned out, she and Nick went alone. On what was, perhaps, the most important journey they ever made together.

They were due to go to Druid's Bottom two days before Christmas, but Auntie Lou was ill. She coughed all morning and her eyes were red-rimmed. After midday dinner, Mr Evans came into the kitchen and looked at her, coughing over the sink. 'You're not fit to go out,' he said. 'Send the children.'

Auntie Lou coughed and coughed. 'I thought I'd go tomorrow instead. Hepzibah will know I'm not coming now it's getting so late. I'll be better tomorrow.'

'I'll want you in the shop, Christmas Eve,' Mr Evans said. 'The children can go. Earn their keep for a change.'

'It'll be a heavy goose, Samuel.'

'They can manage between them.'

There was a short silence. Auntie Lou avoided the children's eyes. Then she said, uneasily, 'It'll be dark before they get there and back.'

'Full moon,' Mr Evans said. He looked at the children, at Nick's horrified face, and then at Auntie Lou. She began to blush painfully. He said in a quiet and ominous voice, 'You've not been putting ideas in their heads, I do hope!'

Auntie Lou looked at the children, too. Her expression begged them not to give her away. Carrie felt impatient with her – no grown-up should be so weak and so silly – but she was sorry as well. She said innocently, 'What ideas, Mr Evans? Of course we'd love to go, we don't mind the dark.'

'There's nothing *to* mind,' she said to Nick as they trudged along the railway line. 'What is there to be scared of? Just a few old trees.'

Nick said nothing; only sighed.

Carrie said, 'All that queer place stuff is just Auntie Lou being superstitious. You know how superstitious she is, touching wood and not walking under ladders and throwing salt over her shoulder when she's spilled some. I'm not surprised Mr Evans gets cross with her sometimes. She's so scared, she'd jump at her own shadow.'

But when they reached the Grove, Carrie felt a little less bold. It was growing dusk; stars were pricking out in the cold sky above them. And it was so quiet, suddenly, that their ears seemed to be singing.

Carrie whispered, 'There's the path down. By that stone.'

Nick's pale face glimmered as he looked up at her. He whispered back, 'You go. I'll wait here.'

'Don't be silly.' Carrie swallowed – then pleaded with him. 'Don't you want a nice mince pie? We might get a mince pie. And it's not far. Auntie Lou said it wasn't far down the hill. Not much more than five minutes.'

Nick shook his head. He screwed up his eyes and put his hands over his ears.

Carrie said coldly, 'All right, have it your own way. But it'll be dark soon and you'll be really scared then. Much more scared by yourself than you would be with me. Druids and ghosts coming to get you! Wild animals too – you don't *know*! I wouldn't be surprised if there were wolves in these mountains. But *I* don't care. Even if I hear them howling and snapping their jaws I shan't hurry!'

And she marched off without looking back. White stones marked the path through the yew trees and in the steep places there were steps cut in the earth and shored up with wood. She hadn't gone far when she heard Nick wailing behind her, 'Carrie, wait for me, *wait* . . .' She stopped and he skidded into her back. 'Don't leave me, Carrie!'

'I thought it was you leaving *me*,' she said, making a joke of it, to comfort him, and he tried to laugh but it turned into a sob in his throat.

He hung on to the back of her coat, whimpering under his breath as she led the way down the path. The yew trees grew densely, some of them covered with ivy that rustled and rattled. Like scales, Carrie thought; the trees were like live creatures with scales. She told herself not to be stupid, but stopped to draw breath. She said, 'Do be quiet, Nick.'

'Why?'

'I don't know,' Carrie said. 'Something . . .'

She couldn't explain it. It was such a strange feeling. As if there was something here, something *waiting*. Deep in the trees or deep in the earth. Not a ghost – nothing so simple. Whatever it was had no name. Something old and huge and nameless, Carrie thought, and started to tremble.

Nick said, 'Carrie . . .'

'Listen.'

'What for?'

'*Sssh* . . .'

No sound at first. Then she heard it. A kind of slow, dry whisper, or sigh. As if the earth were turning in its sleep. Or the huge, nameless thing were breathing.

'Did you hear?' Carrie said. 'Did you *hear*?'

Nick began to cry piteously. Silence now, except for his weeping.

Carrie said, dry-mouthed, 'It's gone now. It wasn't anything. There's nothing there, really.'

Nick gulped, trying hard to stop crying. Then he clutched Carrie. 'Yes there is! There is *now*!'

Carrie listened. It wasn't the sound she had heard before but something quite different. A queer, throaty, chuckling, gobbling sound that seemed to come from somewhere above them, higher up the path. They stood still as stone. The sound was coming closer.

'*Run*,' Carrie said. She began to run, stumbling. The big bag they had brought for the goose caught between her legs and almost threw her down but she recovered her balance, her feet slipping and sliding. She ran, and Nick ran behind her, and the creature, whatever it was, the gobbling *Thing*, followed them. It seemed to be calling to them and Carrie thought of fairy tales she had read – you looked back at something behind you and were caught in its spell! She gasped, 'Don't look back, Nick, whatever you do.'

The path widened and flattened as it came out of the Grove and she caught Nick's hand to make him run faster. Too fast for his shorter legs and he fell on his knees. He moaned, as she pulled him up, 'I can't, I *can't*, Carrie . . .'

She said, through chattering teeth, 'Yes you *can*. Not much farther.'

They saw the house then, its dark, tall-chimneyed bulk looming up, and lights in the windows. One light quite high up and one low down, at the side. They ran, on rubbery legs, through an open gate and across a dirty yard towards the lit window. There was a door but it was shut. They flung themselves against it.

Gobble-Gobble was coming behind them, was crossing the yard.

'Please,' Carrie croaked. 'Please.' Quite sure that it was too late, that the creature would get them.

But the door opened inward, like magic, and they fell through it to light, warmth, and safety.

A warm, safe, lighted place.

Hepzibah's kitchen was always like that, and not only that evening. Coming into it was like coming home on a bitter cold day to a bright, leaping fire. It was like the smell of bacon when you were hungry; loving arms when you were lonely; safety when you were scared. . . .

Not that they stopped being scared at once, that first, frightened time. They were indoors, it was true, but the door was still open. And the woman seemed in no hurry to close it and shut out the dangerous night; she simply stood, looking down at the children and smiling. She was tall with shining hair the colour of copper. She wore a white apron, the sleeves of her dress were rolled up, showing big, fair, freckled arms, and there was flour on her hands.

Carrie saw her, then the room. A big, stone-flagged kitchen, shadowy in the corners but bright near the fire. A dresser with blue and white plates; a scrubbed, wooden table; a hanging oil lamp. And Albert Sandwich, sitting at the table with an open book where the light fell upon it.

He opened his mouth to speak but Carrie had turned. She said, 'Shut the door!' The woman looked puzzled – people were always so *slow*, Carrie thought. She said desperately, 'Miss Evans sent us for the goose. But something chased us. We ran and ran but it chased us. Sort of *gobbling*.'

The woman peered where she pointed, out into the night.

'Oh, shut the *door*,' Carrie cried. 'It'll come *in*.'

The woman smiled broadly. She had lovely, white teeth with a gap in the middle. 'Bless you, love, it's only Mister Johnny. I didn't know he was out.'

'He went to shut up the chickens,' Albert Sandwich said. 'I expect he went for a walk after.'

'But it wasn't a *person*,' Carrie said, speaking slowly to make them understand. She wasn't so frightened now. Albert had spoken so calmly that it made her calm too. She said, 'It didn't talk, it went *gobble-gobble*.'

'That's Mister Johnny's way of talking,' Albert Sandwich said. 'You must admit, Hepzibah, it could frighten someone.' He looked at Carrie, quite sternly. 'Though I expect you frightened him just as much. How would you feel if people ran away from you when you didn't mean to hurt them?'

Hepzibah called softly into the darkness, 'It's all right, Mister Johnny, all right, come on in.' Her voice wasn't Welsh. A different, throatier, accent.

Someone appeared in the doorway and stood close to Hepzibah, as if for protection. A small person in a tweed suit and a spotted bow tie with a shy, scrumpled-up face. He tried to smile but he couldn't smile properly: one side of his mouth seemed dragged down.

Hepzibah said, 'This is Mister Johnny Gotobed, children. Mister Johnny, say how-do-you-do to our visitors, will you?'

He looked at her and made that queer sound in his throat. Chuckle-gobble – only now it did seem like talking. Some strange, unknown language. He rubbed his right hand on his trousers and looked at it. Then held it out, shakily.

Carrie couldn't move. Though he wasn't a ghost she was still too scared to touch that small, shaky hand. But Nick said, 'Hallo, Mister Johnny,' and went up to him as if it were the easiest and most natural thing in the world. 'I'm Nick,' he said. 'Nicholas Peter Willow and I'm just ten. It was my birthday last week. And Carrie, my sister, will be twelve next May.'

'Hch. Harch-a. Chala. Larschla,' Mister Johnny said. He spat a bit as he spoke and Carrie dreaded the moment when she would have to shake hands and be spat at.

But Hepzibah saved her. She said, 'The goose is ready for you. But you'll take a little something first, won't you? Albert, take Carrie to fetch the goose while I set the table.'

Albert took a candle from the dresser and lit it. Carrie followed him, through a door at the back of the kitchen, down a stone passage into a dairy. The goose lay, neatly trussed, on a cold, marble slab. There were speckly eggs in trays on the shelf, slabs of pale, oozy butter, and a big bowl of milk with a skin of cream on top.

Carrie felt hollow with hunger. She said, 'I thought Mr Gotobed was dead. Mr Evans's sister's husband.'

'That's not him,' Albert said. 'Mister Johnny is a sort of distant cousin of *that* Mr Gotobed. He used to live in Norfolk but when his parents died he came here with Hepzibah. She's been his nurse since he was born.' He looked at Carrie as he set the candle down to give himself two free hands for the goose. 'Bit of a shock, I suppose, the first time.'

Holding the bag open so he could put the goose in, Carrie said, 'Is he mad?'

'No more than a lot of people. Just a bit simpler than some. Innocent, is what Hepzibah calls him.' Albert pushed the goose down and tied the string round the top of the bag. 'She's a witch,' he said calmly.

'A *witch*?'

He grinned at her. 'Oh, not what you're thinking of. Not black cats and broomsticks! Just what country people call a wise woman. When I was ill she gave me some herbs made into a medicine and I got better quite quickly. The doctor was amazed – he had thought I was going to die. I never thought that lad would see the spring, was what he told Hepzibah.'

'So that's where you've been. In bed, ill!' Carrie said, and then blushed. This might sound, to Albert, as if she'd been looking for him. She said quickly, 'What's been wrong with you?'

'Pneumonia. Rheumatic fever,' Albert said. 'Just about every medical crime in the calendar. It's lucky I was sent here, to Hepzibah, or I'd be pushing up daisies. Though it wasn't luck, altogether. I told the billeting officer I liked books and he said there was a library here. And there is. A proper library, in a *house*!' He spoke as if this still amazed him. 'Shall I show you?'

They left the goose in the dairy and went back along the passage and through a swing door with baize on one side into a wide, dark hall where a grandfather clock ticked in one corner and a small oil lamp threw shadows. 'Here,' Albert said, opening another door and holding his candle high so that Carrie could see. Books – shelves and shelves of books, reaching up to the ceiling, most of them bound in pale calf with gold lettering on the spines. 'Marvellous, isn't it?' Albert said in a reverent voice as if he were speaking in church. 'And to think no one uses it! Only me!'

60

'Where's Mrs Gotobed?' Carrie asked.

'*Gone* to bed.' Albert laughed and his spectacles flashed. 'She's dying, I think.'

The idea of someone dying, here in this house, frightened Carrie. She looked up at the ceiling and shivered.

Albert said, 'She's been ill for ages. I read to her sometimes when she isn't too tired. Do you like reading?'

'Not much,' Carrie said. This wasn't quite true but all these books made her heart sink. So many words written; it would take a lifetime to read them.

'What do you do then?' Albert asked in a tone of surprise. 'When you're not at school, I mean.'

'I help in the shop sometimes. Mr Evans's shop. Nick's not allowed now, but I am. And I play on the mountains and I slide down the slag heap.'

Albert looked as if he thought these were rather childish occupations. But he said, politely and kindly, 'If you don't care for books much, perhaps you'd like to see the screaming skull. There's an interesting story about it. Untrue, I daresay, but interesting all the same.'

He advanced into the room and set the candle down on a desk. Carrie hung back. 'It sounds horrible.'

'Oh it's only a skull,' Albert said. 'Come and see.'

There was a box on the desk and inside it, resting on velvet, a small, ivory skull. Pearly-smooth and grinning.

'Touch it,' Albert said, and Carrie touched the top lightly. It was warmer than she'd expected. She said, 'What's the story?'

'Ask Hepzibah,' Albert said. 'She tells it better than I would. It's supposed to be the skull of an African boy who was brought here during the slave trade, but I don't believe it. It's not a boy's skull. You just look.'

He picked the skull out of its velvet bed and showed it to Carrie. The bottom jaw was missing and some of the teeth from the top, but the sockets were there. 'It had sixteen teeth in the top jaw,' Albert said, 'which means its wisdom teeth too. And you don't get your wisdom teeth until you're eighteen, at least. I looked it up in *Gray's Anatomy* and that's what it says. And you see those wiggly lines on the top? That's the sutures, where the bones are starting to join up. So it must have been a grown person's skull but it's too small and light for an adult male, so it must have been a woman. What I think is, there's an Iron Age settlement at the top of the Grove, and I think someone found this woman's skull there, and made up a story about it, the way people do.'

He put the skull back and looked at Carrie. 'That's *me* making up a story, of course. I don't *know*. But you can test the age of the bones. I'd like to take this skull to the British Museum one day and get them to test it. The British Museum can find anything out, it's the most marvellous place in the world. Have you been there?'

'Once,' Carrie said. She remembered going with her father one day, and being dreadfully bored. All those old things in glass cases. 'It's very interesting,' she said, to please Albert.

His eyes danced as if he guessed what she really had thought. He put the skull back in its box and the lid on the top. He said, 'Would your brother like to see it?'

'No, he'd be scared,' Carrie said. 'That sort of thing scares him.'

Scared her a little too, though she wouldn't admit it to Albert. Not the skull, but the thought of the live person it had once been: a woman with eyes and hair who was dead now. Just pale, shiny bone in a box in a dark, musty library where the shelves of old books reached up into shadow. She said, 'Shouldn't we go back to the kitchen? I expect tea's ready by now.'

And it was. The cloth on the table was so stiffly starched that it stuck out at the corners. There was a huge plate of mince pies, golden brown and dusted with sugar, a tall jug of milk, a pink ham, and slices of bread thickly spread with the lovely, pale, sweaty butter Carrie had seen in the dairy. Nick was already at the table, tucking in, and Mister Johnny sat beside him; a white napkin round his neck. He chuckled excitedly as Carrie came in and she said, 'Hallo, Mister Johnny, can I sit next to you?'

Albert looked at her approvingly. He said, 'Hepzibah, I've been showing Carrie the skull. Tell her that old tale, will you? She'd like to hear it. Though it's a lot of old nonsense, of course!'

Hepzibah put a brown teapot down on the table and aimed a fake blow at his ear. 'I'll give you nonsense, my lad! Mister Albert Uppity-Know-All. You don't know so much yet, or you'd know that wise people don't mock what they don't understand!'

'Charsh, hcha,' Johnny Gotobed said.

'That's right, Mister Johnny.' Hepzibah bent over him, cutting up the ham on his plate. 'You've got more sense in your little finger than he's got in his clever young head.'

'I'm sorry, Hepzibah,' Albert said. 'Please tell Carrie.'

'Oh, it's a foolish tale, his young Lordship thinks.' Hepzibah sat down, smiling at Carrie and smoothing her copper hair back. She had a rather broad face, pale as cream, and dotted with freckles. Carrie thought she looked beautiful: so warm and friendly and kind.

She said, 'Please, Miss Green.'

'Hepzibah. That's my name.'

'Please, Hepzibah.'

'Well then. Perhaps I might, since you ask me so nicely. Fill up your plate now – go on, you can manage a bit more, growing girl like you. It's not home-cured ham, I'm sorry to say, though it would have been once. They had a good home farm, the Gotobeds. They made their money out of sugar and slaves and then moved here and made a fine place of the house. I heard about them long before I came to live here. When I was in service in Norfolk with Mister Johnny's parents, they used to tell me about their rich cousins in Wales and the screaming skull and the curse on the house. It's a queer old story, too . . .'

She sipped her tea thoughtfully, staring in front of her and frowning a little. Then she put her cup down and began to speak in a soft, sad, dreaming voice that seemed to weave a spell of silence in the room. 'He was brought here, the African boy, when he was ten or so. It was the fashion at that time for rich people to have a little black page, dressed up in silks and satins and riding on the step of their carriage. So they fetched this poor innocent away from his family, across the sea, to a strange land. And of course he cried, as any child might cry, taken from his mother. The Gotobeds weren't hard people, the young ladies gave him sweets and toys and made a real pet of him, but they couldn't comfort him, and in the end they said he could go back home one day. Perhaps they meant it, but he died of a fever his first winter here and it must have seemed to him that they'd broken a promise. So he put a curse on the house. He said, on his death-bed, that they could bury his body but when his flesh had rotted they must dig up his skull and keep it in the house or some dreadful disaster would come. The walls would crumble. And they believed him, people believed in curses then, and they did what he said. The skull has been kept in the library ever since – it only left the house once, when old Mr Gotobed's grandmother was a girl. She couldn't abide the thought of it, sitting there grinning, it gave her bad dreams she said, so she took it one morning and hid it in the stable loft. Nothing happened at all, she waited all day to see, and then went to bed, no doubt very pleased with herself. But in the middle of the night there was a great scream – like a screech owl – and a loud crashing sound. And when the family came running down in their night-clothes, all the crockery was smashed in the kitchen, all the glass in the dining-room, every mirror in the house cracked to pieces! Then of course the girl said what she'd done and they fetched the skull back and had no trouble after . . .'

'With sixteen teeth in its upper jaw,' Albert said. 'Count your teeth, Nick. You're the same age as that boy would have been, see if *you've* got sixteen!'

Nick blinked at him.

Carrie said, 'It's a lovely story, Albert Clever Sandwich, don't you dare spoil it!' Though she thought, secretly, that it was a comfort to know it might not be true. She said in a sentimental voice, 'A lovely *sad* story. Poor little African boy, all that way from home!'

Nick sighed, very deeply. Then he got down from his chair and went to stand by Hepzibah. He put his head on her shoulder and she turned and picked him up and sat him on her broad lap, her arms tight about him. She rocked him gently and he nestled close and put his thumb in his mouth. The room was quiet except for the hiss of the fire. Even Mister Johnny sat still, as if the story had lulled him, though perhaps it was only the soft sound of Hepzibah's voice.

Carrie looked at Nick on Hepzibah's lap and felt jealous. Of Nick, because she would like to be sitting there, she wasn't too big. And of Hepzibah, because she was comforting Nick in a way she knew she could never do.

She said, 'We ought to go, really. Auntie Lou knew we might stay to tea but it's getting late now and she'll start to worry.'

Then she thought of going back, through the dark trees, and her stomach seemed to sink down inside her. That noise she had heard, that deep, sighing breath!

Perhaps what she was feeling showed in her face because Albert said, 'I'll come with you if you like. As far as the railway.'

'Not with your chest, you won't,' Hepzibah said.

Albert grinned. 'I could hardly go without it, could I? Go on, Hepzibah, I'm strong as a horse now and I could do with some air.'

'Not night air,' Hepzibah said. 'Besides, I want you to come and read to Mrs Gotobed while I settle her, it puts her mind at rest for the night. Mister Johnny will see them safe through the Grove.' She smiled at Carrie, her eyes so bright, suddenly, that Carrie felt they saw straight into her mind. Though this was an odd feeling, it wasn't frightening somehow. Hepzibah said, 'You'll be all right with him. No harm of the kind you're afraid of, ever comes near the innocent.'

Carrie said, 'Mr Evans says no harm can ever come to those who trust in the Lord.'

'Perhaps that's another way of saying the same thing,' Hepzibah said. She gave Nick a last hug and tipped him off her lap. 'Come again, love. Both of you, whenever you like. Are you ready, Mister Johnny?'

He seemed to understand her. He was on his feet, holding out his hand to Nick who went to him and took it trustingly.

The Wool-Pack

Cynthia Harnett

Nicholas Fetterlock's father is one of the richest wool merchants in the Cotswolds. In this fascinating novel, set in fifteenth century England, we see how Nicholas starts to learn his father's trade and how his curiosity and courage save his father from ruin and disgrace. The everyday life of Nicholas, his family and their servants, is so vividly described that we can really feel what it must have been like to live at that time. This extract is from the beginning of Cynthia Harnett's exciting story.

NICHOLAS FETTERLOCK lay on his back on the hillside, gazing up into the young leaves of an oak tree.

He was hot and dirty, and it was good to stretch his full length in the shade. All round him from hills far and near came the bleating of sheep – the high anxious cry of lambs and the deeper reassuring answer of the ewes. Farther away he could hear the voices of the village children. They were wool-gathering down near the river, collecting every fragment of fleece that the sheep had left caught on hedges and bushes. Presently they would take it home to their mothers who would wash it and spin it and make it into warm garments for the winter.

Since early morning Nicholas had been helping with the sheep-washing. It was fun pushing the silly sheep, one by one, off the plank into the river and with long poles making them swim some way down stream before they were allowed to scramble out on to clean pasture. He liked working with the men, Giles the shepherd, and Colin, and Tom, and above all with Hal, the shepherd's son, who was his best friend.

At this moment, however, he was deliberately keeping out of sight. He had played truant from a lesson which he detested. He ought to have washed and dressed and presented himself at the office of his father's factor who taught him all the dull business side of the wool trade. But instead of going, clean and prepared, with his quill pens sharpened, he had just peeped in at the door, all dirty as he was. The factor was not there, so he had slipped away, back to the sheep again.

There would be trouble, too, when he went home. His mother would be angry when she saw him in a herdsman's tunic with bare legs, instead of in his proper doublet and hose. To make matters worse, he smelt; he was quite well aware of it. Sheep were smelly things at the best of times, but wet sheep were the smelliest of all. His clothes fairly reeked, and his mother would be bound to notice it.

It would make no difference to her that the sheep belonged to his father, who was one of the richest wool merchants in the Cotswolds. Did not his father keep a shepherd and endless labourers to do the dirty work? she would inquire. Then with an air of disgust, she would sniff at her perfume ball and send him away to change his clothes.

But, with any luck, the storm would not last. It would all be forgotten tomorrow when his father arrived home from Calais, where he had been attending a meeting of the Staple. The wool trade, England's most important industry, was governed by three hundred leading wool merchants, known as the Fellowship of Merchants of the Wool Staple, and it was at Calais that they had their headquarters. Nicholas was not sure what happened at these meetings, to which his father journeyed several times a year, but he knew that the Staple fixed all the prices of wool and made endless strict rules which had to be obeyed by everyone who took part in the trade. It was a fine thing to be a merchant of the Staple, and here in the Cotswolds, where everyone made a living out of sheep, his father was counted a very great man. He did not only buy and sell wool grown by other people, as many other wool traders did; but he kept large flocks of his own on the rolling hills. He had built a fine stone house on the outskirts of the little town of Burford, and some day Nicholas would follow in his footsteps and become a merchant of the Staple too.

Lying comfortably in the shade Nicholas was beginning to get drowsy when he was disturbed by the shrill notes of a reed pipe. That was Hal, giving orders to his dogs. Nicholas sat up and looked about him. The sheep had moved up the hill, and were now grazing quite near by. Among them, facing the other way, stood Hal, busy with his shepherd's pipe.

Nicholas hallooed through his hands. Hal looked round and started up the slope with his long rolling stride. He was a big lanky fellow, half a head taller than Nicholas, though there was only a month or two between them. His hood was pushed back, and his plain good-tempered face was burned to the colour of copper.

'I didn't know you were here, master,' he called. 'I thought you'd gone to your lesson with Master Leach.'

Nicholas frowned. It gave him a shock when Hal addressed him as 'master'. It was something quite new, evidently an order to Hal from his father the shepherd, and it was a reminder that they were both growing up. From babyhood they had been like brothers, for Hal's mother had been Nicholas's nurse.

'Master Leach was out,' said Nicholas briefly. 'I went to his counting-house, but he wasn't there. I didn't wait long, you can stake your life.'

Master Leach the factor – or wool-packer, as was his proper title – was a cold sour man, and both the boys, in common with everyone else, disliked him heartily.

Hal grinned. 'I saw him by the river an hour since,' he said, 'but he's gone back now. He went towards the town. It's lucky that you did not meet him.'

'I'll stay here,' Nicholas decided. 'He won't be likely to come this way. What are you doing? I heard you signal to the dogs "Go seek, go seek".'

'I'm gathering the ewes,' Hal explained. 'I want to count them all tonight and pen them safely. Then they'll be ready for the washing in the morning. The sooner the washing's done, the sooner the shearing will begin. The shearing supper is going to be a grand one this year.' He smacked his lips, rolled his eyes, and rubbed his middle, to indicate the joys of the feast.

Nicholas laughed. Hal made such comic faces; he ought to have been a mountebank at a fair. 'Shall I come and help?' he offered.

'Best not,' said Hal. 'Master Leach might spot you. You'd better stay there till he's gone home.'

He whistled to his collies, Fan and Rolf, and went back to the sheep.

Nothing loath Nicholas lay down again. He was not a bit repentant about playing truant. All the stuff he was supposed to learn from Master Leach was so dreadfully dull. It consisted mostly of long lists, entered in ledgers, of so many bales of clipped wool, called '*sarplers*', and so many sheep skins, called 'wool-fells', to be shipped aboard from London or Sandwich or Southampton, to Calais or to anywhere else abroad that the Staple permitted them to go. He was expected to know all the different grades of wool, their prices, and details of their packing.

These lessons were an extra, for he went every morning to the parson to study reading and writing and Latin grammar. He was willing enough to do that. He liked the parson; there were other boys in his class, and it was a condition of his remaining at home. Otherwise he would have been sent away as an apprentice to London, or else to school at some distant monastery.

He was getting stiff, so he rolled over, and propping his chin on his hands, gazed up the hill.

The old drover's road ran along the ridge from Witney and Oxford in one direction, towards Northleach and far off Gloucester in the other. Against the sky he saw a long line of packhorses pacing eastward, laden with bales of wool. Probably they were from Northleach, five miles away, where the big export merchants came to meet the local wool-men and bargain for the best of the famous 'fine Cotts'. Packhorses were the only means of carrying the wool, since the river Windrush was not suitable for barges; and this string of patient plodding animals might be going even as far as London.

Close at hand an old man with a stick goaded a reluctant ass up the grassy slope. That was hunchback Hubert from Witney, a familiar figure who came every week to collect the yarn spun by the cottage women and carry it to the weavers to be made into blankets.

Suddenly, from behind a clump of trees a solitary horseman came in sight – a tall figure mounted on a piebald horse. Nicholas caught his breath, and lay very still. The sunlight threw up so vividly the black and white patches on the horse that there could be no mistake. It was Master Simon Leach the wool-packer. Evidently he had given up any idea of Nicholas's lesson, locked his counting-house, and was going back to his home at Westwell a couple of miles away. Nicholas watched him as he crossed the road at the top of the hill and vanished down the other side. Then he gave a sigh of relief. As he had often been before, he was thankful for that piebald horse, so easily recognized from a distance. Now he could go home.

But as he sat up and stretched himself a distant gleam of light caught his eye. A little party of horsemen was approaching from the east. They were too far off for him to see what they were, but the glint could only come from the reflection of the sun on armour. There seemed to be about six of them, though only the last four were men-at-arms. Now who could be riding with an armed escort in these days? A few years ago, before the Wars of the Roses were ended, it would have been quite common to see soldiers in armour. But it was nearly eight years since the battle of Bosworth Field, where King Richard the Third had been killed, and King Henry Tudor had put on the crown, and nowadays everything was peaceful.

Nicholas decided that they were merchants, and wealthy ones, too. He noticed that a dog, a tall gazehound, trotted on leash beside the grey horse. They must certainly be people of importance to travel with such an array. He wondered for a moment who they were and where they were going.

All at once, without a second's warning, chaos broke loose. The merchants' horses, which had been so quiet and well-behaved, suddenly reared. There was a stamping of hoofs, a jangle of harness, and sharp cries in a foreign tongue. Nicholas could not make out what had happened until he saw a small dark shadow come streaking like an arrow down the hill towards him. It was a hare, and after it, coursing with all the power of its supple body, came the merchant's gazehound.

Nicholas jumped to his feet, startling the hare. It doubled back, darted down the field and headed straight into the midst of the grazing flock, with the hound close behind it. Sheep stampeded in every direction. The hound lost sight of its quarry. It hesitated, and in the twinkling of an eye the collies were upon it, and all three dogs rolled over and over, biting and snarling in a savage fight.

Nicholas started to run towards them, but dodged just in time as, with a thunder of hoofs, the small man in black galloped by. Hal had rushed upon the scene, crook in hand, and now the horseman swept down upon them all, laying about him with his riding-whip. He lashed out savagely, raining blows indiscriminately, as much upon Hal as upon the dogs. Nicholas tore along the field shouting just as Hal darted out of range with the blood streaming down his face.

By this time the little procession was near enough to be seen clearly. In front rode two fine gentlemen, one tall and elegant on a big grey horse, the other small, dressed in black and slouched in the saddle. Behind them came four guards with steel caps and cuirasses, leading a laden baggage horse.

But the whip had done its work. The sheepdogs drew off and the gazehound freed itself; and, in obedience to the shrill note of a whistle, speeded back towards the top of the hill. Nicholas made a grab at Fan, who was yelping from the lash, while Rolf, starting after the hound but hopelessly outpaced, lay down panting.

The man on horseback trotted round in a circle and came back. His face was sallow and pock-marked, with little eyes that peered under heavy lids, and a large flabby mouth. A black fur-edged gown hung from his high shoulders, and he wore a wide black hat with a long feather.

He halted beside the boys, and looked from one to the other.

'Maybe your cur-dogs have learned a lesson,' he said in a clipped foreign voice. 'Whose sheep are these that you are minding?'

Nicholas had gone white with anger. 'They are my father's sheep,' he replied boldly, 'and my father is Master Thomas Fetterlock, of the Fellowship of the Staple, at your mastership's pleasure. Your dog attacked his sheep, and you have beaten his servant. He shall hear of it when he returns.'

Clearly the stranger was astonished. He looked the boy slowly up and down from head to foot, while Nicholas became more and more acutely aware that his face was dirty and his legs were bare. Then with an unpleasant leering smile, the man swept off his hat in a bow so exaggerated that Nicholas knew that it was done in mockery.

'I ask your pardon that I did not recognize your father's son,' he said pointedly. 'The hound did but course a hare. It is unfortunate that he should have disturbed the sheep. But as it happens our meeting is apt. Let me present myself. On the hill yonder you see my lord, Messer Antonio Bari of Florence, agent of the noble banking house of the Medici. I am his humble secretary. We are on our way to your worshipful father's house, to sup with him.'

Once again he bowed low, as though to someone of importance, and Nicholas, red to the roots of his hair, returned the bow with as much dignity as he could muster. He explained that his father was away on business of the Staple and was not expected home before the morrow.

The secretary smiled again.

'You are behind the times, young sir,' he said. 'Your father is but a few miles off. We met him in Oxford and were honoured with an invitation to sup and sleep at his house in Burford. A messenger has ridden ahead to tell your lady mother.'

Nicholas bowed again with tight shut lips. It was all news to him. He had never heard his father speak of these foreigners. If they were bankers he supposed that they must be Lombards. All bankers seemed to be Lombards.

The secretary, on the point of riding away, hesitated and came back.

'Could you of your goodness direct me to the house of one Master Simon Leach in this neighbourhood?' he asked.

That was easy. Glad to be able to assert himself Nicholas said promptly that Master Leach was his father's packer, that he lived at Westwell, and had just gone home – only a short while ago. He turned to point out the direction when he noticed that the Lombard looked strangely taken aback.

'Your father's packer?' he repeated quickly. 'I did not know. I thank you for your courtesy, young sir.'

He wheeled his horse and with a polite reminder that they would meet again later, he rode swiftly away.

For one moment Nicholas watched him, wondering what had made him break off so abruptly, and what on earth a Lombard banker could want with Leach the packer.

Then he turned to look for Hal.

Hal had gone down to the river to swill water over his head. Nicholas met him coming up again, wiping two ugly red weals tenderly with his old woollen hood.

Nicholas's wrath was bubbling over. 'The cowardly knave,' he cried. 'Are you much hurt? I'd like to see the colour of his blood.'

'He had a face like a toad,' said Hal contemptuously. 'But his plaguey dog scattered the sheep. We must get them in quickly or they will be half across the parish. Do you take Fan and go up the hill, and I will go down with Rolf.'

In their fright the sheep had indeed strayed far and wide. Hal's reed pipe was kept busy guiding the dogs. 'Go seek, go seek.' 'Hold! Hold!' 'Fetch them in, fetch them in.' Fan and Rolf knew the notes as well as Nicholas did. They guided the flock into the fold through a gap in the stone wall, and Hal counted as the sheep passed in, using his father's own special tally rhyme.

Eggum, peggum, penny leggum
Popsolorum Jig:
Eeny, meeny, ficcaty fee
Dil dol domini
Alla beranti, middle di danti,
Ficcaty forni a rusticus.

Nicholas murmured the words under his breath. He had known them from babyhood, though he had no idea what they meant. He'd first learned them from Meg, Hal's mother, when she was his nurse, and they reminded him of the warm stuffy smell of wood smoke, wet wool, and mutton stew in Meg's cottage.

When Hal was satisfied that none of the sheep were missing they closed the gap in the fold with hurdles. Nicholas glanced at the position of the sun. The shadows had not yet begun to lengthen. Supper would not be ready for a couple of hours.

'I'll come home with you,' he announced to Hal. 'I'd just like to see your father's face when you tell him what happened. And he may know why that ugly master should ask the way to Leach's house.'

Hal had not heard the secretary inquire for Leach. He was quite excited about it, and certain that his father would be interested. There was little love lost between the shepherd and the packer. Giles was an old servant, who had started work under Nicholas's grandfather, while Simon Leach was comparatively a newcomer whom Master Fetterlock had brought from London. Leach was trained in all the latest business methods and stood high in his employer's favour. But the master was often away on the business of the Staple in Calais and knew too little of what went on among his Cotswold flocks. Old Giles often shook his head about it, and Nicholas knew that he not only disliked the packer but distrusted him.

The two boys, with the dogs, left the bare hill-side, and turned towards the valley where the silvery Windrush curved among the willows, and where the shepherd's cot lay on a sheltered slope. It was a cosy little house of plastered timber and thatch, set about with barns and pigsties, dovecot and beehives and fenced garden patch.

Nicholas had been reared there with Hal as his foster brother. There had been only one room in those days, a room without a chimney where the smoke billowed round and round before it found its ways out of a trapdoor in the roof. Since then it had been improved by the addition of a big stone chimney built up through the middle of the cottage, so massive that it supported the beams for the floor of a tiny bed-chamber in the angle of the thatched roof. Nicholas remembered how he and Hal as children had delighted in creeping up and down the ladder stair for the excitement of the climb. Hal slept in that little room now, and Nicholas still envied him.

All the happiest memories of his childhood were centred in this tiny cottage. At home he had continually to remember his manners. He might never sit in the presence of his parents without their leave, nor raise his voice, nor speak unless spoken to. His father was indulgent and seldom beat him – far too indulgent his mother said, when in some moment of extreme exasperation she so far forgot her duty as to criticize her husband. But there was no freedom for Nicholas at home as there was here under the shepherd's roof, where he could behave as any ordinary healthy boy, and where, into the bargain, he enjoyed the privileges of being 'the young master'.

On this spring afternoon, smoke was rising from the stone chimney and the shutters were down, leaving the window spaces open in both walls – a sure sign of warm still weather, since if it were cold or stormy only the side away from the wind could be open. A trestle table and a couple of benches stood outside the cottage and through the window space Meg, a plump homely little woman in a shapeless woollen gown, was setting on the table spoons made of sheeps' bone, some wooden bowls, and a pitcher of baked clay.

When she saw the boys she came to the door.

'There has been a message for you, young master,' she called to Nicholas. 'Your lady mother sent to look for you because there is to be company to sup.' Then she caught sight of Hal, and forgot Nicholas. 'God save us, boy, look at your head. What have you been at?'

While she mixed a poultice of bread and sour milk and slapped it on her son's brow, he and Nicholas told of the dog fight and the scattered sheep. She listened with little clucking noises of anger and dismay.

'A plague on all foreign knaves,' she cried. 'I wish the dogs had gone for him instead of for his hound. A shame that you must sup with him at your father's table, Master Nicholas. I've been making some of your favourite little cakes on the griddle too, and now, with a feast to come, you'll not be able to eat them.'

Promising cheerfully that no feast could spoil his appetite for her cakes, Nicholas followed her indoors. A table, fashioned roughly from a tree trunk, held the remains of Meg's cooking, a big bed was built into the wall, and on pegs by the door hung the shepherd's cloak, the tarbox and searing iron with which he doctored his flock, his lantern and spare crook. It was all warmly familiar, and Nicholas stooped to pet one of the delicate lambs that lay bedded on hay in a corner.

Over the fire, a griddle swung from a hook. Meg swept two or three hot crisp little cakes from it into the boys' out-stretched hands, and stood laughing to watch the old game of 'Catching the devil with hot tongs' as they tossed them about till they were cool enough for their teeth to tackle. Then burned tongues had to be soothed with draughts of ewe's milk, and once more the sense of home possessed Nicholas. In his mother's house they drank only cow's milk.

He was still draining the mug when a joyful clamour from Fan and Rolf announced that their master, Giles, had come home. He had been, Meg said, to help her brother the barber-chirugeon at his shop in the town. It was part of a barber's business to extract teeth, set broken limbs, and perform any small operation needed by the townsfolk. Sometimes when the case was a difficult one, or the patient full of fight, Nash, the barber, appealed to his brother-in-law. Like most shepherds Giles had learned wisdom in the folds, and an ailing human was not, in his eyes, very different from an ailing sheep. He was also a strong man, and accustomed to holding down struggling ewes.

As Nicholas heard the shepherd's voice, he set down his mug, dropped a hasty kiss on Meg's apple cheek, and went outside.

Hal now wore a bandage so, of course, his father inquired what was the matter, and once more they told their story.

Giles, a tall old man with a furrowed face and shaggy grizzled hair, sat down on the bench by the window, then, with a side glance towards 'the young master', half got up again till Nicholas also seated himself.

At first the boys' tale amused him, but gradually the smile faded from his face, and when Nicholas came to the part about Leach, he thumped the table with his fist.

'The Lombards!' he cried. 'Leach in the hands of the Lombards? By Heaven, I might have guessed it.'

Nicholas looked at him blankly. He had expected Giles to enjoy a bit of gossip, but he had not anticipated a storm.

'What do the Lombards do?' he asked doubtfully. 'I'm always hearing people talk of Lombards, and everyone seems to hate them, but, to tell the truth, I don't understand why. They are foreigners from North Italy, that much I know. His mastership out on the hill said that they were bankers.'

'*Bankers?*' snorted Giles. 'That's too sweet a name for it, master. *Usurers* would be better; and Holy Church condemns all usury. They ride round the country lending money at vast interest to any who are in difficulties – that is if they have something to offer in pledge. People say they have half the traders of England in their power. They buy wool too, direct from the growers, and ship it abroad as they will, which is more than an Englishman may do. The Staple itself cannot stop them because they hold their licences direct from the King. 'Tis said that even he is in their debt and dare refuse them nothing.'

Nicholas frowned. He was still not sure what all these words meant – 'usury' and 'interest' – though he saw plainly enough that it had something to do with borrowing money and having to pay back more than you borrowed. But if these Lombards were as bad as all that, would his father have invited them to sup? He said this to Giles.

The old shepherd shook his head.

'Your father is a great merchant, sir. Doubtless he knows what he is about. And I've heard that some of the Lombard bankers are fine lords.' He turned on Nicholas a pair of keen blue eyes. 'But all the same, Master Nicholas, I'd like to know what they want with Simon Leach.'

There was a pause while Meg filled her husband's bowl with steaming mutton broth. He crossed himself, broke off a hunk of barley bread, dipped it and sucked it thoughtfully.

'Have you seen Leach's new barn, young master? He has built for himself a big stone barn, right out on the wolds. Now Leach is a member of the Guild of Wool-packers, and by law wool-packers are not allowed to trade in wool for themselves. Would you tell me, then, what he wants with a great new barn?'

This certainly was a poser. Nicholas said he thought that Leach had some sheep of his own.

'He may have a dozen ewes for his own needs,' Giles admitted testily, 'but no man builds a barn like that for a dozen ewes. It is always locked. What does he keep inside it? No, Master Nicholas, say what you will, there are things afoot in these parts that I like not. The old labourers are gone. It is Leach's business to find others. He is engaging strange men from distant parts. Some of them scarce know one end of a sheep from the other.'

'Have you told this to my father?' inquired Nicholas.

The shepherd shook his head. 'You well know, sir, that your worshipful father is not an easy man. He is just and true in every word, and a kind master, but he does not like to take advice. The man Leach has won his favour and he will not hearken to me. All the same as soon as the shearing is safely past I will seek to speak with him again.'

At mention of the shearing both boys cheered up. The sheep shearing was the great event of the Cotswold year. All the local wool-dealers, as well as the agents of the big Staple merchants, came riding round the farms taking samples of the wool and bidding for the proceeds of the clip. Sometimes a fleece was sold even before it left the sheep's back. And when it was all over there was the shearing supper given by every master for his men, with lots to eat and drink, and singing and dancing far into the night.

Last year was the first time that Nicholas had been allowed to remain at the supper with the men, instead of going home early with the women and children, and he, as well as Hal, was looking forward eagerly to this year's feast. He began to question Giles. When would the clip begin? How long would it last?

But before the shepherd could answer, the sound of a distant bell came floating along the valley. It was the clock from the tower of Burford Church striking the hour of five. Nicholas started to his feet, remembering that the Lombards were coming to supper, and, what was more, that his father would be home. He must change his clothes, and if he did not hurry, he would be late.

The White Mountains

John Christopher

The world has been invaded by the Masters, mysterious beings from another planet. They, and their monster machines the Tripods, control the human population by 'Capping' them – fitting strange metal caps over everyone's head at the age of thirteen.
In John Christopher's superb story, twelve year old Will Parker rebels against the rule of the Tripods and tries to escape to the White Mountains where he is told a resistance movement exists.

APART from the one in the church tower, there were five clocks in the village that kept reasonable time, and my father owned one of them. It stood on the mantelshelf in the parlour, and every night before he went to bed he took the key from a vase, and wound it up. Once a year the clockman came from Winchester, on an old jogging pack-horse, to clean and oil it and put it right. Afterwards he would drink camomile tea with my mother, and tell her the news of the city and what he had learnt in the villages through which he had passed. My father, if he were not busy milling, would stalk out at this time, with some contemptuous remark about gossip; but later, in the evening, I would hear my mother passing the stories on to him. He did not show much enthusiasm, but he listened to them.

My father's great treasure, though, was not the clock, but the Watch. This, a miniature clock with a dial less than an inch across and a circlet permitting it to be worn on the wrist, was kept in a locked drawer of his desk; and only brought out to be worn on ceremonial occasions, like Harvest Festival, or a Capping. The clockman was only allowed to see to it every third year, and at such times my father stood by, watching him as he worked. There was no other Watch in the village, nor in any of the villages round about. The clockman said there were a number in Winchester, but none as fine as this. I wondered if he said it to please my father, who certainly showed pleasure in the hearing, but I believe it truly was of very good workmanship. The body of the Watch was of a steel much superior to anything they could make at the forge in Alton, and the works inside were a wonder of intricacy and skill. On the front was printed 'Anti-magnetique', and 'Incabloc', which we supposed must have been the name of the craftsman who made it in olden times.

The clockman had visited us the week before, and I had been permitted to look on for a time while he cleaned and oiled the Watch. The sight fascinated me, and after he had gone I found my thoughts running continually on this treasure, now locked away again in its drawer. I was, of course, forbidden to touch my father's desk, and the notion of opening a locked drawer in it should have been unthinkable. Nonetheless, the idea persisted. And after a day or two, I admitted to myself that it was only the fear of being caught that prevented me.

On Saturday morning, I found myself alone in the house. My father was in the mill-room, grinding, and the servants – even Molly who normally did not leave the house during the day – had been brought in to help. My mother was out visiting old Mrs Ash, who was sick, and would be gone an hour at least. I had finished my homework, and there was nothing to stop me going out into the bright May morning and finding Jack. But what completely filled my mind was the thought that I had this opportunity to look at the Watch, with small chance of detection.

The key, I had observed, was kept with the other keys in a small box beside my father's bed. There were four, and the third one opened the drawer. I took out the Watch, and gazed at it. It was not going, but I knew one wound it and set the hands by means of the small knob at one side. If I were to wind it only a couple of turns it would run down quite soon – just in case my father decided to look at it later in the day. I did this, and listened to its quiet rhythmic ticking. Then I set the hands by the clock. After that it only remained for me to slip it on my wrist. Even notched to the first hole, the leather strap was loose; but I was wearing the Watch.

Having achieved what I had thought was an ultimate ambition, I found, as I think is often the case, that there remained something more. To wear it was a triumph, but to be seen wearing it . . . I had told my cousin, Jack Leeper, that I would meet him that morning, in the old ruins at the end of the village. Jack, who was nearly a year older than myself and due to be presented at the next Capping, was the person, next to my parents, that I most admired. To take the Watch out of the house was to add enormity to disobedience, but having already gone so far, it was easier to contemplate it. My mind made up, I was determined to waste none of the precious time I had. I opened the front door, stuck the hand with the Watch deep into my trouser pocket, and ran off down the street.

The village lay at a cross-roads, with the road in which our house stood running alongside the river (this giving power for the mill, of course) and the second road crossing it at the ford. Beside the ford stood a small wooden bridge for foot travellers, and I pelted across, noticing that the river was higher than usual from the spring rains. My Aunt Lucy was approaching the bridge as I left it at the far end. She called a greeting to me, and I called back, having first taken care to veer to the other side of the road. The baker's shop was there, with trays of buns and cakes set out, and it was reasonable that I should be heading that way: I had a couple of pennies in my pocket. But I ran on past it, and did not slacken to a walk until I had reached the point where the houses thinned out and at last ended.

The ruins were a hundred yards further on. On one side of the road lay Spiller's meadow, with cows grazing, but on my side there was a thorn hedge, and a potato field beyond. I passed a gap in the hedge, not looking in my concentration on what I was going to show Jack, and was startled a moment later by a shout from behind me. I recognized the voice as Henry Parker's.

Henry, like Jack, was a cousin of mine – my name is Will Parker – but, unlike Jack, no friend. (I had several cousins in the village: people did not usually travel far to marry.) He was a month younger than I, but taller and heavier, and we had hated each other as long as I could remember. When it came to fighting, as it very often did, I was outmatched physically, and had to rely on agility and quickness if I were not going to be beaten. From Jack I had learned some skill in wrestling which, in the past year, had enabled me to hold my own more, and in our last encounter I had thrown him heavily enough to wind him and leave him gasping for breath. But for wrestling one needed the use of both hands. I thrust my left hand deeper into the pocket and, not answering his call, ran on towards the ruins.

He was closer than I had thought, though, and he pounded after me, yelling threats. I put a spurt on, looked back to see how much of a lead I had, and found myself slipping on a patch of mud. (Cobbles were laid inside the village, but out here the road was in its usual poor condition, aggravated by the rains.) I fought desperately to keep my footing, but would not, until it was too late, bring out my other hand to help balance myself. As a result, I went slithering and sprawling and finally fell. Before I could recover, Henry was kneeling across me, holding the back of my head with his hand and pushing my face down into the mud.

This activity would normally have kept him happy for some time, but he found something of greater interest. I had instinctively used both hands to protect myself as I fell, and he saw the Watch on my wrist. In a moment he had wrenched it off, and stood up to examine it. I scrambled to my feet, and made a grab, but he held it easily above his head and out of my reach.

I said, panting: 'Give that back!'

'It's not yours,' he said. 'It's your father's.'

I was in agony in case the Watch had been damaged, broken maybe, in my fall, but even so I attempted to get my leg between his, to drop him. He parried, and, stepping back, said:

'Keep your distance.' He braced himself, as though preparing to throw a stone. 'Or I'll see how far I can fling it.'

'If you do,' I said, 'you'll get a whipping for it.'

There was a grin on his fleshy face. 'So will you. And your father lays on heavier than mine does. I'll tell you what: I'll borrow it for a while. Maybe I'll let you have it back this afternoon. Or tomorrow.'

'Someone will see you with it.'

He grinned again. 'I'll risk that.'

I made a grab at him: I had decided that he was bluffing about throwing it away. I almost got him off balance, but not quite. We swayed and struggled, and then crashed together and rolled down into the ditch by the side of the road. There was some water in it, but we went on fighting, even after a voice challenged us from above. Jack – for it was he who had called to us to get up – had to come down and pull us apart by force. This was not difficult for him. He was as big as Henry, and tremendously strong also. He dragged us back up to the road, got to the root of the matter, took the Watch off Henry, and dismissed him with a clip across the back of the neck.

I said tearfully: 'Is it all right?'

'I think so.' He examined it, and handed it to me. 'But you were a fool to bring it out.'

'I wanted to show it to you.'

'Not worth it,' he said briefly. 'Anyway, we'd better see about getting it back. I'll lend a hand.'

Jack had always been around to lend a hand, as long as I could remember. It was strange, I thought, as we walked towards the village, that in just over a week's time I would be on my own. The Capping would have taken place, and Jack would be a boy no longer.

Jack stood guard while I put the Watch back and returned the drawer key to the place where I had found it. I changed my wet and dirty trousers and shirt, and we retraced our steps to the ruins. No one knew what these buildings had once been, and I think one of the things that attracted us was a sign, printed on a chipped and rusted metal plate:

We had no idea what Volts had been, but the notion of danger, however far away and long ago, was exciting. There was more lettering, but for the most part the rust had destroyed it. . LECT . . CITY: we wondered if that were the city it had come from.

Further along was the den Jack had made. One approached it through a crumbling arch; inside it was dry, and there was a place to build a fire. Jack had made one before coming out to look for me, and had skinned, cleaned and skewered a rabbit ready for us to grill. There would be food in plenty at home – the midday meal on a Saturday was always lavish – but this did not prevent my looking forward greedily to roast rabbit with potatoes baked in the embers of the fire. Nor would it stop me doing justice to the steak pie my mother had in the oven. Although on the small side, I had a good appetite.

We watched and smelled the rabbit cooking in companionable silence. We could get on very well together without much conversation, though normally I had a ready tongue. Too ready, perhaps – I knew that a lot of the trouble with Henry arose because I could not avoid trying to get a rise out of him whenever possible.

Jack was not much of a talker under any circumstances, but to my surprise, after a time he broke the silence. His talk was inconsequential at first, chatter about events that had taken place in the village, but I had the feeling that he was trying to get round to something else, something more important. Then he stopped, stared in silence for a second or two at the crisping carcase, and said:

'This place will be yours, after the Capping.'

It was difficult to know what to say. I suppose if I had thought about it at all, I would have expected that he would pass the den on to me, but I had not thought about it. One did not think much about things connected with the Cappings, and certainly did not talk about them. For Jack, of all people, to do so was surprising, but what he said next was more surprising still.

'In a way,' he said, 'I almost hope it doesn't work. I'm not sure I wouldn't rather be a Vagrant.'

I should say something about the Vagrants. Every village generally had a few – at that time there were four in ours, as far as I knew – but the number was constantly changing as some moved off and others took their place. They occasionally did a little work, but whether they did or not the village supported them. They lived in the Vagrant House, which in our case stood on the corner where the two roads crossed and was larger than all but a handful of houses (my father's being one). It could easily have accommodated a dozen Vagrants, and there had been times when there had been almost that many there. Food was supplied to them – it was not luxurious, but adequate – and a servant looked after the place. Other servants were sent to lend a hand when the House filled up.

What was known, though not discussed, was that the Vagrants were people for whom the Capping had proved a failure. They had Caps, as normal people did, but they were not working properly. If this were going to happen, it usually showed itself in the first day or two following a Capping: the person who had been Capped showed distress, which increased as the days went by, turning at last into a fever of the brain. In this state, they were clearly in much pain. Fortunately the crisis did not last long; fortunately also, it happened only rarely. The great majority of Cappings were entirely successful. I suppose only about one in twenty produced a Vagrant.

When he was well again, the Vagrant would start his wanderings. He, or she; because it happened occasionally with girls, although much more rarely. Whether it was because they saw themselves as being outside the community of normal people, or because the fever had left a permanent restlessness in them, I did not know. But off they would go and wander through the land, stopping a day here, as long as a month there, but always moving on. Their minds, certainly, had been affected. None of them could settle to a train of thought for long, and many had visions, and did strange things.

They were taken for granted, and looked after, but, like the Cappings, not much talked about. Children, generally, viewed them with suspicion and avoided them. They, for their part, mostly seemed melancholy, and did not talk much even to each other. It was a great shock to hear Jack say he half wished to be a Vagrant, and I did not know how to answer him. But he did not seem to need a response. He said:

'The Watch – do you ever think what it must have been like in the days when things like that were made?'

I had, from time to time, but it was another subject on which speculation was not encouraged, and Jack had never talked in this way before. I said:

'Before the Tripods?'

'Yes.'

'Well, we know it was the Black Age. There were too many people, and not enough food, so that people starved, and fought each other, and there were all kinds of sicknesses, and . . .'

'And things like the Watch were made – by men, not the Tripods.'

'We don't know that.'

'Do you remember,' he asked, 'four years ago, when I went to stay with my Aunt Matilda?'

I remembered. She was his aunt, not mine, even though we were cousins: she had married a foreigner. Jack said:

'She lives at Bishopstoke, on the other side of Winchester. I went out one day, walking, and I came to the sea. There were the ruins of a city that must have been twenty times as big as Winchester.'

I knew of the ruined great-cities of the ancients, of course. But these, too, were little talked of, and then with disapproval and a shade of dread. Not one would dream of going near them. It was disquieting even to think of looking at one, as Jack had done. I said:

'Those were the cities where all the murdering and sickness was.'

'So we are told. But I saw something there. It was the hulk of a ship, rusting away so that in places you could see right through it. And it was bigger than the village. Much bigger.'

I fell silent. I was trying to imagine it, to see it in my mind as he had seen it in reality. But my mind could not accept it.

Jack said: 'And that was built by men. Before the Tripods came.'

Again I was at a loss for words. In the end, I said lamely:

'People are happy now.'

Jack turned the rabbit on the spit. After a while, he said:

'Yes. I suppose you're right.'

The weather stayed fine until Capping Day. From morning till night people worked in the fields, cutting the grass for hay. There had been so much rain earlier that it stood high and luxuriant, a promise of good winter fodder. The Day itself, of course, was a holiday. After breakfast, we went to church, and the parson preached on the rights and duties of manhood, into which Jack was to enter. Not of womanhood, because there was no girl to be Capped. Jack, in fact, stood alone, dressed in the white tunic which was prescribed. I looked at him, wondering how he was feeling, but whatever his emotions were, he did not show them.

Not even when, the service over, we stood out in the street in front of the church, waiting for the Tripod. The bells were ringing the Capping Peal, but apart from that all was quiet. No one talked or whispered or smiled. It was, we knew, a great experience for everyone who had been Capped. Even the Vagrants came and stood in the same rapt silence. But for us children, the time lagged desperately. And for Jack, apart from everyone, in the middle of the street?

I felt for the first time a shiver of fear, in the realization that at the next Capping I would be standing there. I would not be alone, of course, because Henry was to be presented with me. There was not much consolation in that thought.

At last we heard, above the clang of bells, the deep staccato booming in the distance, and there was a kind of sigh from everyone. The booming came nearer and then, suddenly, we could see it over the roofs of the houses to the south: the great hemisphere of gleaming metal rocking through the air above the three articulated legs, several times as high as the church. Its shadow came before it, and fell on us when it halted, two of its legs astride the river and the mill. We waited, and I was shivering in earnest now, unable to halt the tremors that ran through my body.

Sir Geoffrey, the Lord of our Manor, stepped forward and made a small stiff bow in the direction of the Tripod; he was an old man, and could not bend much nor easily. And so one of the enormous burnished tentacles came down, gently and precisely, and its tip curled about Jack's waist, and it lifted him up, up, to where a hole opened like a mouth in the hemisphere, and swallowed him.

In the afternoon there were games, and people moved about the village, visiting, laughing and talking, and the young men and women who were unmarried strolled together in the fields. Then, in the evening, there was the Feast, with tables set up in the street since the weather held fair, and the smell of roast beef mixing with the smells of beer and cyder and lemonade, and all kinds of cakes and puddings. Lamps were hung outside the houses; in the dusk they would be lit, and glow like yellow blossoms along the street. But before the Feast started, Jack was brought back to us.

There was the distant booming first, and the quietness and waiting, and the tread of the gigantic feet, shaking the earth. The Tripod halted as before, and the mouth opened in the side of the hemisphere, and then the tentacle swept down and carefully set Jack by the place which had been left for him at Sir Geoffrey's right hand. I was a long way away, with the children at the far end, but I could see him clearly. He looked pale, but otherwise his face did not seem any different. The difference was in his white shaved head, on which the darker metal tracery of the Cap stood out like a spider's web. His hair would soon grow again, over and round the metal, and, with thick black hair such as he had, in a few months the Cap would be almost unnoticeable. But it would be there all the same, a part of him now till the day he died.

This, though, was the moment of rejoicing and making merry. He was a man, and tomorrow would do a man's work and get a man's pay. They cut the choicest fillet of beef and brought it to him, with a frothing tankard of ale, and Sir Geoffrey toasted his health and fortune. I forgot my earlier fears, and envied him, and thought how next year I would be there, a man myself.

I did not see Jack the next day, but the day after that we met when, having finished my homework, I was on my way to the den. He was with four or five other men, coming back from the fields. I called him, and he smiled and, after a moment's hesitation, let the others go on. We stood facing each other, only a few yards from the place where, little more than a week earlier, he had separated Henry and me. But things were very different.

I said: 'How are you?'

It was not just a polite question. By now, if the Capping were going to fail, he would be feeling the pains and discomfort which would lead, in due course, to his becoming a Vagrant. He said:

'I'm fine, Will.'

I hesitated, and blurted out: 'What was it like?'

He shook his head. 'You know it's not permitted to talk about that. But I can promise you that you won't be hurt.'

I said: 'But why?'

'Why what?'

'Why should the Tripods take people away, and Cap them? What right have they?'

'They do it for our good.'

'But I don't see why it has to happen. I'd sooner stay as I am.'

He smiled. 'You can't understand now, but you will understand when it happens. It's . . .' He shook his head. 'I can't describe it.'

'Jack,' I said, 'I've been thinking.' He waited, without much interest. 'Of what you said – about the wonderful things that men made, before the Tripods.'

'That was nonsense,' he said, and turned and walked on to the village. I watched him for a time and then, feeling very much alone, made my way to the den.

The Eighteenth Emergency

Betsy Byars

Mouse and his friend Ezzie have worked out ways to escape from most of life's dangers. For example: 'Emergency Four – Crocodile Attack. When attacked by a crocodile, prop a stick in its mouth and the crocodile is helpless.' But now Marv Hammerman, the biggest boy in the school, is after Mouse and he can't think of a way out of this particular emergency. In this extract Mouse (Benjie to his mother) tells Ezzie his troubles.

'Hey, Mouse!' It was Ezzie.

He got up from the sofa quickly and went to the window. 'What?' he called back.

'Come on down.'

His mother said in the kitchen, 'You've got to eat.'

'I've got to eat, Ezzie.'

'Well, hurry up. I'll wait.'

He stood at the window and watched Ezzie sit down on the steps. The dog had finished with his Cracker Jacks and was now sitting in front of Ezzie, looking at him hopefully. The smell of chicken and noodles was coming from one of the windows, and the dog thought it was coming from Ezzie. The dog wanted some chicken and noodles so badly that his nose had started to run.

Ezzie patted the dog once. 'I haven't got anything,' he told him. 'And quit looking at me.' Once the dog had looked at Ezzie so long that Ezzie had gone in the house and fixed him a devilled egg sandwich. 'I haven't got anything,' Ezzie said again and turned his head away. Ezzie had named the dog Garbage Dog because of his eating habits. 'Go *on*.' Slowly Garbage Dog got up. He circled once like a radar finder and then began slowly to move in the direction of the chicken and noodles.

'Come to supper,' Mouse's mother called. He went into the kitchen where his mother was putting the food on the table. She sat down, spread a paper napkin on her lap and said, 'Why doesn't Ezzie help you with those boys?'

'What?'

'Why doesn't Ezzie help you fight those boys?' she repeated, nodding her head towards the window.

'Oh, Mom.'

'I mean it. If there were *two* of you, then those boys would think twice before—'

'Oh, Mom!' He bent over his plate and began to smash his lima beans with his fork. He thought about it for a moment, of stepping in front of Marv Hammerman and Tony Lionni and the boy in the black sweat shirt and saying in a cool voice, 'I think I'd better warn you that I've got my friend with me.'

'Who's your friend?'

'*This* is my friend.' At that Ezzie would step out from the shadows and stand with him.

Marv Hammerman would look at them, sizing them up, the two of them, this duo his mother had created for strength. Then with a faint smile Hammerman would reach out, grab them up like cymbals and clang them together. When Hammerman set them down they would twang for forty-five minutes before they could stumble off.

'Well, I know what I'm talking about, that's all,' his mother said. 'If you could get Ezzie to help you—'

'All right, Mom, I'll ask him.'

He ate four lima beans and looked at his mother. 'Is that enough? I'm not hungry.'

'Eat.'

He thought he was going to choke. Emergency Five – Being Choked by a Boa Constrictor. When you were being strangled by a boa constrictor, Ezzie had said, what you had to do was taunt the boa constrictor and get him to *bite* you instead of *strangle* you. His bite, Ezzie admitted, was a little painful but the strangulation was worse.

This had seemed a first-rate survival measure at the time. Now he had trouble imagining him and Ezzie in the jungle being squeezed by the boa constrictor. He tried to imagine Ezzie's face, pink and earnest, above the boa constrictor's loop. He tried to hear Ezzie's voice taunting, 'Sure you can strangle, but can you bite? Let's see you try to bite us!'

'Hey, Mouse, you coming?' Ezzie had opened the door to the hall now, and his voice came up the stairs as if through a megaphone.

'I'll eat the rest later,' Mouse said. He was already out of his chair, moving towards the door.

'Oh, all right,' his mother said, 'go on.'

He ran quickly out of the apartment and down the stairs. Ezzie was waiting for him outside, sitting down. As soon as he saw Mouse, Ezzie got up and said, 'Hey, what happened? Where'd you go after school?'

Mouse said, 'Hammerman's after me.'

Ezzie's pink mouth formed a perfect O. He didn't say anything, but his breath came out in a long sympathetic wheeze. Finally he said, '*Marv* Hammerman?' even though he knew there was only one Hammerman in the world, just as there had been only one Hitler.

'Yes.'

'Is after *you*?'

Mouse nodded, sunk in misery. He could see Marv Hammerman. He came up in Mouse's mind the way monsters do in horror movies, big and powerful, with the same cold, unreal eyes. It was the eyes Mouse really feared. One look from those eyes, he thought, just one look of a certain length – about three seconds – and you knew you were his next victim.

'What did you do?' Ezzie asked. 'Or did you do anything?'

'At least, Mouse thought, Ezzie understood that. If you were Marv Hammerman, you didn't need a reason. He sat down on the steps and squinted up at Ezzie. 'I did something,' he said.

'What?' Ezzie asked. His tongue flicked out and in so quickly it didn't even moisten his lips. 'What'd you do? You bump into him or something?'

Mouse shook his head.

'Well, what?'

Mouse said, 'You know that big chart in the upstairs hall at school?'

'What'd you say? I can't even hear you, Mouse. You're muttering.' Ezzie bent closer. 'Look at me. Now what did you say?'

Mouse looked up, still squinting. He said, 'You know that big chart outside the history room? In the hall?'

'Chart?' Ezzie said blankly. 'What chart, Mouse?'

'This chart takes up the whole wall, Ez, how could you miss it? It's a chart about early man, and it shows man's progress up from the apes, the side view of all those different kinds of prehistoric men, like Cro-Magnon man and Homo erectus. *That* chart.'

'Oh, yeah, I saw it, so go on.'

Mouse could see that Ezzie was eager for him to get on to the good part, the violence. He slumped. He wet his lips. He said, 'Well, when I was passing this chart on my way out of history – and I don't know why I did this – I really don't. When I was passing this chart, Ez, on my way to math –' He swallowed, almost choking on his spit. 'When I was passing this chart, Ez, I took my pencil and I wrote Marv Hammerman's name on the bottom of the chart and then I drew an arrow to the picture of Neanderthal man.'

'What?' Ezzie cried, '*What?*' He could not seem to take it in. Mouse knew that Ezzie had been prepared to sympathize with an accident. He had almost been the victim of one of those himself. One day at school Ezzie had reached for the handle on the water fountain a second ahead of Marv Hammerman. If Ezzie hadn't glanced up just in time, seen Hammerman and said quickly, 'Go ahead, I'm not thirsty,' then this sagging figure on the steps might be him. 'What did you do it for, Mouse?'

'I don't know.'

'You crazy or something?'

'I don't know.'

'Marv Hammerman!' Ezzie sighed. It was a mournful sound that seemed to have come from a culture used to sorrow. 'Anybody else in the school would have been better. I would rather have the principal after me than Marv Hammerman.'

'I know.'

'Hammerman's big, Mouse. He's flunked a lot.'

'I know,' Mouse said again. There was an unwritten law that it was all right to fight anyone in your own grade. The fact that Hammerman was older and stronger made no difference. They were both in the sixth grade.

'Then what'd you do it for?' Ezzie asked.

'I don't know.'

'You must want trouble,' Ezzie said. 'Like my grandfather. He's always provoking people. The bus driver won't even pick him up any more.'

'No, I don't want trouble.'

'Then, why did you—'

'I don't *know*.' Then he sagged again and said, 'I didn't even know I had done it really until I'd finished. I just looked at the picture of Neanderthal man and thought of Hammerman. It does look like him, Ezzie, the sloping face and the shoulders.'

'Maybe Hammerman doesn't know you did it though,' Ezzie said. 'Did you ever think of that? I mean, who's going to go up to Hammerman and tell him his name is on the prehistoric man chart?' Ezzie leaned forward. 'Hey, Hammerman,' he said, imitating the imaginary fool, 'I saw a funny thing about you on the prehistoric man chart! Now, who in their right mind is going to—'

'He was right behind me when I did it,' Mouse said.

'What?'

'He was right behind me,' Mouse said stiffly. He could remember turning and looking into Hammerman's eyes. It was such a strange, troubling moment that Mouse was unable to think about it.

Ezzie's mouth formed the O, made the sympathetic sigh. Then he said, 'And you don't even know what you did it for?'

'No.'

Ezzie sank down on the steps beside Mouse. He leaned over his knees and said, 'You ought to get out of that habit, that writing names and drawing arrows, you know that? I see those arrows everywhere. I'll be walking down the street and I'll look on a building and I'll see the word DOOR written in little letters and there'll be an arrow pointing to the door and I know you did it. It's crazy, labelling stuff like that.'

'I never did that, Ez, not to a door.'

'Better to a door, if you ask me,' Ezzie said, shaking his head. He paused for a moment, then asked in a lower voice, 'You ever been hit before, Mouse? I mean, hard?'

Mouse sighed. The conversation had now passed beyond the question of whether Hammerman would attack. It was now a matter of whether he, Mouse Fawley, could survive the attack. He said thickly, remembering, 'Four times'.

'Four times in one fight? I mean, you stood up for four hits, Mouse?' There was grudging admiration in his voice.

Mouse shook his head. 'Four hits – four fights.'

'You went right down each time? I mean POW and you went down, POW and you went down, POW and you went—'

'Yes!'

'Where did you take these hits?' Ezzie asked, straightening suddenly. Ezzie had never taken a single direct blow in his life because he was a good dodger. Sometimes his mother chased him through the apartment, striking at him while he dodged and ducked, crying, 'Look out, Mom, look out now! You're going to hit me!'

He asked again, 'Where were you hit?'

Mouse said, 'In the stomach.'

'All four times?'

'Yeah.' Mouse suddenly thought of his stomach as having a big red circular target on it with HIT HERE printed in the centre.

'Who hit you?'

'Two boys in Cincinnati when I was on vacation, and a boy named Mickey Swearinger, and somebody else I don't remember.' He lowered his head because he remembered the fourth person all right, but he didn't want to tell Ezzie about it. If he had added the name of Viola Angotti to the list of those who had hit him in the stomach, Ezzie's face would have screwed up with laughter. 'Viola Angotti hit you? No fooling, Viola Angotti?' It was the sort of thing Ezzie could carry on about for hours. 'Viola Angotti. *The* Viola Angotti?'

And Mouse would have had to keep sitting there saying over and over, 'Yes, Viola Angotti hit me in the stomach. Yes, *the* Viola Angotti.' And then he would have to tell Ezzie all about it, every detail, how one recess long ago the boys had decided to put some girls in the school trash cans. It had been one of those suggestions that stuns everyone with its rightness. Someone had said, 'Hey, let's put those girls over there in the trash cans!' and the plan won immediate acceptance. Nothing could have been more appropriate. The trash cans were big and had just been emptied, and in an instant the boys were off chasing the girls and yelling.

It had been wonderful at first, Mouse remembered. Primitive blood had raced through his body. The desire to capture had driven him like a wild man through the school yard, up the sidewalk, everywhere. He understood what had driven the cave man and the barbarian, because this same passion was driving him. Putting the girls in the trash cans was the most important challenge of his life. His long screaming charge ended with him red-faced, gasping for breath – and with Viola Angotti pinned against the garbage cans.

His moment of triumph was short. It lasted about two seconds. Then it began to dim as he realized, first, that it *was* Viola Angotti, and, second, that he was not going to be able to get her into the garbage can without a great deal of help.

He cried, 'Hey, you guys, come on, I've got one,' but behind him the school yard was silent. Where was everybody? he had wondered uneasily. As it turned out, the principal had caught the other boys, and they were all being marched back in the front door of the school, but Mouse didn't know this.

He called again, 'Come on, you guys, get the lid off this garbage can, will you?' And then, when he said that, Viola Angotti had taken two steps forward. She said, 'Nobody's putting *me* in no garbage can.' He could still remember how she had looked standing there. She had recently taken the part of the Statue of Liberty in a class play, and somehow she seemed taller and stronger at this moment than when she had been in costume.

He cried, 'Hey, you guys!' It was a plea. 'Where are you?'

And then Viola Angotti had taken one more step, and with a faint sigh she had socked him in the stomach so hard that he had doubled over and lost his lunch. He hadn't known it was possible to be hit like that outside a boxing ring. It was the hardest blow he had ever taken. Viola Angotti could be heavyweight champion of the world.

As she walked past his crumpled body she had said again, 'Nobody's putting me in no garbage can.' It had sounded like one of the world's basic truths. The sun will rise. The tides will flow. Nobody's putting Viola Angotti in no garbage can.

Later, when he thought about it, he realized that he had been lucky. If she had wanted to, Viola Angotti could have capped her victory by tossing his rag-doll body into the garbage can and slamming down the lid. Then, when the principal came out on to the playground calling, 'Benjamin Fawley! Has anybody seen Benjamin Fawley?' he would have had to moan. 'I'm in here.' He would have had to climb out of the garbage can in front of the whole school. His shame would have followed him for life. When he was a grown man, people would still be pointing him out to their children. '*That*'s the man that Viola Angotti stuffed into the garbage can.'

Now he thought that Marv Hammerman could make Viola Angotti's blow seem like a baby's pat. He wanted to double over on the steps.

Ezzie said, 'You ought to watch out for your stomach like a fighter, protect your body. There's a lot of valuable stuff in there.'

'I know.'

'The trick of it,' Ezzie said, 'is moving quickly, ducking, getting out of the way.' Ezzie did a few quick steps, his feet flashing on the sidewalk. 'You dance, Mouse, like this.' Mouse suddenly remembered that Ezzie had once told him that if you were ever bitten by a tarantula (Emergency Six) you had to start dancing immediately. Ezzie said you were supposed to do this special Italian folk dance, but any quick lively steps would probably do.

Mouse had a picture of himself doing this lively dance in front of Hammerman. Hammerman would watch for a moment. There would be no expression on his face. The dance would reach a peak. Mouse's arms and legs would be a blur of motion. And then Hammerman would reach down, a sort of slow graceful movement like he was bowling, and come up effortlessly right into Mouse's stomach. Mouse leaned forward, shielding his body with his arms. He cleared his throat. 'Did anybody ever hit you, Ezzie?'

Ezzie stopped dancing. 'Sure.'

'Who?'

'Well, relatives mostly. You can't hardly walk through my living-room without somebody trying to hit you – for any little thing. I accidentally step on my sister's feet – she's got long feet, Mouse, she can't hardly buy ordinary shoes, and she takes it as an insult if you step on one of them. She's fast too, Mouse. That's how I learned about getting out of the way.'

'But nobody like Hammerman ever hit you?'

'No.' He sounded apologetic.

Mouse sighed. Above him his mother called, 'Benjie, come up now. I want you to do something for me.'

'I got to go.' Mouse still sat there. He hated to leave the warmth of Ezzie's understanding. Ezzie didn't want to leave either. Mouse had taken on a fine tragic dimension in his eyes, and there was something about being with a person like that that made him feel good.

Ezzie had felt the same way about their teacher last fall when he had told them he had to go to the hospital. For the first time, Mr Stein in his baggy suit had seemed a fine tragic figure, bigger than life. Ezzie would have done anything for Mr Stein that day. But then, when Mr Stein came limping back the next week – it turned out he had had some bone spurs removed from his heels – he had been his normal size.

'Benjie, come up now,' his mother called again.

'I'm coming.'

'Did you tell your mom about Hammerman being after you?' Ezzie asked.

'Yeah.'

'What'd she say?'

He tried to think of the most impossible statement his mother had made. 'She said I'll laugh about it in a week or two.'

'Laugh about it?'

'Yeah, through my bandages.'

Ezzie's face twisted into a little smile. 'Hey, remember Al Armsby when he had those broken ribs? Remember how he would beg us not to make him laugh? And I had this one joke about a monkey and I would keep telling it and keep telling it and he was practically on his knees begging for mercy and—'

Mouse got slowly to his feet. 'Well, I better go,' he said.

Ezzie stopped smiling. 'Hey, wait a minute. Listen, I just remembered something. I know a boy that Hammerman beat up, and he said it wasn't so bad.'

'Who?'

'A friend of my brother's. I'll find out about it and let you know.'

Charlie & the Chocolate Factory

Roald Dahl

Mr Willy Wonka is the most extraordinary chocolate maker in the world, but nobody knows how his fantastic sweets are made because no workers ever go into his chocolate factory and no one ever comes out! Then one day Mr Wonka announces that he has hidden five golden invitations inside five Wonka chocolate bars. The lucky children who discover these golden tickets will be allowed to visit him in his factory. And, what is more, these children will receive a free life-time's supply of sweets! Charlie Bucket is one of the lucky winners, and this extract from Roald Dahl's fantastic story begins as Charlie and his Grandpa Joe wait, with the other four golden ticket holders, for the factory gates to open.

THE sun was shining brightly on the morning of the big day, but the ground was still white with snow and the air was very cold.

Outside the gates of Wonka's factory, enormous crowds of people had gathered to watch the five lucky ticket holders going in. The excitement was tremendous. It was just before ten o'clock. The crowds were pushing and shouting, and policemen with arms linked were trying to hold them back from the gates.

Right beside the gates, in a small group that was carefully shielded from the crowds by the police, stood the five famous children, together with the grown-ups who had come with them.

The tall bony old figure of Grandpa Joe could be seen standing quietly among them, and beside him, holding tightly on to his hand, was little Charlie Bucket himself.

All the children, except Charlie, had both their mothers and fathers with them, and it was a good thing that they had, otherwise the whole party might have got out of hand. They were so eager to get going that their parents were having to hold them back by force

102

to prevent them from climbing over the gates. 'Be patient!' cried the fathers. 'Be still! It's not *time* yet! It's not ten o'clock!'

Behind him, Charlie Bucket could hear the shouts of the people in the crowd as they pushed and fought to get a glimpse of the famous children.

'There's Violet Beauregarde!' he heard someone shouting. 'That's her all right! I can remember her face from the newspapers!'

'And you know what?' somebody else shouted back. 'She's still chewing that dreadful old piece of gum she's had for three months! You look at her jaws! They're still working on it!'

'Who's the big fat boy?'

'That's Augustus Gloop!'

'So it is!'

'Enormous, isn't he!'

'Fantastic!'

'Who's the kid with a picture of The Lone Ranger stencilled on his windcheater?'

'That's Mike Teavee! He's the television fiend!'

'He must be crazy! Look at all those toy pistols he's got hanging all over him!'

'The one *I* want to see is Veruca Salt!' shouted another voice in the crowd. 'She's the girl whose father bought up half a million chocolate bars and then made the workers in his peanut factory unwrap every one of them until they found a Golden Ticket! He gives her anything she wants! Absolutely anything! She only has to start screaming for it and she gets it!'

'Dreadful, isn't it?'

'Shocking, I call it!'

'Which do you think is her?'

'That one! Over there on the left! The little girl in the silver mink coat!'

'Which one is Charlie Bucket?'

'Charlie Bucket? He must be that skinny little shrimp standing beside the old fellow who looks like a skeleton. Very close to us. Just there! See him?'

'Why hasn't he got a coat on in this cold weather?'

'Don't ask me. Maybe he can't afford to buy one.'

'Goodness me! He must be freezing!'

Charlie, standing only a few paces away from the speaker, gave Grandpa Joe's hand a squeeze, and the old man looked down at Charlie and smiled.

Somewhere in the distance, a church clock began striking ten.

Very slowly, with a loud creaking of rusty hinges, the great iron gates of the factory began to swing open.

The crowd became suddenly silent. The children stopped jumping about. All eyes were fixed upon the gates.

'*There he is!*' somebody shouted. '*That's him!*'

And so it was!

Mr Wonka was standing all alone just inside the open gates of the factory.

And what an extraordinary little man he was!

He had a black top hat on his head.

He wore a tail coat made of a beautiful plum-coloured velvet.

His trousers were bottle green.

His gloves were pearly grey.

And in one hand he carried a fine gold-topped walking cane.

Covering his chin, there was a small, neat, pointed black beard – a goatee. And his eyes – his eyes were most marvellously bright. They seemed to be sparkling and twinkling at you all the time. The whole face, in fact, was alight with fun and laughter.

And oh, how clever he looked! How quick and sharp and full of life! He kept making quick jerky little movements with his head, cocking it this way and that, and taking everything in with those bright twinkling eyes. He was like a squirrel in the quickness of his movements, like a quick clever old squirrel from the park.

Suddenly, he did a funny little skipping dance in the snow, and he spread his arms wide, and he smiled at the five children who were clustered near the gates, and he called out, 'Welcome, my little friends! Welcome to the factory!'

His voice was high and flutey. 'Will you come forward one at a time, please,' he called out, 'and bring your parents. Then show me your Golden Ticket and give me your name. Who's first?'

The big fat boy stepped up. 'I'm Augustus Gloop,' he said.

'Augustus!' cried Mr Wonka, seizing his hand and pumping it up and down with terrific force. 'My *dear* boy, how *good* to see you! Delighted! Charmed! Overjoyed to have you with us! And *these* are your parents? How *nice*! Come in! Come in! That's right! Step through the gates!'

Mr Wonka was clearly just as excited as everybody else.

'My name,' said the next child to go forward, 'is Veruca Salt.'

'My *dear* Veruca! How *do* you do? What a pleasure this is! You *do* have an interesting name, don't you? I always thought that a veruca was a sort of wart that you got on the sole of your foot! But I must be wrong, mustn't I? How pretty you look in that lovely mink coat! I'm so glad you could come! Dear me, this is going to be *such* an exciting day! I *do* hope you enjoy it! I'm sure you *will*! I *know* you will! Your father? How *are* you, Mr Salt? And Mrs Salt? Overjoyed to see you! Yes, the ticket is *quite* in order! Please go in!'

The next two children, Violet Beauregarde and Mike Teavee, came forward to have their tickets examined and then to have their arms practically pumped off their shoulders by the energetic Mr Wonka.

And last of all, a small nervous voice whispered, 'Charlie Bucket.'

'Charlie!' cried Mr Wonka. 'Well, well, well! So *there* you are! You're the one who found your ticket only yesterday, aren't you? Yes, yes. I read *all* about it in this morning's papers! *Just* in time, my dear boy! I'm so glad! So happy for you! And this? Your grandfather? Delighted to meet you, sir! Overjoyed! Enraptured! Enchanted! All right! Excellent! Is everybody in now? Five children? Yes! Good! Now will you please follow me! Our tour is about to begin! But *do* keep together! *Please* don't wander off by yourselves! I shouldn't like to lose any of you at *this* stage of the proceedings! Oh, dear me, no!'

Charlie glanced back over his shoulder and saw the great iron entrance gates slowly closing behind him. The crowds on the outside were still pushing and shouting. Charlie took a last look at them. Then, as the gates closed with a clang, all sight of the outside world disappeared.

'Here we are!' cried Mr Wonka, trotting along in front of the group. 'Through this big red door, please! *That's* right! It's nice and warm inside! I have to keep it warm inside the factory because of the workers! My workers are used to an *extremely* hot climate! They can't stand the cold! They'd perish if they went outdoors in this weather! They'd freeze to death!'

'But who *are* these workers?' asked Augustus Gloop.

'All in good time, my dear boy!' said Mr Wonka, smiling at Augustus. 'Be patient! You shall see everything as we go along! Are all of you inside? Good! Would you mind closing the door? Thank you!'

Charlie Bucket found himself standing in a long corridor that stretched away in front of him as far as he could see. The corridor was so wide that a car could easily have been driven along it. The walls were pale pink, the lighting was soft and pleasant.

.'How lovely and warm!' whispered Charlie.

'I know. And what a marvellous smell!' answered Grandpa Joe, taking a long deep sniff. All the most wonderful smells in the world seemed to be mixed up in the air around them — the smell of roasting coffee and burnt sugar and melting chocolate and mint and violets and crushed hazelnuts and apple blossom and caramel and lemon peel. . . .

And far away in the distance, from the heart of the great factory, came a muffled roar of energy as though some monstrous gigantic machine were spinning its wheels at breakneck speed.

'Now *this*, my dear children,' said Mr Wonka, raising his voice above the noise, 'this is the main corridor. Will you please hang your coats and hats on those pegs over there, and then follow me. *That's* the way! Good! Everyone ready! Come on, then! Here we go!' He trotted off rapidly down the corridor with the tails of his plum-coloured velvet coat flapping behind him, and the visitors all hurried after him.

It was quite a large party of people, when you came to think of it. There were nine grown-ups and five children, fourteen in all. So you can imagine that there was a good deal of pushing and shoving as they hustled and bustled down the passage, trying to keep up with the swift little figure in front of them. 'Come *on*!' cried Mr Wonka. 'Get a move on, please! We'll *never* get round today if you dawdle like this!'

Soon, he turned right off the main corridor into another slightly narrower passage.

Then he turned left.

Then left again.

Then right.

Then left.

Then right.

Then right.

Then left.

The place was like a gigantic rabbit warren, with passages leading this way and that in every direction.

'Don't you let go my hand, Charlie,' whispered Grandpa Joe.

'Notice how all these passages are sloping downwards!' called out Mr Wonka. 'We are now going underground! *All* the most important rooms in my factory are deep down below the surface!'

'Why is that?' somebody asked.

'There wouldn't be *nearly* enough space for them up on top!' answered Mr Wonka. 'These rooms we are going to see are *enormous*! They're larger than football fields! No building in the *world* would be big enough to house them! But down here, underneath the ground, I've got *all* the space I want. There's no limit – so long as I hollow it out.'

Mr Wonka turned right.

He turned left.

He turned right again.

The passages were sloping steeper and steeper downhill now.

Then suddenly, Mr Wonka stopped. In front of him, there was a shiny metal door. The party crowded round. On the door, in large letters, it said:

THE CHOCOLATE ROOM

'An important room, this!' cried Mr Wonka, taking a bunch of keys from his pocket and slipping one into the keyhole of the door. '*This* is the nerve centre of the whole factory, the heart of the whole business! And so *beautiful*! I *insist* upon my rooms being beautiful! I can't *abide* ugliness in factories! *In* we go, then! But *do* be careful, my dear children! Don't lose your heads! Don't get over-excited! Keep very calm!'

Mr Wonka opened the door. Five children and nine grown-ups pushed their ways in – and *oh*, what an amazing sight it was that now met their eyes!

They were looking down upon a lovely valley. There were green meadows on either side of the valley, and along the bottom of it there flowed a great brown river.

What is more, there was a tremendous waterfall halfway along the river – a steep cliff over which the water curled and rolled in a solid sheet, and then went crashing down into a boiling churning whirlpool of froth and spray.

Below the waterfall (and this was the most astonishing sight of all), a whole mass of enormous glass pipes were dangling down into the river from somewhere high up in the ceiling! They really were *enormous*, those pipes. There must have been a dozen of them at least, and they were sucking up the brownish muddy water from the river and carrying it away to goodness knows where. And because they were made of glass, you could see the liquid flowing and bubbling along inside them, and above the noise of the waterfall, you could hear the never-ending suck-suck-sucking sound of the pipes as they did their work.

Graceful trees and bushes were growing along the riverbanks – weeping willows and alders and tall clumps of rhododendrons with their pink and red and mauve blossoms. In the meadows there were thousands of buttercups.

'*There!*' cried Mr Wonka, dancing up and down and pointing his gold-topped cane at the great brown river. 'It's *all* chocolate! Every drop of that river is hot melted chocolate of the finest quality. The *very* finest quality. There's enough chocolate in there to fill *every* bathtub in the *entire* country! *And* all the swimming pools as well! Isn't it *terrific*? And just look at my pipes! They suck up the chocolate and carry it away to all the other rooms in the factory where it is needed! Thousands of gallons an hour, my dear children! Thousands and thousands of gallons!'

The children and their parents were too flabbergasted to speak. They were staggered. They were dumbfounded. They were bewildered and dazzled. They were completely bowled over by the hugeness of the whole thing. They simply stood and stared.

'The waterfall is *most* important!' Mr Wonka went on. 'It mixes the chocolate! It churns it up! It pounds it and beats it! It makes it light and frothy! No other factory in the world mixes its chocolate by waterfall! But it's the *only* way to do it properly! The *only* way! And do you like my trees?' he cried, pointing with his stick. 'And my lovely bushes? Don't you think they look pretty? I told you I hated ugliness! And of course they are *all* eatable! All made of something different and delicious! And do you like my meadows? Do you like my grass and my buttercups? The grass you are standing on, my dear little ones, is made of a new kind of soft, minty sugar that I've just invented! I call it swudge! Try a blade! Please do! It's delectable!'

Automatically, everybody bent down and picked one blade of grass – everybody, that is, except Augustus Gloop, who took a big handful.

And Violet Beauregarde, before tasting her blade of grass, took the piece of world-record-breaking chewing-gum out of her mouth and stuck it carefully behind her ear.

'Isn't it *wonderful*!' whispered Charlie. 'Hasn't it got a wonderful taste, Grandpa?'

'I could eat the whole *field*!' said Grandpa Joe, grinning with delight. 'I could go around on all fours like a cow and eat every blade of grass in the field!'

'Try a buttercup!' cried Mr Wonka. 'They're even *nicer!*'

Suddenly, the air was filled with screams of excitement. The screams came from Veruca Salt. She was pointing frantically to the other side of the river. '*Look!* Look over there!' she screamed. 'What *is* it? He's moving! He's walking! It's a little *person!* It's a little *man!* Down there below the waterfall!'

Everybody stopped picking buttercups and stared across the river.

'*She's right, Grandpa!*' cried Charlie. 'It *is* a little man! Can you *see* him?'

'I see him, Charlie!' said Grandpa Joe excitedly.

And now everybody started shouting at once.

'There's *two* of them!'

'My gosh, so there is!'

'There's more than two! There's one, two, three, four, five!'

'What are they *doing?*'

'Where do they *come* from?'

'Who *are* they?'

Children and parents alike rushed down to the edge of the river to get a closer look.

'Aren't they *fantastic!*'

'No higher than my knee!'

'Look at their funny long hair!'

The tiny men – they were no larger than medium-sized dolls – had stopped what they were doing, and now they were staring back across the river at the visitors. One of them pointed towards the children, and then he whispered something to the other four, and all five of them burst into peals of laughter.

'But they can't be *real* people,' Charlie said.

'Of course they're real people,' Mr Wonka answered. 'They're Oompa-Loompas.'

Born Free

Joy Adamson

The Adamsons adopt Elsa the lioness and her two sisters when they are a few weeks old because their mother has been killed. The other two cubs are sent away from the reserve in Kenya (where George and Joy Adamson live) to a zoo in Holland, but Joy Adamson keeps Elsa and eventually decides to try to return her to the wild. Letting a lion 'go wild' might sound easy, but it has many dangers, especially for the animal itself. In this extract Joy Adamson describes some of the events which persuade her that it might be possible to set Elsa free and how she and her husband begin to organise the 'first release'.

ELSA has charming manners at all times; no matter for how short a time we have been separated, she will greet us ceremoniously, walking from one to the other, rubbing her head against us while miaowing in a low moan. Invariably, I come first, then George, followed by Nuru, and whoever happens to be near is afterwards greeted in the same way. She knows at once who likes her and reacts affectionately. She tolerates justifiably nervous guests, but those who are really scared have a hard time. Not that she has ever done them any harm but she delights in thoroughly terrifying them.

Since she was a tiny cub she has known just how to use her weight. But now she had become much more effective. Whenever she wanted to stop us, she flung herself with all her force at our feet, pressing her body against our shins and thus knocking us over.

Soon after our return from a safari to Lake Rudolf when we took her out for her evening walks she began to display a growing restlessness. Sometimes she refused to return with us, and she spent the night out in the bush. Usually we succeeded in getting her back by going to fetch her in the Land-Rover. In fact, she soon decided that it was a waste of energy to walk home when a car had been specially brought to fetch her. So she would jump on to the canvas roof and loll at her ease, and from this vantage point she could watch out for game as we drove along. This was a very satisfactory arrangement from her point of view but, unfortunately, the manufacturers had not designed the roof as a couch for a lioness. As a result the supports began to give way under the strain and we found Elsa gradually subsiding on top of us. So George had to rig up extra supports and reinforce the canvas.

When she was not with us, Nuru was still always in charge of Elsa; one day we wanted to film him with her and told him that he should wear something rather smarter than his usual tattered shirt and trousers. In a few minutes he reappeared in a startling, close-fitting cream-coloured jacket, with braid and frogging down the front, which he had bought for his wedding. We thought that he looked just like a professional lion tamer in it. Elsa took one look at him and made at once for the bush; from there she peeped out from behind a shrub until she had established his identity. Then she came up to him and gave him a smack as though to say, 'What the devil do you mean by giving me such a fright?'

115

Nuru and Elsa had many adventures together; for instance, one day Nuru told us that while they were resting under a bush a leopard approached them down wind. Elsa watched eagerly and, although tense with excitement, kept still and controlled herself, except for her tail, until the leopard was nearly on top of her. Then suddenly the animal noticed the switching tail and bolted like lightning, nearly over-running Nuru in its flight.

Elsa was now twenty-three months old and her voice broke to a deep growl. Now she began looking for a mate. Normally she followed us on our walks wherever we went, but for two days she had seemed determined to cross the valley. On this particular afternoon, she led us in *her* direction, and we soon found the fresh pugmarks of a lion. At dark, she refused to return. As we were near a car track, we went back to get the Land-Rover, and George set off in it while I stayed at home in case she took a short cut back. When he reached the place where we had left her, George shouted to her for some time, but there was no response – only the hills echoed his calls. . . . He drove on for another mile, calling at intervals. Then, hoping that Elsa had already come home, he returned. I told him I had waited for two long hours, but that there was still no sign of her, so he left again and some time after he had gone I heard a shot. Until he came back I was very anxious, and then most upset by what he had to tell me.

He had driven out and called for a good half-hour, but Elsa had not shown up. Then he had stopped the car in an opening in the bush, wondering where to look next. Suddenly, some two hundred yards behind the car there had been a great uproar of lions quarrelling. Then, the next moment a lioness flashed by with another in hot pursuit. As they shot past, George seized his rifle and put a bullet under the second animal, assuming, probably rightly, that she was a jealous lioness, bent on Elsa's destruction. Then he jumped into the car and gave chase. He drove along a narrow lane between dense thornbush, flashing a spotlight from side to side, until he was brought up short by a lion and two lionesses, who only very reluctantly moved out of his way, giving vent to loud roars.

Now he had come to fetch me; we drove back to the scene, but though we called desperately for Elsa – called and called – no familiar sound came in answer. But presently, as if in derision, the lion chorus started up a few hundred yards away. We drove towards them until we could see the glint of three pairs of eyes. There was nothing more to be done. So, with heavy hearts, we turned for home. Would Elsa be killed by a jealous lioness? However, to our great relief, we had not gone more than a mile along the track when we came upon Elsa, sniffing at a bush. She utterly ignored us. We tried to persuade her to join us but she remained where we had found her, gazing wistfully into the bush in the direction in which the lions had last been heard. Presently they started calling again, and approached. Thirty yards behind us was a dry river bed, and here the pride stopped, growling vigorously.

It was now well after midnight. Elsa sat in the moonlight between the lions and us; both parties called her to their side. Who was going to win the contest? Suddenly Elsa moved towards the lions and I shouted, 'Elsa, *no*, don't go there, you'll get killed.' She sat down again, looking at us and looking back at her own kind, undecided what to do. For an hour the situation did not alter, then George fired two shots over the lions; this had the effect of sending them off in silence. Then, as Elsa had still not made up her mind, we drove slowly back, hoping that she might follow us; and so she did. Very reluctantly, she walked parallel with the car, looking back many times, till finally she hopped on to the roof and we brought her back to safety. When we arrived home she was very thirsty and exhausted and drank without stopping.

What had happened during the five hours which Elsa had spent with the lions? Would a wild pride accept her in spite of the human smell which she carried? Why had she returned with us instead of joining her own kind? Was it because she was frightened of the fierce lioness? These were some of the questions we asked ourselves. The fact remained that she had come to no harm as a result of this experience.

But after this adventure the call of the wild evidently grew stronger and stronger. Often she did not return with us at dark and we spent many evenings looking for her. In the dry season water was our main hold on her, for this she could only get at the house.

Rocks were her favourite place, and she always chose the top of a cliff or some other safe position as her look-out. Once, in spite of hearing a leopard 'coughing' close by, we had to leave her on such a rock. Next morning she returned with several bleeding scratches and we wondered whether the leopard was responsible for them.

Another time, after sunset, she followed the laughing cries of a hyena; soon these increased to hysterical shrieks to which Elsa replied by loud growls. George rushed to see what was happening and was just in time to shoot one of two hyenas which were closing in on Elsa. After this she pulled her 'kill' into a bush, dragging it between her front legs as she had often done with a groundsheet when she was a cub. But, although she was now two years old, her teeth could not yet penetrate the skin of a hyena, and she did not know what to do with her quarry.

At this age giraffes still remained her favourite friends. She would stalk them, using every stratagem of her kind, but invariably they would spot her before she got too close; this was mainly because Elsa seemed unable to control her tail. Her body would freeze without so much as the twitch of an ear, but the conspicuous black tassel on her tail would never keep still. Once the giraffes had spotted her, there would be a competition to see who would be the boldest among them. One by one, in a half-circle, they would edge forward, giving vent to low, long-drawn snorts, until Elsa could contain herself no longer and would make a rush and put the herd to flight. On two occasions she made a sustained chase after a huge old bull; only after they had gone about a mile the giraffe, either winded or fed up with being chased, turned at bay. Elsa then circled him closely, keeping just out of reach of the mighty pounding forelegs, a blow from which could easily have smashed her skull.

Soon after her adventure with the lions Nuru reported that, when in the morning he tried to follow her, Elsa had growled at him repeatedly. Obviously she wished him to remain behind, while she walked determinedly into the hills. So, in spite of the increasing heat, she had trotted off quickly until he lost her tracks in the rocks. In the afternoon, we followed her spoor, but soon lost it and could only call to her from the foot of the cliffs. A reply came, a strange growl, unlike Elsa's voice but undoubtedly that of a lion. Soon afterwards we saw her struggling downhill, over the boulders, calling in her familiar way. When she reached us she flung herself exhausted on to the ground, panting and very excited. We had brought water with us and she could not have enough of it. Now we noticed several bleeding claw marks on her hind legs, shoulders and neck and also two bleeding perforations on her forehead, which were definitely made by teeth and not by claws.

As soon as she had recovered a little, she greeted us in her customary manner, as well as purring at each of us in turn in a most startling way, as though to say, 'Listen to what I have learned.'

When she had assured herself of our admiration, she threw herself on the ground again and fell fast asleep for two hours. She had obviously just been with a lion when we had interfered by calling to her.

Two days later she spent a whole day and night away, and when we followed her spoor we found her in the company of a lioness; both having laid up several times together.

From this time onwards, Elsa spent more and more nights away. We tried to induce her to come home by driving near to her favourite places and calling to her. Occasionally she came, more often she did not. Sometimes she was away, without food or water, for two or three days. Water was still some hold over her, but soon the rains were due and we realised that when they came we should lose all control of her. This raised a problem which we had to solve; it was one which was made more urgent by the fact that our long overseas leave was due in May. Elsa was now twenty-seven months old, almost full grown. We had always known that we could not keep her free indefinitely at Isiolo. Our original idea had been to send her to join her sisters at the Rotterdam Zoo, and we had even made the necessary arrangements in case an emergency should arise. But now she had taken her future into her own paws and her latest developments were decisive in altering our plans for her. Because we had been so fortunate in bringing her up in her natural environment and because she seemed so much at home in the bush and was accepted by wild animals, we felt that she might well prove to be the exception to the rule that a pet will be killed by its own kind because of its human smell and ignorance of bush life. To release Elsa back to the wild would be an experiment well worth trying.

We intended to spend two or three weeks with her. Then, if all went well, we would take our long leave.

Next we had to consider, *where* to release Elsa? Unfortunately Isiolo was far too populated for us to let her go wild there. But we knew of an area which for most of the year was devoid of inhabitants and livestock but had an abundance of game, especially lion.

We received permission to take Elsa to this place and made the necessary arrangements. The rains were expected any day, so we had no time to lose if she were to reach her possible future home before they began.

In order to get to this area we should have to travel three hundred and forty miles, crossing the highlands on our way and also the great rift valley, going through relatively thickly populated country where there were many European farms. Because we feared that Elsa might be embarrassed by gaping crowds and inquisitive Africans at every halt, and also to avoid the heat of the day, we decided to travel by night. We settled to start about seven in the evening, but Elsa had other ideas. Before setting off we took her out for her usual walk to her favourite rocks, across the valley from our house. There I photographed her for the last time in her home. She is genuinely camera-shy and always hates being filmed or sketched. As soon as she sees one of those awful shiny boxes focused on her she invariably turns her head, or covers it with a paw, or just walks away. On this last day at Isiolo she had to endure a lot from our Leica and plainly got thoroughly fed up with it. So finally she took her revenge. When, for a moment, I left the camera unguarded, she leapt up, sprang upon it and galloped away with it over the rocks. That, we thought, was the end of our precious Leica. For more than an hour we tried every device to rescue it, but as we tried each new trick we had invented for the purpose, she shook it more provokingly between her teeth or chewed at it, holding it firmly between her paws. Finally we recovered it, and miraculously it was not badly damaged.

By then, it was time to get back to the house and start off on the long journey, but just then Elsa sat herself on a rock and gazed across the valley in the contemplative manner of her kind and nothing would move her. Obviously she had no intention of walking back and expected the car to be brought for her. All hope of making an early start was gone. George went home, fetched the car and came back to the foot of the hills where we had left Elsa, but she was no longer there and had apparently gone for her evening stroll. He called to her, but there was no response. Not until eleven at night did she reappear, jump on the roof of the Land-Rover and consent to be driven home.

= ⚬ ◄⊙◄ ⦿ ►⊙► ⚬ =

It was after midnight when we had at last secured Elsa in her travelling crate and started off. In the hope of making the trip easier for her I gave her a tranquilliser; we had been told by the vet that the drug was harmless and that the effect would last about eight hours. To give Elsa all the moral support I could, I travelled with her in the open lorry. During the night we passed through country that is 8,000 feet above sea level, and the cold was icy. Owing to the effect of the tranquilliser Elsa was only semi-conscious, yet even in this state every few minutes she stretched her paws out through the bars of the crate, to assure herself that I was still there. It took us seventeen hours to reach our destination. The effect of the tranquilliser did not wear off until an hour after we had arrived.

It was late in the afternoon by the time we reached our destination; there we were met by a friend who is the Game Warden of this district. We pitched camp on a superb site at the base of a thousand-foot escarpment overlooking a vast plain of open bush country, through which a belt of dark vegetation marks the course of a river. As we were at an altitude of 5,000 feet, the air was fresh and brisk. Immediately in front of our camp lay open grassland sloping towards the plain, on which herds of Thomson's gazelle, topi, wildebeeste, Burchell's zebra, roan antelope, kongoni, and a few buffalo were grazing. It was a game paradise. While the tents were being pitched we took Elsa for a stroll and she rushed at the herds, not knowing which to follow, for in every direction there were animals running. As if to shake off the effects of the ghastly journey, Elsa lost herself among these new playmates, who were rather astonished to find such a strange lion in their midst; one who rushed foolishly to and fro without any apparent purpose. Soon, however, Elsa had had enough and trotted back to camp and her dinner.

Our plan was this; we would spend the first week taking Elsa, perched on the roof of the Land-Rover, round the new country, thus getting her used to it and to the animals, many of which belonged to species which do not live in the Northern Frontier and she had therefore never seen. During the second week we intended to leave her overnight, while she was active in the bush, and to visit and feed her in the mornings when she was sleepy. Afterwards we would reduce her meals, in the hope that this would encourage her to kill on her own, or to join a wild lion.

On the morning after our arrival we started our programme. First we took off her collar, as the symbol of liberation. Elsa hopped on to the roof of the Land-Rover and we went off. After only a few hundred yards we saw a lioness walking parallel to us downhill. We drove closer to her. Elsa displayed much excitement, jumped off her seat and, making low moaning noises, cautiously followed this new friend. But as soon as the lioness stopped and turned round, her courage failed her and she raced back as fast as she could to the safety of the car. The lioness continued her purposeful walk, and we soon detected six cubs waiting for her on a small ant-hill in tall grass.

We drove on and surprised a hyena chewing a bone. Elsa jumped off and chased the startled animal, who had only time to grasp her bone and lumber away. In spite of her ungainliness, the hyena made good her escape but lost her bone in the process.

Later we passed through herd after herd of different antelope, whose curiosity seemed to be aroused by the sight of a Land-Rover with a lion on it and allowed us, provided that we remained in the car and did not talk, to approach within a few yards of them. All the time Elsa watched carefully, but did not attempt to leave the car unless she spotted an animal off guard, grazing with its back towards her, or fighting; then she would get down quietly and creep forward with her belly close to the ground, taking advantage of every bit of cover, and thus advance towards her victim. But as soon as the animal showed any suspicion, she either froze to immobility or, if the situation seemed better handled in another way, she pretended to be uninterested, licked her paws, yawned, or even rolled on her back, until the animal was reassured. Then she would at once start stalking again. But however cunning she was, she never got close enough to kill.

The Owl Service

Alan Garner

It all begins when Alison hears noises in the roof of the old Welsh house. They seem to be too loud for mice or rats. Gwyn goes up into the loft to have a look and finds a pile of plates – in fact a whole dinner service – decorated with an unusual pattern. Peculiar things start to happen when Alison traces the design from the plates and finds it makes the shape of an owl. The paper owls and the pattern on the plates both disappear and it seems that strange and powerful forces are being unleashed in the quiet Welsh valley. Here is the opening of Alan Garner's superb and disturbing novel.

'How's the bellyache, then?'

Gwyn stuck his head round the door. Alison sat in the iron bed with brass knobs. Porcelain columns showed the Infant Bacchus and there was a lump of slate under one leg because the floor dipped.

'A bore,' said Alison. 'And I'm too hot.'

'Tough,' said Gwyn. 'I couldn't find any books, so I've brought one I had from school. I'm supposed to be reading it for Literature, but you're welcome: it looks deadly.'

'Thanks anyway,' said Alison.

'Roger's gone for a swim. You wanting company, are you?'

'Don't put yourself out for me,' said Alison.

'Right,' said Gwyn. 'Cheerio.'

He rode sideways down the banisters on his arms to the first floor landing.

'Gwyn!'
'Yes? What's the matter? You OK?'
'Quick!'
'You want a basin? You going to throw up, are you?'
'Gwyn!'
He ran back. Alison was kneeling on the bed.
'Listen,' she said. 'Can you hear that?'
'That what?'
'That noise in the ceiling. Listen.'
The house was quiet. Mostyn Lewis-Jones was calling after the
sheep on the mountain: and something was scratching in the ceiling
above the bed.
'Mice,' said Gwyn.
'Too loud,' said Alison.
'Rats, then.'
'No. Listen. It's something hard.'
'They want their claws trimming.'
'It's not rats,' said Alison.
'It is rats. They're on the wood: that's why they're so loud.'

'I heard it the first night I came,' said Alison, 'and every night since: a few minutes after I'm in bed.'

'That's rats,' said Gwyn. 'As bold as you please.'

'No,' said Alison. 'It's something trying to get out. The scratching's a bit louder each night. And today – it's the loudest yet – and it's not there all the time.'

'They must be tired by now,' said Gwyn.

'Today – it's been scratching when the pain's bad. Isn't that strange?'

'You're strange,' said Gwyn. He stood on the bed, and rapped the ceiling. 'You up there! Buzz off!'

The bed jangled as he fell, and landed hard, and sat gaping at Alison. His knocks had been answered.

'Gwyn! Do it again!'

Gwyn stood up.

Knock, knock.

Scratch, scratch.

Knock.

Scratch.

Knock knock knock.

Scratch scratch scratch.

Knock – knock knock.

Scratch – scratch scratch.

Gwyn whistled. 'Hey,' he said. 'These rats should be up the Grammar at Aberystwyth.' He jumped off the bed. 'Now where've I seen it? – I know: in the closet here.'

Gwyn opened a door by the bedroom chimney. It was a narrow space like a cupboard, and there was a hatch in the ceiling.

'We need a ladder,' said Gwyn.

'Can't you reach if you stand on the washbasin?' said Alison.

'Too chancy. We need a pair of steps and a hammer. The bolt's rusted in. I'll go and fetch them from the stables.'

'Don't be long,' said Alison. 'I'm all jittery.'

' "Gwyn's Educated Rats": how's that? We'll make a packet on the telly.'

He came back with the step ladder, hammer and a cage trap.

'My Mam's in the kitchen, so I couldn't get bait.'

'I've some chocolate,' said Alison. 'It's fruit and nut.'

'Fine,' said Gwyn. 'Give it us here now.'

He had no room to strike hard with the hammer, and rust and old paint dropped in his face.

'It's painted right over,' he said. 'No one's been up for years. Ah. That's it.'

The bolt broke from its rust. Gwyn climbed down for Alison's
torch. He wiped his face on his sleeve, and winked at her.

'That's shut their racket, anyway.'

As he said this the scratching began on the door over his head,
louder than before.

'You don't have to open it,' said Alison.

'And say goodbye to fame and fortune?'

'Don't laugh about it. You don't have to do it for me. Gwyn, be
careful. It sounds so sharp: strong and sharp.'

'Who's laughing, girlie?' He brought a dry mop from the landing
and placed the head against the door in the ceiling. The scratching
had stopped. He pushed hard, and the door banged open. Dust
sank in a cloud.

'It's light,' said Gwyn. 'There's a pane of glass let in the roof.'

'Do be careful,' said Alison.

' "Is there anybody there? said the Traveller" – Yarawarawara-
warawara!' Gwyn brandished the mop through the hole. 'Nothing,
see.'

He climbed until his head was above the level of the joists. Alison
went to the foot of the ladder.

'A lot of muck and straw. Coming?'

'No,' said Alison. 'I'd get hayfever in that dust. I'm allergic.'

'There's a smell,' said Gwyn: 'a kind of scent: I can't quite – yes:
it's meadowsweet. Funny, that. It must be blowing from the river.
The slates feel red hot.'

'Can you see what was making the noise?' said Alison.

Gwyn braced his hands on either side of the hatch and drew his
legs up.

'It's only a place for the water tanks, and that,' he said. 'No
proper floor. Wait a minute, though!'

'Where are you going? Be careful.' Alison heard Gwyn move
across the ceiling.

In the darkest corner of the loft a plank lay over the joists, and on it was a whole dinner service: squat towers of plates, a mound of dishes, and all covered with grime, straw, droppings and blackened pieces of birds' nests.

'What is it?' said Alison. She had come up the ladder and was holding a handkerchief to her nose.

'Plates. Masses of them.'

'Are they broken?'

'Nothing wrong with them as far as I can see, except muck.

They're rather nice – green and gold shining through the straw.'

'Bring one down, and we'll wash it.'

Alison saw Gwyn lift a plate from the top of the nearest pile, and then he lurched, and nearly put his foot through the ceiling between the joists.

'Gwyn! Is that you?'

'Whoops!'

'Please come down.'

'Right. Just a second. It's so blooming hot up here it made me go sken-eyed.'

He came to the hatch and gave Alison the plate.

'I think your mother's calling you,' said Alison.

Gwyn climbed down and went to the top of the stairs.

'What you want, Mam?'

'Fetch me two lettuce from the kitchen garden!' His mother's voice echoed from below. 'And be sharp now!'

'I'm busy!'

'You are not!'

Gwyn pulled a face. 'You clean the plate,' he said to Alison. 'I'll be right back.' Before he went downstairs Gwyn put the cage trap into the loft and closed the hatch.

'What did you do that for? You didn't see anything, did you?' said Alison.

'No,' said Gwyn. 'But there's droppings. I still want to know what kind of rats it is can count.'

Roger splashed through the shallows to the bank. A slab of rock stood out of the ground close by him, and he sprawled backwards into the foam of meadowsweet that grew thickly round its base. He gathered the stems in his arms and pulled the milky heads down over his face to shield him from the sun.

Through the flowers he could see a jet trail moving across the sky, but the only sounds were the river and a farmer calling sheep somewhere up the valley.

The mountains were gentle in the heat. The ridge above the house, crowned with a grove of fir trees, looked black against the summer light. He breathed the cool sweet air of the flowers. He felt the sun drag deep in his limbs.

Something flew by him, a blink of dark on the leaves. It was heavy, and fast, and struck hard. He felt the vibration through the rock, and he heard a scream.

Roger was on his feet, crouching, hands wide, but the meadow was empty, and the scream was gone: he caught its echo in the farmer's distant voice and a curlew away on the mountain. There was no one in sight: his heart raced, and he was cold in the heat of the sun. He looked at his hands. The meadowsweet had cut him, lining his palm with red beads. The flowers stank of goat.

He leaned against the rock. The mountains hung over him, ready to fill the valley. 'Brrr——' He rubbed his arms and legs with his fists. The skin was rough with gooseflesh. He looked up and down the river, at the water sliding like oil under the trees and breaking on the stones. 'Now what the heck was that? Acoustics? Tricky acoustics? And those hills – they'd addle anyone's brains.' He pressed his back against the rock. 'Don't you move. I'm watching you. That's better——Hello?'

There was a hole in the rock. It was round and smooth, and it went right through from one side to the other. He felt it with his hand before he saw it. Has it been drilled on purpose, or is it a freak? he thought. Waste of time if it isn't natural: crafty precision job, though. 'Gosh, what a fluke!' He had lined himself up with the hole to see if it was straight, and he was looking at the ridge of fir trees above the house. The hole framed the trees exactly. . . . 'Brrrr, put some clothes on.'

Roger walked up through the garden from the river.

Huw Halfbacon was raking the gravel on the drive in front of the house, and talking to Gwyn, who was banging lettuces together to shake the earth from the roots.

'Lovely day for a swim,' said Huw.

'Yes,' said Roger. 'Perfect.'

'Lovely.'

'Yes.'

'You were swimming?' said Huw.

'That's why I'm wearing trunks,' said Roger.

'It is a lovely day for that,' said Huw. 'Swimming.'

'Yes.'

'In the water,' said Huw.

'I've got to get changed,' said Roger.

'I'll come with you,' said Gwyn. 'I want to have a talk.'

'That man's gaga,' said Roger when they were out of hearing.
'He's so far gone he's coming back.'

They sat on the terrace. It was shaded by its own steepness, and
below them the river shone through the trees. 'Hurry up, then,' said
Roger. 'I'm cold.'

'Something happened just now,' said Gwyn. 'There was scratching in the loft over Alison's bedroom.'

'Mice,' said Roger.

'That's what I said. But when I knocked to scare them away –
they knocked back.'

'Get off!'

'They did. So I went up to have a look. There's a pile of dirty
plates up there: must be worth pounds.'

'Oh? That's interesting. Have you brought them down?'

'One. Alison's cleaning it. But what about the scratching?'

'Could be anything. These plates, though: what are they like?
Why were they up there?'

'I couldn't see much. I asked Huw about them.'

'Well?'

'He said, "Mind how you are looking at her." '

'Who? Ali? What's she got to do with it?'

'Not Alison. I don't know who he meant. When I told him I'd
found the plates he stopped raking for a moment and said that:
"Mind how you are looking at her." Then you came.'

'I tell you, the man's off his head. ——Why's he called
Halfbacon, anyway?'

'It's the Welsh: Huw Hannerhob,' said Gwyn. 'Huw Halfbacon:
Huw the Flitch: he's called both.'

'It suits him.'

'It's a nickname,' said Gwyn.

'What's his real name?'

'I don't think he knows. Roger? There's one more thing. I don't
want you to laugh.'

'OK.'

'Well, when I picked up the top plate, I came over all queer. A sort of tingling in my hands, and everything went muzzy – you know how at the pictures it sometimes goes out of focus on the screen and then comes back? It was like that: only when I could see straight again, it was different somehow. Something had changed.'

'Like when you're watching a person who's asleep, and they wake up,' said Roger. 'They don't move, nothing happens, but you know they're awake.'

'That's it!' said Gwyn. 'That's it! Exactly! Better than what I was trying to say! By, you're a quick one, aren't you?'

'Can you tell me anything about a rock with a hole through it down by the river?' said Roger.

'A big slab?' said Gwyn.

'Yes, just in the meadow.'

'It'll be the Stone of Gronw, but I don't know why. Ask Huw. He's worked at the house all his life.'

'No thanks. He'd give me the London Stockmarket Closing Report.'

'What do you want to know for, anyway?' said Gwyn.

'I was sunbathing there,' said Roger. 'Are you coming to see how Ali's managed with your plate?'

'In a sec,' said Gwyn. 'I got to drop these in the kitchen for Mam. I'll see you there.'

Roger changed quickly and went up to Alison. His bedroom was immediately below hers, on the first floor.

She was bending over a plate which she had balanced on her knees. The plate was covered with a sheet of paper and she was drawing something with a pencil.

'What's this Gwyn says you've found?' said Roger.

'I've nearly finished,' said Alison. She kept moving the paper as she drew. 'There! What do you think of that?' She was flushed.

Roger took the plate and turned it over. 'No maker's mark,' he said. 'Pity. I thought it might have been a real find. It's ordinary stuff: thick: not worth much.'

'Thick yourself! Look at the pattern!'

'Don't you see what it is?'

'An abstract design in green round the edge, touched with a bit of rough gilding.'

'Roger! You're being stupid on purpose! Look at that part. It's an owl's head.'

'—Yes? I suppose it is, if you want it to be. Three leafy heads with this kind of abstract flowery business in between each one. Yes: I suppose so.'

'It's not abstract,' said Alison. 'That's the body. If you take the design off the plate and fit it together it makes a complete owl. See. I've traced the two parts of the design, and all you do is turn the head right round till it's the other way up, and then join it to the top of the main pattern where it follows the rim of the plate. There you are. It's an owl – head, wings and all.'

'So it's an owl,' said Roger. 'An owl that's been sat on.'

'You wait,' said Alison, and she began to cut round the design with a pair of scissors. When she had finished she pressed the head forward, bent and tucked in the splayed legs, curled the feet and perched the owl on the edge of her candlestick.

Roger laughed. 'Yes! It is! An owl!'

It was an owl: a stylised, floral owl. The bending of its legs had curved the back, giving the body the rigid set of an owl. It glared from under heavy brows.

'No, that's really good,' said Roger. 'How did you think it all out – the tracing, and how to fold it?'

'I saw it as soon as I'd washed the plate,' said Alison. 'It was obvious.'

'It was?' said Roger. 'I'd never have thought of it. I like him.'

'Her,' said Alison.

'You can tell? OK. Her. I like her.' He tapped the owl's head with the pencil, making the body rock on its perch. 'Hello there!'

'Don't do that,' said Alison.

'What?'

'Don't touch her.'

'Are you all right?'

'Give me the pencil. I must make some more,' said Alison.

'I put the lettuce by the sink,' Gwyn called. 'I'm going to see Alison.'

'You wait, boy,' said his mother. 'Them lettuce need washing. I only got one pair of hands.'

Gwyn slashed the roots into the pig bucket and ran water in the sink. His mother came through from the larder. She was gathering herself to make bread. Gwyn tore the leaves off the lettuce and flounced them into the water. Neither of them spoke for a long time.

'I told you be sharp with them lettuce,' said his mother. 'You been back to Aber for them?'

'I was talking,' said Gwyn.

'Oh?'

'To Roger.'

'You was talking to Halfbacon,' said his mother. 'I got eyes.'

'Well?'

'I told you have nothing to do with him, didn't I?'

'I only stopped for a second.'

'You keep away from that old fool, you hear me? I'm telling you, boy!'

'He's not all that old,' said Gwyn.

'Don't come that with me,' said his mother. 'You want a backhander? You can have it.'

'There's slugs in this lettuce,' said Gwyn.

'You was speaking Welsh, too.'

'Huw doesn't manage English very clever. He can't say what he means.'

'You know I won't have you speaking Welsh. I've not struggled all these years in Aber to have you talk like a labourer. I could have stayed in the valley if I'd wanted that.'

'But Mam, I got to practise! It's exams next year.'

'If I'd known you was going to be filled with that squit you'd never have gone the Grammar.'

'Yes, Mam. You keep saying.'

'What was you talking about, then?'

'I was only asking Huw if he could tell me why those plates were in the roof above Alison's room.'

The silence made Gwyn look round. His mother was leaning against the baking board, one hand pressed to her side.

'You not been up in that roof, boy.'

'Yes. Alison was – a bit bothered, so I went up, and found these plates. I didn't touch – only one. She's cleaning it.'

'That Alison!' said Gwyn's mother, and made for the stairs, scraping her floury arms down her apron. Gwyn followed.

They heard Alison and Roger laughing. Gwyn's mother knocked at the bedroom door, and went in.

Alison and Roger were playing with three flimsy cut out paper models of birds. One was on the candlestick, and the other two were side by side on a chair back. The plate Gwyn had brought from the loft was next to Alison's pillows and covered with scraps of paper. Alison pushed the plate behind her when Gwyn's mother came in.

'Now, Miss Alison, what's this about plates?'

'Plates, Nancy?'

'If you please.'

'What plates, Nancy?'

'You know what I mean, Miss Alison. Them plates from the loft.'

'What about them?'

'Where are they?'

'There's only one, Mam,' said Gwyn.

'Gwyn!' said Alison.

'I'll trouble you to give me that plate, Miss.'

'Why?'

'You had no right to go up there.'

'I didn't go.'

'Nor to send my boy up, neither.'

'I didn't send him.'

'Excuse me,' said Roger. 'I've things to do.' He ducked out of the room.

'I'll thank you not to waste my time, Miss Alison. Please to give me that plate.'

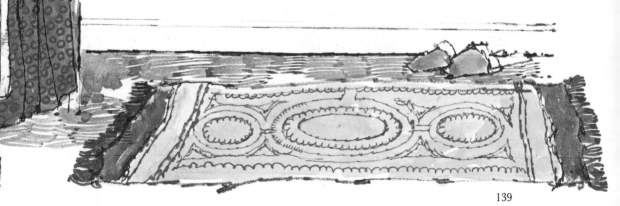

'Nancy, you're hissing like an old goose.'

'Please to give me that plate, Miss Alison.'

'Whose house is this, anyway?' said Alison.

Gwyn's mother drew herself up. She went over to the bed and held out her hand. 'If you please. I seen where you put it under your pillow.'

Alison sat stiffly in the bed. Gwyn thought that she was going to order his mother from the room. But she reached behind her and pulled out the plate, and threw it on the bed. Gwyn's mother took it. It was a plain white plate, without decoration.

'Very well, Miss Alison. Ve-ry well!'

Nancy went from the room with the plate in her hand. Gwyn stood at the door and gave a silent whistle.

'You ever played Find the Lady, have you?' he said. ' "Now you see it, now you don't". Who taught you that one, girlie?'

'You've caused a right barny,' said Roger. 'Nancy's been throwing her apron over her head and threatening I don't know what, your mother's had a fit of the vapours, and now Nancy's on her dignity. She's given my Dad her notice three times already.'

'Why doesn't he accept it?' said Alison.

'You should know Dad by now,' said Roger. 'Anything for a quiet life: that's why he never gets one. But you'd a nerve, working that switch on her. Pity she knew the plates were decorated. How did you manage it?'

'I didn't,' said Alison.

'Come off it.'

'I didn't. That was the plate I traced the owls from.'

'But Gwyn says you gave Nancy an ordinary white one.'

'The pattern disappeared.'

Roger began to laugh, then stopped.

'You're serious, aren't you?'

Alison nodded.

'Ali, it's not possible,' said Roger. 'The plate was glazed: the pattern was under the glaze. It couldn't rub off.'

'But it did,' said Alison.

'But it couldn't, little step-sister. I'll show you.'

Roger climbed the ladder and opened the trap door.

'It's too dark. Where's your torch?'

'Here,' said Alison. 'Can you see the plates? They're in a corner over to your left.'

'Yes. I'll bring a couple to prove they're all the same.'

'Bring more. As many as you can. Let's have them. Hand them down to me.'

'Better not,' said Roger: 'after the tizz. But I don't think these'll be missed.'

'Mind the joists,' said Alison. 'Gwyn nearly fell through the ceiling there. It was queer.'

'I bet it was!'

'No. Really queer. He slipped when he touched the plate, and he went all shadowy. Just for a second it didn't look like Gwyn.'

'It's the darkest part of the loft,' said Roger.

They washed the plates and took them to the window. Roger scrubbed the glaze with a nail brush. 'The glaze is shot,' he said. He picked at it with his finger nail. 'It comes off easily.'

'All right,' said Alison. 'I want to trace these owls before the light goes. I'm making them properly this time, out of stiff paper.'

'Not more!' said Roger. 'Why do you want more? Where are the three you did earlier?'

'I couldn't find them.'

'If you're going to start that drawing again, I'm off,' said Roger. 'When you've done one you've done them all. Shall I take your supper things down?'

'I've not had supper,' said Alison.

'Hasn't Dad been up with your tray?'

'No.'

Roger grinned. 'Your mother sent him to do the stern father act.'

'He's not come.'

'Good old Dad,' said Roger.

Roger went downstairs and out through the kitchen to the back of the house. He listened at the door of a long building that had once been the dairy but was now a billiard-room. He heard the click of ivory.

Roger opened the door. His father was playing snooker by himself in the dusk. A supper tray was on an armchair.

'Hello, Dad,' said Roger.

'Jolly good,' said father.

'I'll light the lamps for you.'

'No need. I'm only pottering.'

Roger sat on the edge of the chair. His father moved round the table, trundling the balls into the pockets, under the eyes of the falcons and buzzards, otters, foxes, badgers and pine martens that stared from their glass cases on the wall.

'Don't they put you off your game?' said Roger.

'Ha ha; yes.'

'This room was the dairy, wasn't it?'

'Oooh, yes, I dare say.'

'Gwyn was telling me. He thinks it might have been the original house before that – an open hall, with everybody living together.'

'Really?' said his father. 'Fancy that.'

'It often happens, Gwyn says. The original house becomes an outbuilding.'

'Damn,' said Roger's father. 'I'm snookered.' He straightened up and chalked his cue. 'Yes: rum old place, this.'

'It's that olde worlde wall panelling that gets me,' said Roger. 'I mean, why cover something genuine with that phoney stuff?'

'I thought it was rather tasteful, myself,' said his father.

'All right,' said Roger. 'But why go and pebble-dash a piece of the wall? Pebble-dash! Inside!' A rectangle of wall near the door was encrusted with mortar.

'I've seen worse than that,' said his father. 'When I started in business I was on the road for a few years, and there was one Bed-and-Breakfast in Kendal that was grey pebble-dashed all over inside. Fifteen-watt bulbs, too, I remember, in every room. We called it Wookey Hole.'

'But at least it was all over,' said Roger. 'Why just this piece of wall?'

'Damp?'

'The walls are a yard thick.'

'Still,' said his father, 'it must be some weakness somewhere. It's cracked.'

'Is it? It wasn't this morning.'

'Right across, near the top.'

'That definitely wasn't there this morning,' said Roger. 'I was teaching Gwyn billiards. We tried to work out what the pebble-dash was for. I looked very closely. It wasn't cracked.'

'Ah, well it is now,' said his father. 'Not much use doing any more tonight. Let's pack up.'

They collected the balls, stacked the cues and rolled the dust sheet over the table.

'Would you like me to take Ali her supper?' said Roger.

'Yes – er: no: no: I said I would: I'd better. Margaret thinks I ought. She's a bit upset by the fuss.'

'How's Nancy?'

'Phew! That was a real up-and-downer while it lasted! But I think we've managed. A fiver cures most things. She's dead set against some plates or other – I didn't understand what any of it was about. No: I'd better go and chat up old Ali.'

Alison was cutting out the last owl when she heard her step-father bringing the supper tray. She had arranged the plates on the mantelpiece and had perched the owls about the room as she finished them. He pushed the door open with his shoulder and came in backwards.

'Grub up!'

'Thanks, Clive,' said Alison. 'What is it?'

'Nancy's Best Limp Salad, with sheep-dip mayonnaise.' He put the tray by the bed and lit the lamp. 'I say, these are jolly fellows. What are they?'

'Owls. I made them.'

'They're rather fun.'

'Yes.'

'Well – er: how are the gripes?'

'Much better, thanks.'

'Good. Up and about in the morning?'

'What sort of a day did you and Mummy have?' said Alison.

'Didn't catch anything, and one of the waders leaked, but I've great hopes of tomorrow. Old Halfwhatsit says he knows a stretch of the river where they always bite.'

'I bet he didn't say where it is.'

'Er – no. No, he didn't.'

'Have you been sent to tell me off about Nancy?'

'What? Oh. Ha ha,' said Clive.

'I don't know why she was going on like that,' said Alison, 'and I didn't see it had anything to do with her. Gwyn found some of those plates in the loft, and she came storming up as if she owned the place.'

'Yes. Well. Old Nance, eh? You know——'

'But she went berserk, Clive!'

'Too true. We had a basinful when we came home, I'll tell you!

Your mother's very upset. She says you ought to – oh well, skip it.'

'But it's my house, isn't it?' said Alison.

'Ah yes.'

'Well then.'

'It's a bit dodgy. If your father hadn't turned it over to you before he died your mother would've had to sell this house to clear the death duties. Morbid, but there it is.'

'But it's still my house,' said Alison. 'And I don't have to take orders from my cook.'

'Fair do's,' said Clive. 'Think of your mother. It was hard enough to get someone to live in all summer. If Nance swept out we'd never find a replacement, and your mother would have to cope by herself. She'd be very upset. And it is the first time we've all been together – as a family, and – and – you know?'

'Yes, Clive. I suppose so.'

'That's my girl. Now eat your supper. ——Hello: sounds as if we've mice in the roof.'

'Don't wait, Clive,' said Alison. 'I'm not hungry. I'll eat this later, and bring the tray down in the morning. Tell Mummy not to worry.'

'That's my girl. God bless.'

145

Mrs Frisby and the Rats of NIMH

Robert C. O'Brien

Mrs Frisby, a widowed field mouse, and her four children have their winter home in a farmer's garden. When young Timothy Frisby falls ill, Mrs Frisby risks encountering the cat Dragon to visit the wise, old, white mouse Mr Ages. He gives her some medicine but warns her Timothy might die if he is moved within three weeks. Only a few days later however, Mrs Frisby sees the farmer getting ready to plough the garden, which will destroy their home! In desperation, she asks the advice of the owl who, learning she is the widow of Jonathan Frisby, tells her to go to the rats who live under the rose bush for help. There she meets Mr Ages (who has broken his ankle), and the rat Justin.

The tunnel led gently downwards, and after the first dozen steps they were in darkness. Mrs Frisby could see nothing at all. Behind her Mr Ages limped along; ahead she could hear the scuffle of Justin's footsteps. She followed the sound blindly. Then she heard his voice.

'Just walk straight forward, Mrs Frisby. There's nothing to trip over, and nothing to bump into. If you get off course, you'll feel the wall.' He added: 'The dark part doesn't last long.'

Now what did he mean by that? She thought it over for a minute or two as she walked and had just decided to ask him, when to her surprise she saw ahead of her a faint glow. A light! But how could there be a light down so far? 'There, we're through it,' said Justin cheerfully. 'I know that blackout bit must be annoying the first time, but it's necessary.'

'But aren't we under the ground?'

'Oh yes. About three feet down by now, I'd guess.'

'Then how can it be light?'

'I could tell you,' Justin said, 'but if you'll wait fifteen seconds, you'll see for yourself.'

In a few more steps the tunnel – Mrs Frisby could now discern, dimly, its shape and direction – took a turn to the right, and she did see for herself. She stopped in astonishment.

Ahead of her stretched a long, well-lit hallway. Its ceiling and walls were a smoothly curved arch, its floor hard and flat, with a soft layer of carpet down the middle. The light came from the walls, where every foot or so on both sides a tiny light bulb had been recessed and the hole in which it stood, like a small window, had been covered with a square of coloured glass – blue, green or yellow. The effect was that of stained-glass windows in sunlight.

Justin was watching her and smiling. 'Do you like it? The carpet and the coloured glass we don't really need. Some of the wives did that on their own, just for looks. They cut the glass, believe it or not, from old bottles. The carpet was a piece of trim they found somewhere.'

'It's beautiful,' Mrs Frisby said. 'But how . . .'

'We've had electricity for years now.'

'Five,' said Mr Ages.

'Five,' said Justin agreeably. 'The lights' – they were the very small, very bright twinkling kind – 'we found on trees. In fact, most of our lights come from trees. Not until after Christmas, of course – about New Year. The big light bulbs we have trouble handling.'

Mrs Frisby was familiar with electricity (her husband, who knew all kinds of thing, had once explained it to her). At night she had seen the lamps shining in Mr Fitzgibbon's house, and at Christmas time the lights that his sons strung on a pine tree outside.

'You mean you just took them?' she asked.

'We were careful to take only a few from each tree,' said Mr Ages.

'It was like picking fruit,' Justin said rather dreamily. 'The annual light bulb harvest. We had to go quite far up the road before we had enough. Even so, it took two Christmases.'

'Justin,' said Mr Ages, 'I think we'd better get on.'

They continued along the corridor, which curved always slightly to the right, so Mrs Frisby could never really tell how long it was, and which soon began to incline more steeply into the ground. Mrs Frisby noticed that the air, which should have been dank and damp so deep underground, was on the contrary fresh and clean, and she thought she could even detect a very faint breeze blowing past her ears as she moved.

In a few more minutes the hall widened abruptly into a large oval chamber. Here the lights were set in the ceiling; at the far end, Mrs Frisby could see, the long tunnel continued and looked as if it slanted upward again – perhaps to another entrance, a back door. Was this, then, their destination, the main hall of the rats? But if so, where were all the other rats? The room was entirely empty – not even a stick of furniture.

'A storeroom,' said Justin. 'Sometimes full. Now empty.'

Then she saw that off one side of the chamber there was a stairway leading down, and beside it a small door. Justin led them to the door.

'For freight only,' he said with a grin at Mr Ages. 'But considering your limp, I think we can make an exception. The stairs wouldn't be easy.'

Mrs Frisby looked at the stairway. It went down in a spiral and each step was neatly inlaid with a rectangular piece of slate. She could not tell how far down it led, since after the first turn of the spiral she could see no more, but she had a feeling it was a long way down. As Justin said, it would be hard for Mr Ages.

Justin opened the door. It led into a square room that looked like a cupboard.

'After you,' he said. Mrs Frisby went in, the others followed, and the door swung shut. On the wall were two knobs. Justin pushed one of them, and Mrs Frisby, who had never been in a lift before, gasped and almost fell as she felt the floor suddenly sink beneath her feet. Justin reached out a hand to steady her.

'It's all right,' he said. 'I should have warned you.'

'But we're falling!'

'Not quite. We're going down, but we've got two strong cables and an electric motor holding us.'

Still, Mrs Frisby held her breath during the rest of the descent, until finally the small lift came to a gentle stop and Justin opened the door. Then she breathed again and looked out.

The room before her was at least three times as big as the one they had just left, and corridors radiated from it in as many directions as petals from a daisy. Directly opposite the lift an open arch led into what looked like a still larger room – seemingly some kind of an assembly hall, for it had a raised platform at one end.

And now there were rats. Rats by dozens – standing and talking in groups of twos and threes and fours, rats walking slowly, rats hurrying, rats carrying papers. As Mrs Frisby stepped from the elevator, it became obvious that strangers were a rarity down there, for the hubbub of a dozen conversations stopped abruptly, and all heads turned to look at her. They did not look hostile, nor were they alarmed – since her two companions were familiar to them – but merely curious. Then, as quickly as it had died out, the sound of talking began again, as if the rats were too polite to stand and stare. But one of them, a lean rat with a scarred face, left his group and walked towards them.

'Justin. Mr Ages. And I see we have a guest.' He spoke graciously, with an air of quiet dignity, and Mrs Frisby noticed two more things about him. First, the scar on his face ran across his left eye, and over this eye he wore a black patch, fastened by a cord around his head. Second, he carried a satchel – rather like a handbag – by a strap over his shoulders.

'A guest whose name you will recognize,' said Justin. 'She is Mrs Jonathan Frisby. Mrs Frisby, this is Nicodemus.'

'A name I recognize indeed,' said the rat called Nicodemus. 'Mrs Frisby – are you perhaps aware of this? – your late husband was one of our greatest friends. You are welcome here.'

'Thank you,' said Mrs Frisby, but she was more puzzled than ever. 'In fact, I did not know that you knew my husband. But I'm glad to hear it, because I've come to ask your help.'

'Mrs Frisby has a problem,' said Mr Ages. 'An urgent one.'

'If we can help you, we will,' said Nicodemus. He asked Mr Ages: 'Can it wait until after the meeting? An hour? We were just ready to begin again.'

Mr Ages considered. 'An hour will make no difference, I think.'

Nicodemus said: 'Justin, show Mrs Frisby to the library, where she can be comfortable until the meeting is over.'

By this time the last of the other assembled rats had made their way into the large meeting hall, where they sat facing the raised platform. Nicodemus followed them, pulling some papers and a small reading glass from the satchel at his side as he walked to the front of the room.

Justin led Mrs Frisby in another direction, down a corridor to their left, and again she had the impression of a faint, cool breeze against her face. She realized that the corridor she had walked in up above was merely a long entrance-way, and that the halls around her were the rats' real living quarters. The one down which Justin led her was lined with doors, one of which he opened.

'In here,' he said. The room they entered was big, square, well lit, and had a faint musty smell. 'It's reasonably comfortable, and if you like to read ...' he gestured at the walls. They were lined with shelves from floor to ceiling, and on the shelves stood – Mrs Frisby dredged in her memory. 'Books,' she said. 'They're books.'

'Yes.' said Justin. 'Do you read much?'

'Only a little,' said Mrs Frisby. 'My husband taught me. And the children ...' She started to tell him how. Laboriously scratching letters in the earth with a stick – it seemed so long ago. But Justin was leaving.

'Excuse me – I've got to go to the meeting. I hate meetings, but this one's important. We're finishing up the schedule for the Plan.' he pronounced it with a capital P.

'The Plan?'

But he was out of the door, closing it gently behind him.

Mrs Frisby looked around her. The room – the library, Nicodemus had called it – had, in addition to its shelves of books, several tables with benches beside them, and on these were stacked more books, some of them open.

Books. Her husband, Jonathan, had told her about them. He had taught her and the children to read (the children had mastered it quickly, but she herself could barely manage the simplest words; she had thought perhaps it was because she was older). He had also told her about electricity. He had known these things – and so, it emerged, did the rats. It had never occurred to her until now to wonder *how* he knew them. He had always known so many things, and she had accepted that as a matter of course. But who had taught him to read? Strangely, it also emerged that he had known the rats. Had they taught him? What had been his connection with them? She remembered his long visits with Mr Ages. And Mr Ages knew the rats, too.

She sighed. Perhaps when the meeting was over and she had had a chance to talk to Nicodemus – and had told him about Timothy and Moving Day – perhaps when that was settled, he could explain all this to her.

She noticed at the far end of the room a section of wall where there were no bookshelves. There was, instead, a blackboard, covered with words and numbers written in white chalk. There were pieces of chalk and an eraser in a rack at the bottom of it. The blackboard stood near the end of the longest of the tables. Was the library also used as a classroom? When she looked at the blackboard and, rather laboriously, read what was written on it, she saw that it was not. It was, rather, a conference room. At the top of the board, in large letters, were printed the words: THE PLAN OF THE RATS OF NIMH.

Mrs Frisby spelled it out slowly: The Plan of the Rats of Nimh. What, or where, was Nimh? The name had a strange and faraway sound. Had these rats, then, come here from somewhere else? Did that explain why they had books and electric lights and wires and an electric motor? Yet they had been here – or at least there had been rats here – for as long as she could remember. Still, that was not so very long.

She wondered what other things they had. Suddenly she had an almost overwhelming desire to look around – to see what was behind the other doors and down the other corridors. She went to the door, opened it, and looked out into the hall. It was entirely deserted and silent, except that when she listened carefully she could hear a faint humming in the distance, as if something were running – another motor?

She started out into the hall, and then changed her mind. Better not. Nicodemus had been friendly – they had all been friendly – but explicit. He had said she was to wait in the library. And she was not there to pry but to get help. She went back into the library, closed the door, and sat on one of the benches. The books on the table were mostly paperbacks – small enough so that the rats could handle them easily enough, but too big for her; so she sat in front of the blackboard and looked at it again.

Beneath the title across the top, in neatly chalked handwriting, were columns of words and figures;

SCHEDULE

January:
Group 1 (10): Oats.   30 loads = 2 bu.
Group 2 (10): Wheat.   30 loads = 2 bu.
Group 3 (10): Corn.   20 loads = 1½ bu.
Group 4 (10): Misc. seeds   Est. 10 loads total

The rest of the blackboard was filled with more rows of figures, each headed by the name of a month: February, March, April, May, and so on until the end of July. At the bottom a separate square was ruled off:

Ploughs (Arthur's group) (14)

Plough No. 2. Complete: Jan. 1
Plough No. 3. Complete: Feb. 10
Plough No. 4. Complete: Mar. 20

Mrs Frisby stared at all this, trying to make head or tail of it, but she could not. It was quite incomprehensible.

She was still puzzling over it when the door opened and a rat came in. It was a girl-rat, small and quite young, judging by her looks. She was carrying a pencil and some papers and looking at the papers as she walked, so that she did not see Mrs Frisby at first. When she did she gasped and dropped the papers, scattering them on the floor. Her eyes opened wide.

'Who are you?' she asked. 'I don't know you. How did you get in?' She backed towards the door.

'It's all right,' said Mrs Frisby. 'I'm a friend of Mr Ages.' The rat was very young indeed, only a child.

'But why are you in here? Who let you in?'

'Nicodemus. He told me to wait here.'

The girl-rat looked doubtful. 'You might be a spy.'

'A spy! How could I be? A spy from where?'

'I don't know. From outside. Maybe from Nimh?'

'I don't even know what Nimh is.'

'That's what you *say*.'

'But I don't. What is it?' asked Mrs Frisby, feeling slightly annoyed.

'It's a place.' The girl-rat, her alarm apparently subsiding, began

picking up her scattered papers. 'I'm supposed to be practising my reading.'

'What kind of a place?'

'It's where we came from. I don't know too much about it. I've never been there.'

'How can you come from there if you've never been there?'

'My father and mother did. I was born afterwards. I think it's white. Anyway, I know one thing. We don't want to go back. We don't want to get caught.'

So, Mrs Frisby thought – that sounds as if, whatever Nimh was, the rats had escaped from it to come here. But she realized that she was not likely to get very clear information from such a child. Again, she hoped that Nicodemus would explain it.

'Did Nicodemus come from Nimh, too?'

'Yes.'

'And Justin?'

'Yes. You know Justin?'

'Yes.'

'I suppose you're not a spy,' said the girl-rat. She sounded mildly disappointed. Then she added irrelevantly: 'Justin's not married.' She climbed on one of the benches and opened a book. 'He's the best one of all. He's not even afraid of Dragon.' She read in the book for perhaps thirty seconds, picked up her pencil, then put it down again. 'I'm too young to get married.'

'I suppose so,' said Mrs Frisby. 'For a while yet. But that won't last long.'

'That's what my mother says. But it *seems* long. And Justin might marry somebody else.'

'Maybe not,' said Mrs Frisby, who could see beyond the tip of her nose. 'He's pretty young himself yet. What's your name?'

'Isabella.'

'It's a pretty name.'

'It's all right. Only my brother calls me Izzy. I don't like that.'

'I don't wonder. Where's your brother?'

'At the meeting. He's older. All the men are at the meeting. But my mother didn't go. The mothers don't always go. She's in the grain room, packing grain.'

'Packing grain?'

'For the Plan. She doesn't like the Plan, though.'

The Plan again.

'What is the Plan? Why doesn't she like it?'

'It's just – the Plan. For where we're going to live and all that. She doesn't like it because she says it's too hard – no more electric lights, no more refrigerator, no more running water. But she isn't deserting or anything. Not like Jenner. We didn't like Jenner.'

'Who's Jenner?'

'He was in the group, but he quit. Maybe he went back to Nimh. We don't know.'

Mrs Frisby was gradually getting a picture of life in the rat colony – a somewhat confusing one because Isabella was a child, but nonetheless certain things were apparent: They had a grain room (presumably for food storage); the females sometimes went to meetings and sometimes not; Nicodemus seemed to be the leader; they had a Plan for the future that some rats did not like; and one, named Jenner, had deserted. Or had others gone with him? She was about to ask Isabella when the library door opened and Nicodemus, Justin, and Mr Ages entered. Another rat came with them, a stranger.

The strange rat was named Arthur. He was stocky, square and muscular, with bright, hard eyes. He looked efficient.

'You might call him our chief engineer,' said Nicodemus to Mrs Frisby, 'as, indeed, you might call Justin the captain of the guard – if we had any such titles, but we don't. Mr Ages thought Arthur should come along, though he didn't say why. So we still don't know what your problem is.'

Isabella was gone. She had dropped her papers on the floor again when the others had entered, and Justin, to her intense confusion and visible delight, had helped her pick them up.

'Hello, Izzy,' he said. 'How's the reading coming?'

'It's fine,' she said. 'I finished the Third Reader last week. Now I'm on the Fourth.'

'The Fourth Reader already! You're getting quite grown up!' At that she had almost dropped the papers a third time and made a dash for the door. It did not matter, Mrs Frisby noticed, if Justin called her Izzy – just so long as he called her something.

Nicodemus closed the door behind her, then sat down on one of the benches, facing Mrs Frisby; the others sat down, too, Mr Ages stretching his splinted leg in front of him. Nicodemus took the reading glass from his satchel, opened it, and through it gravely examined Mrs Frisby's face. 'You will forgive the glass and the scrutiny,' he said. 'When I lost my left eye, I also damaged the right one; I can see little close-up without the glass – indeed, not very much even with it.' At length he folded the glass and put it on the table.

'Now,' he said, 'what is it we can do to help you?'

So Mrs Frisby recounted once more the events that had led to her coming there, and at the end repeated what the owl had advised her to say – 'move the house into the lee of the stone.'

She added: 'I don't understand just what he meant by that. Jeremy – the crow – says it means the side where there's no wind. But what good would that do?'

'I think I know what he meant,' said Nicodemus. 'In a broad sense, lee means the sheltered side. A bird, flying over Mr Fitzgibbon's garden, would notice something most of us would miss.'

He reached down into his satchel and took out a sheet of paper and a pencil; he opened the reading glass again. As he talked, he drew a sketch:

'When a farmer ploughs a field with a big rock in it, he ploughs around the rock – close on each side, leaving a triangle of unploughed land on each end.

'Mrs Frisby's house is beside the rock, and will get ploughed up – and probably crushed, as the owl said. But if we can move it a few feet – so that it lies buried *behind* the rock – in the lee – then she and her children can stay in it as long as they need to.

'From the air, the way the owl sees it, the garden would look like that.' He inspected the sketch through the reading glass and then placed it on the table.

Mrs Frisby climbed up on the bench and looked at it. It was a rough map, showing the garden, the big stone near the middle, and the way the furrows made by the plough would curve around it, rather like waves around a boat.

'Show me where your house is buried,' said Nicodemus. Mrs Frisby pointed to the spot on the sketch.

'I know where that cement block is,' said the rat named Arthur. 'In fact, I thought about bringing it in, but I decided it was too long a haul. They had it tied on top of the harrow for weight, and it fell off just as they were finishing the garden.'

'Can you move it,' asked Nicodemus, pointing at the sketch, 'To this spot right there, and bury it again?'

'Yes,' said Arthur. 'That shouldn't be hard.'

Mrs Frisby was delighted; looking at the map, it all became clear, and she could see what a beautifully simple idea it was. When Mr Fitzgibbon ploughed, he would go right past their house; they would not have to move until Timothy was well and until the weather was truly warm. She remembered again what her husband had said – how easy to unlock a door when you have the key. She had found the key. Or rather, the owl had found it.

Nicodemus asked Arthur: 'How long will it take?'

'Depends. With a party of ten, a couple of hours. With twenty, maybe an hour.'

'We can spare twenty. But it's still too long.' He looked worried.

So did Arthur. 'Yes,' he said. 'We'll have to work at night – but even so . . . There's just no cover at all. It's wide open.'

'We'll have to take care of Dragon,' said Justin.

'Yes,' said Mr Ages, 'and with this leg, I can't do it. I'd never make it to the bowl, much less get back again.'

Mrs Frisby, looking at their baffled faces, felt her delight subsiding. Obviously something was wrong.

'I don't understand,' she said. 'I know about Dragon, of course, but . . .'

'At night,' said Justin, 'Dragon prowls the farmyard like a tiger. And you don't see him until he's on top of you.'

'Then you can't move my house after all.'

'Well,' Justin said, 'ordinarily . . .' He turned to Nicodemus. 'Should I explain it to her?'

'Yes,' said Nicodemus.

'Ordinarily,' said Justin, 'when we have a long project to do at night – sometimes even by day – we make sure Dragon won't bother us: We put sleeping powder in his food. Mr Ages makes it. It doesn't do the cat any harm; but he stays extremely drowsy for the next eight hours or so. We station a sentry to watch him, and we're free to work.'

'You did it yesterday!' cried Mrs Frisby, remembering the figures toiling with the wire through the grass, remembering how strangely disinterested Dragon had seemed when he saw her. 'I saw the cat sleeping in the yard.'

'Yes,' said Justin, 'but today Mr Ages has a broken leg.'

'Then he can't make the powder?'

'It isn't that,' said Mr Ages. 'I've plenty of powder.'

'The trouble is,' said Justin, 'it's Mr Ages who puts it in Dragon's dinner bowl, inside the farm kitchen. With his leg broken, he can't move fast enough.'

'But why Mr Ages?' said Mrs Frisby. 'Can't someone else do it?'

'I'd be glad to do it myself,' said Justin, 'but I'm too big.'

'You see,' Nicodemus explained, 'Mrs Fitzgibbon feeds the cat in the morning and in the evening, and his bowl is always kept in the same place – next to a cabinet in one corner of the kitchen. There's a very shallow space between the floor and the bottom of the cabinet. A few years ago when we conceived the idea of putting Dragon to sleep, we cut a hole in the floor just behind the cabinet – if we put it anywhere else they'd see it. To reach the bowl, Mr Ages crawls under the cabinet. When he gets to the edge, he makes a quick dash to the bowl, drops in the powder, and dashes back out of sight. But with a broken leg, he can't dash.'

'We might try leaving some bait outside the house,' said Justin. 'That worked once.'

'Once out of a dozen tries,' said Nicodemus. 'It isn't dependable, and we don't have much time. To be safe, we ought to move that block tonight.'

'If we had some catfood . . .' said Justin, thinking aloud. 'He might eat that, even on the porch, because he knows it's his. Maybe tonight I could go in through the attic and down to the kitchen . . .'

'No use,' said Mr Ages. 'They keep it in a metal cabinet up on the wall. You couldn't get it without a crew. And that would make too much noise.'

'Anyway,' said Nicodemus, 'it would put off moving the block until tomorrow night.'

'Then,' Justin said, 'I guess what we do is stake our scouts wherever we can, try to keep track of Dragon, and hope for the best. Some nights he doesn't go near the garden at all. We might be lucky.'

'Or we might not,' said Arthur. 'I don't like it. We can't dig that block out without some noise, you know.'

Mrs Frisby interrupted quietly. 'There is another way,' she said. 'If Mr Ages can get into the kitchen, so can I. If you will give me the powder and show me the way, I will try to put it in Dragon's bowl.'

Justin said quickly: 'No. It's no job for a lady.'

'You forget,' Mrs Frisby said. 'I'm Timothy's mother. If you, and Arthur, and others in your group can take risks to save him, surely I can, too. And consider this: I don't want any of you to be hurt – maybe even killed – by Dragon. But even more, I don't want the attempt to fail. Perhaps the worst that will happen to you, with luck, is that you will have to scatter and run, and leave my house unmoved. But then what will happen to us? Timothy, at least, will die. So if there is no one else to put the cat to sleep, I must do it.'

Nicodemus considered, and then spoke:

'She's right, of course. If she chooses to take the risk, we can't deny her the right.' To Mrs Frisby he added: 'But you should know that the danger is great. It was in the same kitchen yesterday, running from Dragon's bowl, that Mr Ages got his leg broken. And it was in doing the same thing, last year, that your husband died.'

Horned Helmet

Henry Treece

*Beorn is only a boy when his father dies leaving him to be a slave to the
evil and cruel Glam. His mother had been carried off the year before by
Viking raiders so Beorn is entirely alone. He tries to run away but is
chased along the shore by Glam and is only a hand's breadth away from
capture when both he and Glam run straight into a band of Vikings.
Henry Treece's fierce and exciting story opens in Iceland (where Beorn
lives) at the beginning of the eleventh century. At this time Vikings
travelled the world in their longships seeking plunder. As this extract
shows, Beorn goes with the Vikings to face all the dangers and hardships
of their battle-filled lives.*

At first, Beorn thought this man must be Thor himself. From his
dull iron helmet with the boar's crest, to the gold rings on his
fingers, and the decorated sword-belt about his body, he looked a
god, or a hero at least. His face was broad, and as brown as a piece of
leather. His hair was a rusty red and his eyes as blue as the summer
sky. His square beard jutted as stiffly as though it were carved from
whalebone. His mighty spear was thrust out in front of him.

What Beorn noticed most, though, was that the iron point of the
spear never shook the slightest bit. And it was aimed at Glam's
heart now. Glam was twittering like a partridge disturbed on the
nest and his voice was not coming out very strongly. He was saying,
'Peace be with you, master. I am only chasing my slave. The little
outlaw is trying to run away from a thrashing.'

The red man with the spear said, 'Do you blame him? And who is
to give the thrashing?'

Glam answered, 'I am, master. It is my right.'

The man said, 'What have you done, slave, to merit a thrashing from this big fellow?'

Glam tried to answer, raising his voice above Beorn's, but the man with the spear stepped forward a pace and kicked out, sprawling him on the beach. Then the man said to Glam, 'I am a Jomsviking out of Jomsburg in Vendland. My name is Starkad, and, apart from my master, Jarl Skallagrim, no man disobeys when I command. If I say to a seal, "Speak now," then that seal speaks. If I say to a rock, "Dance for me," then the rock dances. Yet you, a stinking hound of a stinking island, dressed in a stinking cowhide that should have gone on to the midden three years ago, you dare to speak first when I am talking to this boy. How do you explain that?'

He bent a little and put the point of his spear against Glam's ribs, just by his heart, and pushed so that the blade went through the horse-hide a little way. Glam lay back so hard on the pebbles that he looked as though he wanted to burrow into the earth. The big man leaned a little more on the ash-spear, and held Glam there.

Beorn was amazed to hear that Glam was crying now, just as he himself had been only a short while before; and this made him even more afraid. For if a man like Glam was crying, then this Jomsviking must be more terrible than any wolf or bear.

Then the man who called himself Starkad said sharply to Beorn, 'Well, I am waiting, slave. What did you do to cause your master so much anger that he comes sliding down the shale-slope like a madman to catch you?'

Beorn noticed that many men, all in iron helmets, and holding spears, were standing by the ship now, and he felt foolish to speak in such brave company. But Starkad was glaring at him with his pale eyes so fearfully that Beorn whispered, 'I am no slave, sir. I am free-born and a farmer's son. This man claims me because my father would not fight him, but jumped over a cliff instead.'

Glam began to cry out, 'His father was a coward. He burned my barn, then he would not face me with the axe.'

Beorn got angry then and began to shout that his father was crippled in the axe-arm, and that, anyway, it was the lightning that had burned Glam's barn. Starkad listened to them both, his features never moving. Only his blue eyes shifted, from one to the other, and his stiff red beard flickered a time or two as the land-breeze caught it.

He said, 'Whether it was lightning or not, if the man died, then that was his punishment, surely?'

Beorn called out.

'This man burned down our house, too, viking. So I have neither father nor house to go to.'

Starkad said coldly, 'It seems that strange bargains are driven in Iceland these days. I have always heard that you Icelanders were wild dogs with a law of your own. To me, it seems that this man has a very good bargain if he gets a cripple to fling himself over a cliff, then burns that man's house down and takes his son as a slave – all because lightning fired his own barn.'

Glam was yelling out, 'I claim my rights, Jomsviking. I will not let you or anyone, not even Odin, cheat me of my rights.'

When he said this, the Jomsviking's eyes stretched themselves so wide that Beorn thought they would jump out because the lids could not keep them in any longer. It was almost as though Glam had struck the man on the face.

There was an awful quietness then, as the man began to press a little harder on his spear end. Glam started to struggle again and whimper like a trapped fox-cub. Then, from the prow of the longship, a voice called out, 'This fool still speaks of Odin. He is a heathen, then, and does not know that the White-Christ is master in the north today. He does not know the trouble our old king, Harald Bluetooth, once went to, teaching the heathen about the true God.'

Beorn looked past Starkad at the man who spoke from the ship. He was very tall and thin, and had long grey plaits on either side of his head, coming down from below a gilded war-helm. In his bronze-studded belt he carried two swords; one long, one short. In his right hand, a tall ash-spear; on his left arm, a round hide buckler plated with silver strips. His heavy cloak of red wool flared out behind him, like a storm cloud in the setting sun.

The men about the ship, on the shore, began to clap their hands together and shout out, 'Jarl Skallagrim! Jarl Skallagrim!'

Even Starkad seemed rather small beside this splendid man on the ship. And Beorn was scarcely surprised when Glam held out his hands wide and called in a shrill voice, 'I meant no harm, lord. I spoke of Odin only because we poor folk here have always held him as our master. We know no better, lord; we are poor fools, lord. You will see that we mean no harm to the White-Christ, or to old King Bluetooth.'

Jarl Skallagrim smiled like winter, with his grey hair riding the wind about him like a snow cloud. He said bitterly, 'We call at this forsaken midden of a place, to pick up a keg or two of fresh water, and a sheep or two to fill our bellies, voyaging, and we have to listen to a madman who is so afraid to die that he will praise any god or any king in return for his miserable life!'

Starkad called back over his broad shoulder, 'What with him, Jarl? Slave or spear-point?'

Jarl Skallagrim turned his back and began to walk down the deck.

'Neither,' he said, just above the hissing of the sea. 'I want no thing like him aboard *Reindeer*; nor should you want his dog-blood on your point, to eat it away with its poison and blunt it. He is a heathen and that's that. Bind him hand and foot with thongs, and put him into the first rock-pool that will hold him. Not a very deep pool, though. He needs time to think on God before he drowns at the next tide.'

Beorn did not watch while the men did this. Starkad stood looking at him coldly, and said, 'Why do you mourn, boy? He was your enemy.'

Beorn answered, 'I do not like anyone to be hurt, Jomsviking.'

Starkad smiled for the first time and said, 'Then you should have been born into another world than this. Everyone gets hurt, as you should know by now. But why mourn? If this dog keeps howling long enough, someone will come down and take him out of the pool, more's the pity!'

When the other Jomsvikings came back from putting Glam down, and his cries had started echoing along the shore, Starkad turned and began to walk towards the longship, for it was time to catch the ebb-tide and be away.

Beorn was still kneeling among the pebbles when the men strained to push off with the long oars. Now he felt lost indeed. He would almost have been glad to have Glam beside him, for at least that would be some sort of company, bad as it was.

And when the boy had begun to feel that he was shut off from all men, Starkad came to the prow and called to him sharply, 'Well, must we wait here all day for you? Are you afraid to wet your feet and come aboard?'

No dog ever ran to his master as fast as Beorn ran to that ship, gasping as he plunged waist-deep in the cold salt water. Then a black-bearded Jomsviking leaned over the side and hauled him in, grumbling a little that the boy brought so much water into the ship with him.

=◦<◎<◁◉▷◎▷◦=

Reindeer was a vessel of black oak with its planks overlapping one another, sixty paces from prow to the after-cabin, and twenty paces across the beam. Her dragon-head was cased in thin gold, beaten into the chisel-grooves of the wood. Garnets, as big as a man's thumb-joint, were set in the mask for eyes, and the curling tongue was hammered out of red bronze.

Beorn badly wanted to go up on to the prow-platform and see the dragon-head and touch it, but the watch-out man frowned at him, and he shrank away.

Once they had pulled offshore and *Reindeer* was riding the Iceland Sea like a nutshell, Starkad took the steerboard, and drove the longship like a rider spurring a stallion. He had no eyes for Beorn, but stared ahead.

Jarl Skallagrim only came down amidships, among the sea-chests, once a day. At other times he was shut in the after-cabin with a man named Thorgaut, trying to learn Latin. It was hard going, for the Jarl was getting over-aged for such things. Often the teacher, who wore wolf-skin and iron byrnie or war-shirt like the rest of the rovers, got angry with him and made him say words over and over again before he was satisfied. The Jarl was very slow at his Latin, though fast enough at spear-play and sword-work. Beorn was glad he didn't have to learn Latin. It made no sense at all to him, as far as he could hear.

There was only one man who would talk to Beorn at first; a man out of Hedeby, called Gauk the Guardian. When Beorn asked why a man should twist his brains at Latin, which was a right dog's tongue, Gauk the Guardian said it was because the word of the White-Christ was set down in Latin; or if that didn't suit you, it could be got at in Greek – but that was worse. It was like trying to read the thorns in a bush.

This Gauk the Guardian was a friendly enough man, who had had a family of his own, in his youth, but they had got lost in a fire when some Franks came up to bring Christ to the Danes by force. Before he joined the viking community at Jomsburg, he had been a butcher. He told Beorn that there wasn't so much difference; they both used axes.

Some of the Jomsvikings got angry with Beorn for running up and down *Reindeer*, especially when they were playing chess and he accidentally knocked their boards sideways. They shouted at him and told him to jump into the sea and swim home to Iceland, where he belonged.

But Gauk took pity on him, and let him help with one of the sheep that they had taken from the hill above the shore. Some of the joints Gauk hung on hide thongs over the side, letting them trail in the water to keep cool and salted for when they were needed. Other pieces were put into buckets of sea-water on deck. The meat the vikings wanted to keep longest was buried in hot ash, in the fire that Gauk lit in a flat iron pan on the after platform. When this was baked a dark brown, Gauk lifted the deck-planks, near the mast-stepping, and put the meat down in the dark there, over the keel, among all the swords and spears. These weapons were thick with pig-fat, to keep them from rusting, so when mutton came up from under-deck, it tasted more like pig-meat than it should have done. But the men were so hungry before they reached Orkney that no one complained.

One night, as they lay under the tent on deck, with the Pole star behind them, Gauk told Beorn that *Reindeer* made a run up to Iceland almost every year, just to see if there was anything worth taking. He said that most of the northland was picked clean now, by one or another, and that if things didn't improve, the Jomsvikings would be running *Reindeer* down the rivers to Miklagard next season, to see if the Greeks had anything they didn't want, in their famous city where the Emperor lived.

Beorn said, 'If you come to Iceland every year, why have I not seen you before?'

Gauk the Guardian laughed and said, 'Because when we come, all the folk go indoors till we have sailed away. Your folk must have kept you under the bed, or in a coffer-chest. That's why you haven't seen us. Folk usually know when we are about; they light bonfires on the hills to tell one another to stay in. Oh, yes, we know all about it! But we pay no heed. In fact, we often find our way by these bonfires at night! In the old days, when vikings were really fierce fellows, shipmen like us would go ashore and burn a whole town down for lighting those bonfires; but not today, now that we know about the White-Christ. Now, we do not even pick slaves up, as often as we used. We mainly take things like cups and swords and money-chests.'

Beorn said, 'When you used to pick slaves up, did you ever take any from Thorstead, master?'

Gauk scratched his head and considered a while. Then he said, 'Oh, aye, only a year or two ago, in a fit of absent-mindedness, we picked up a woman who was down on the shore, gathering weed and driftwood for her fire. She was a pleasant woman, though she wept to leave her husband and her son, and kept us all awake.'

Beorn said then, 'I think that was my mother. Where did you take her, Gauk?'

Gauk wrapped the blanket round him and said, 'God knows, lad. It could have been Norway, or Scotland, or down to Mull. We called at all those places that year, along the route the old Irish monks used to take. It was a bad year for trade; we got hardly enough to keep the bones from poking through our hides.'

Beorn took the man's hand and said, 'Try to remember, Gauk. Where did you set this woman down?'

But Gauk could not remember. He began to get so cross then that Beorn stopped asking, and went to sleep, to dream of his mother, and then his father jumping over the cliff.

One day, when he was feeling more lonely than ever, because the men would not let him run up and down between the sea-chests, and Gauk had cut his finger chopping up a sheep and was lying down brooding, Beorn went to Starkad at the steerboard and said, 'Master, where are we bound for?'

Starkad was like a hound, smelling his direction. He took a long time to bring his eyes down to Beorn.

He said, 'Unless we strike land soon, we are bound for the bottom, like a hundred more that are on the high seas out of sight of land today. Two of the planks on the larboard side need caulking with tar, and that we can't do until we can get ashore. Haven't you heard the water bubbling below decks at night? We're sinking inch by inch, boy. So that's where we are bound for.'

He spoke so calmly that Beorn thought he was joking. But two nights later the water began to come up through the deck and all the men got on to their sea-chests to keep dry. Then Beorn knew that Starkad had meant it.

Jarl Skallagrim stopped working at his Latin and came among the men. He wore a thick frieze jacket now, and a catskin cap, like any other sailor. His fine clothes were put away in his own sea-chest in the after-cabin. If it had not been for his dagger with the gold handle, no one could have told that he was a great sea-lord.

He asked the man at the prow, 'Did you spy land before the dark came on?'

The man shook his head. So Jarl Skallagrim asked Starkad,

'How far have we settled in the last day?'

Starkad said, 'A hand's length, Jarl. One of my hands; they are longer than most other men's.'

Skallagrim smiled and said, 'Then we can expect to keep afloat for two days more, if you don't mind rowing with the water round your necks. There should be land somewhere ahead of us, judging by the stars.'

One of the men said, 'I was in the water, on a skerry off Shetland, for three days, with the salt in one ear and out the other at every turn of the tide. Apart from the gulls that kept standing on my head, it was not so bad.'

Jarl Skallagrim said, 'You must put your leather hat on, Hrut, when we go down this time. It is no pleasure to have birds standing on one's head. Their claws are sharp.'

Then he passed down the longship and ordered a man to fetch up the thick barley-beer from the forehold. That night no one slept, with the sea about their ankles, and the beer passing round in an iron helmet for all to share. Gauk saw to it that Beorn drank with the grown men, to keep his heart up. He had never tasted thick barley-beer before. It was sweet and had a honey flavour. Before long he was feeling that he did not much mind about the sea coming into *Reindeer*.

Then Beorn remembered a silly Icelandic song his father used to sing, so he got up on a chest and sang it, without being asked, even.

> Snorre Pig had a curly tail,
> A curly tail, a curly tail,
> His head was as round as the top of a pail.
> Hey up, for Snorre Pig!
>
> Snorre Pig had big brown eyes,
> Big brown eyes, big brown eyes,
> And he was the Jarl of all the sties.
> Hey up, for Snorre Pig!
>
> When Snorre Pig met a lady sow,
> A lady sow, a lady sow,
> He'd smile and bend his knee full low;
> Hey up, for Snorre Pig!
>
> But when he met another boar,
> Another boar, another boar,
> He'd tread him into the farmyard floor;
> Hey up, for Snorre Pig!

Beorn sang his song in a clear high voice, with the barley-beer warm in his head, and the sea-wind cold on his cheek; and when he had finished, Jarl Skallagrim said, 'That is what I call poetry! You have no idea what a change it is after all the Latin I have been reading with friend Thorgaut. I like your Snorre Pig, boy, and you shall sing about him every night till *Reindeer* goes down. Pigs are not good things to mention out at sea, I know, but your Snorre is no common pig. Even if he does us no good, I feel that he is such a gentleman he will do us no harm.'

Beorn said, 'Thank you, Jarl. I could sing about him even better if I had a pair of mutton-bone clappers to beat time with.'

Jarl Skallagrim turned to Gauk and said, 'See that the boy has his bone clappers tomorrow.'

Gauk went one better than that, and made a drum for Beorn, of thin sheepskin stretched tight over an old embroidery-frame that he had picked up from somewhere, perhaps Spain, Gauk forgot where. So after that, Beorn sang to the drum, and the men became more friendly to him. Even Starkad smiled at him once – and that was a great deal, for when Starkad smiled a man's head usually fell on to the floor.

And the song must have brought some luck at least, for two days later they sighted a little island off Shetland, and got into a cove there, with the sea up to their waists now, only just in time.

A shipwright named Einar lived there, and he not only caulked the seams with good black pitch and rags, he also told them that the herring had come inshore south along the Scotland-coast, thicker than for ten years.

This made the Jomsvikings so glad that Beorn asked Gauk why. Gauk said, 'When herring come inshore, the coast-folk get excited, and they all go out in their little boats, their cobles and curraghs, and forget to lock their doors, or even leave guards in the villages. So, the thing to do is land a little higher up the coast, and then go overland and take the pickings. Fair's fair – they get the herring; we get the gold! Nothing comes of nothing in this world, lad. A man must pay for what he gets. So, they must pay for the herring.'

After they had this news, and the ship was watertight, *Reindeer* could hardly wait to be off again. She seemed to know the herring were inshore, and tugged at her mooring like a war-horse that smells iron.

So, two months after they had left Iceland, they stood offshore from a Scottish wick, where they could see the blue smoke rising from the clustered houses of a village, and see the tarred skin-boats, the curraghs, coming out in shoals to drag in the herring.

Starkad allowed himself to say, 'It must have been our lucky day when we found you on the shore, Icelander. I had thoughts of throwing you to the fishes, as we came down through the Ice Sea, but after that pig-song of yours, and now the herring-tidings, I am at the edge of changing my mind, and letting you live. How would that suit you, Icelander?'

Beorn had got more used to this strange man now, and knew when he was jesting, so he smiled and nodded, and even dared to answer, 'That suits me well, Master Starkad, I am in your debt.'

But when he said this, Starkad's face went dark red, and he said angrily, 'Never admit that you are in a man's debt, you donkey! No Jomsviking ever does that. A true man is in no one's debt but his own. Never forget that. All is between himself and God, himself and the king.'

He spoke so furiously that white froth came on to his lips, as though he might fall down in a fit. Beorn had not been so frightened since the day Glam chased him on to the headland.

Little House on the Prairie

Laura Ingalls Wilder

This is the story of how, about a century ago, Laura and her family left their home in the woods of Wisconsin U.S.A., for a new life out West in Indian country. Laura and her parents, her sisters Mary and baby Carrie, and their bulldog Jack, set off in a covered wagon. Along the way they exchange their horses for two strong mustangs – Pet and Patty. They travel into wild and lonely country where there are no roads, no shops, no houses and very few other settlers. In these two chapters from this well-loved story, Laura Ingalls Wilder describes how her father builds their new home in the middle of the open prairie.

LAURA and Mary were up next morning earlier than the sun. They ate their breakfast of cornmeal mush with prairie-hen gravy, and hurried to help Ma wash the dishes. Pa was loading everything else into the wagon and hitching up Pet and Patty.

When the sun rose, they were driving on across the prairie. There was no road now. Pet and Patty waded through the grasses, and the wagon left behind it only the tracks of its wheels.

Before noon, Pa said, 'Whoa!' The wagon stopped.

'Here we are, Caroline!' he said. 'Right here we'll build our house.'

Laura and Mary scrambled over the feed-box and dropped to the ground in a hurry. All around them there was nothing but grassy prairie spreading to the edge of the sky.

Quite near them, to the north, the creek bottoms lay below the prairie. Some darker green tree-tops showed, and beyond them bits of the rim of earthen bluffs held up the prairie's grasses. Far away to the east, a broken line of different greens lay on the prairie, and Pa said that was the river.

'That's the Verdigris River,' he said, pointing it out to Ma.

Right away, he and Ma began to unload the wagon. They took out everything and piled it on the ground. Then they took off the wagon-cover and put it over the pile. Then they took even the wagon-box off, while Laura and Mary and Jack watched.

The wagon had been home for a long time. Now there was nothing left of it but the four wheels and the parts that connected them. Pet and Patty were still hitched to the tongue. Pa took a bucket and his axe, and sitting on this skeleton wagon, he drove away. He drove right down into the prairie, out of sight.

'Where's Pa going?' Laura asked, and Ma said, 'He's going to get a load of logs from the creek bottoms.'

It was strange and frightening to be left without the wagon on the High Prairie. The land and the sky seemed too large, and Laura felt small. She wanted to hide and be still in the tall grass, like a little prairie chicken. But she didn't. She helped Ma, while Mary sat on the grass and minded Baby Carrie.

First Laura and Ma made the beds, under the wagon-cover tent. Then Ma arranged the boxes and bundles, while Laura pulled all the grass from a space in front of the tent. That made a bare place for the fire. They couldn't start the fire until Pa brought wood.

There was nothing more to do, so Laura explored a little. She did not go far from the tent. But she found a queer little kind of tunnel in the grass. You'd never notice it if you looked across the waving grass-tops. But when you came to it, there it was – a narrow, straight, hard path down between the grass stems. It went out into the endless prairie.

Laura went along it a little way. She went slowly, and more slowly, and then she stood still and felt queer. So she turned around and came back quickly. When she looked over her shoulder there wasn't anything there. But she hurried.

When Pa came riding back on a load of logs, Laura told him about that path. He said he had seen it yesterday. 'It's some old trail,' he said.

That night by the fire Laura asked again when she would see a papoose, but Pa didn't know. He said you never saw Indians unless they wanted you to see them. He had seen Indians when he was a boy in New York State, but Laura never had. She knew they were wild men with red skins, and their hatchets were called tomahawks.

Pa knew all about wild animals, so he must know about wild men, too. Laura thought he would show her a papoose some day, just as he had shown her fawns, and little bears, and wolves.

For days Pa hauled logs. He made two piles of them, one for the house and one for the stable. There began to be a road where he drove back and forth to the creek bottoms. And at night on their picket-lines Pet and Patty ate the grass, till it was short and stubby all around the log-piles.

Pa began the house first. He paced off the size of it on the ground, then with his spade he dug a shallow little hollow along two sides of that space. Into these hollows he rolled two of the biggest logs. They were sound, strong logs, because they must hold up the house. They were called sills.

Then Pa chose two more strong, big logs, and he rolled these logs on to the ends of the sills, so that they made a hollow square. Now with his axe he cut a wide, deep notch near each end of these logs. He cut these notches out of the top of the log, but with his eye he measured the sills, and he cut the notches so that they would fit around half of the sill.

When the notches were cut, he rolled the log over. And the notches fitted down over the sill.

That finished the foundation of the house. It was one log high. The sills were half buried in the ground, and the logs on their ends fitted snugly to the ground. At the corners, where they crossed, the notches let them fit together so that they were no thicker than one log. And the two ends stuck out beyond the notches.

Next day Pa began the walls. From each side he rolled up a log, and he notched its ends so that it fitted down over the end logs.

Then he rolled up logs from the ends, and notched them so that they fitted down over the side logs. Now the whole house was two logs high.

The logs fitted solidly together at the corners. But no log is ever perfectly straight, and all logs are bigger at one end than at the other end, so cracks were left between them all along the walls. But that did not matter, because Pa would chink those cracks.

All by himself, he built the house three logs high. Then Ma helped him. Pa lifted one end of a log on to the wall, then Ma held it while he lifted the other end. He stood up on the wall to cut the notches, and Ma helped roll and hold the log while he settled it where it should be to make the corner perfectly square.

So, log by log, they built the walls higher, till they were pretty high, and Laura couldn't get over them any more. She was tired of watching Pa and Ma build the house, and she went into the tall grass, exploring. Suddenly she heard Pa shout, 'Let go! Get out from under!'

The big, heavy log was sliding. Pa was trying to hold up his end of it, to keep it from falling on Ma. He couldn't. It crashed down. Laura saw Ma huddled on the ground.

She got to Ma almost as quickly as Pa did. Pa knelt down and called Ma in a dreadful voice, and Ma gasped, 'I'm all right.'

The log was on her foot. Pa lifted the log and Ma pulled her foot from under it, Pa felt her to see if any bones were broken.

'Move your arms,' he said. 'Is your back hurt? Can you turn your head?' Ma moved her arms and turned her head.

'Thank God,' Pa said. He helped Ma to sit up. She said again, 'I'm all right, Charles. It's just my foot.'

Quickly Pa took off her shoe and stocking. He felt her foot all over, moving the ankle and the instep and every toe. 'Does it hurt much?' he asked.

Ma's face was grey and her mouth was a tight line. 'Not much,' she said.

'No bones broken,' said Pa. 'It's only a bad sprain.'

Ma said cheerfully: 'Well, a sprain's soon mended. Don't be so upset, Charles.'

'I blame myself,' said Pa. 'I should have used skids.'

He helped Ma to the tent. He built up the fire and heated water. When the water was as hot as Ma could bear, she put her swollen foot into it.

It was providential that the foot was not crushed. Only a little hollow in the ground had saved it.

Pa kept pouring more hot water into the tub in which Ma's foot was soaking. Her foot was red from the heat and the puffed ankle began to turn purple. Ma took her foot out of the water and bound strips of rag tightly round and round the ankle. 'I can manage,' she said.

She could not get her shoe on. But she tied more rags around her foot, and she hobbled on it. She got supper as usual, only a little more slowly. But Pa said she could not help to build the house until her ankle was well.

He hewed out skids. These were long, flat slabs. One end rested on the ground, and the other end rested on the log wall. He was not going to lift any more logs; he and Ma would roll them up these skids.

But Ma's ankle was not well yet. When she unwrapped it in the evenings, to soak it in hot water, it was all purple and black and green and yellow. The house must wait.

Then one afternoon Pa came merrily whistling up the creek road. They had not expected him home from hunting so soon. As soon as he saw them he shouted, 'Good news!'

They had a neighbour, only two miles away on the other side of the creek. Pa had met him in the woods. They were going to trade work and that would make it easier for everyone.

'He's a bachelor,' said Pa, 'and he says he can get along without a house better than you and the girls can. So he's going to help me first. Then as soon as he gets his logs ready, I'll go over and help him.'

They need not wait any longer for the house, and Ma need not do any more work on it.

'How do you like that, Caroline?' Pa asked, joyfully; and Ma said, 'That's good, Charles. I'm glad.'

Early next morning Mr Edwards came. He was lean and tall and brown. He bowed to Ma and called her 'Ma'am' politely. But he told Laura that he was a wild-cat from Tennessee. He wore tall boots and a ragged jumper, and a coon-skin cap, and he could spit tobacco juice farther than Laura had ever imagined that anyone could spit tobacco juice. He could hit anything he spat at, too. Laura tried and tried, but she could never spit so far or so well as Mr Edwards could.

He was a fast worker. In one day he and Pa built those walls as high as Pa wanted them. They joked and sang while they worked, and their axes made the chips fly.

On top of the walls they set up a skeleton roof of slender poles. Then in the south wall they cut a tall hole for a door, and in the west wall and the east wall they cut square holes for windows.

Laura couldn't wait to see the inside of the house. As soon as the tall hole was cut, she ran inside. Everything was striped there. Stripes of sunshine came through the cracks in the west wall, and stripes of shadow came down from the poles overhead. The stripes of shade and sunshine were all across Laura's hands and her arms and her bare feet. And through the cracks between the logs she could see stripes of prairie. The sweet smell of the prairie mixed with the sweet smell of cut wood.

Then, as Pa cut away the logs to make the window hole in the west wall, chunks of sunshine came in. When he finished, a big block of sunshine lay on the ground inside the house.

Around the door hole and the window holes Pa and Mr Edwards nailed thin slabs against the cut ends of the logs. And the house was finished, all but the roof. The walls were solid and the house was large, much larger than the tent. It was a nice house.

Mr Edwards said he would go home now, but Pa and Ma said he must stay to supper. Ma had cooked an especially good supper because they had company.

There was stewed jack rabbit with white-flour dumplings and plenty of gravy. There was a steaming hot, thick cornbread flavoured with bacon fat. There was molasses to eat on the

cornbread, but because this was a company supper they did not
sweeten their coffee with molasses. Ma brought out the little paper
sack of pale brown store sugar.

Mr Edwards said he surely did appreciate that supper.

Then Pa brought out his fiddle.

Mr Edwards stretched out on the ground, to listen. But first Pa
played for Laura and Mary. He played their very favourite song,
and he sang it. Laura liked it best of all because Pa's voice went
down deep, deep, deeper in that song.

> 'Oh, I am a Gipsy King!
> I come and go as I please!
> I pull my old nightcap down,
> And take the world at my ease.'

Then his voice went deep, deep down, deeper than the very
oldest bullfrog's.

> 'Oh!
>   I am
>   a
>   Gyp-
>   sy
>   KING!'

They all laughed. Laura could hardly stop laughing.

'Oh, sing it again, Pa! Sing it again!' she cried, before she
remembered that children must be seen and not heard. Then she
was quiet.

Pa went on playing, and everything began to dance. Mr
Edwards rose up on one elbow, then he sat up, then he jumped up
and he danced. He danced like a jumping-jack in the moonlight,
while Pa's fiddle kept on rollicking and his foot kept tapping the
ground, and Laura's hands and Mary's hands were clapping
together and their feet were patting, too.

'You're the fiddlin'est fool that ever I see!' Mr Edwards shouted admiringly to Pa. He didn't stop dancing, Pa didn't stop playing. He played 'Money Musk' and 'Arkansas Traveller', 'Irish Washer-woman', and the 'Devil's Hornpipe'.

Baby Carrie couldn't sleep in all that music. She sat up in Ma's lap, looking at Mr Edwards with round eyes, and clapping her little hands and laughing.

Even the firelight danced, and all around its edge the shadows were dancing. Only the new house stood still and quiet in the dark, till the big moon rose and shone on its grey walls and the yellow chips around it.

Mr Edwards said he must go. It was a long way back to his camp on the other side of the woods and the creek. He took his gun, and said good night to Laura and Mary and Ma. He said a bachelor got mighty lonesome, and he surely had enjoyed this evening of home life.

'Play, Ingalls!' he said. 'Play me down the road!' So while he went down the creek road and out of sight, Pa played, and Pa and Mr Edwards and Laura sang with all their might.

> 'Old Dan Tucker was a fine old man;
> He washed his face in the frying-pan,
> He combed his hair with a wagon wheel,
> And died of the toothache in his heel.
>
> 'Git out of the way for old Dan Tucker!
> He's too late to get his supper!
> Supper's over and the dishes washed,
> Nothing left but a piece of squash!
>
> 'Old Dan Tucker went to town,
> Riding a mule, leading a houn' . . .'

Far over the prairie rang Pa's big voice and Laura's little one, and faintly from the creek bottoms came a last whoop from Mr Edwards.

> 'Git out of the way for old Dan Tucker!
> He's too late to get his supper!'

When Pa's fiddle stopped, they could not hear Mr Edwards any more. Only the wind rustled in the prairie grasses. The big, yellow moon was sailing high overhead. The sky was so full of light that not one star twinkled in it, and all the prairie was a shadowy mellowness.

Then from the woods by the creek a nightingale began to sing.

Everything was silent, listening to the nightingale's song. The bird sang on and on. The cool wind moved over the prairie and the song was round and clear above the grasses' whispering. The sky was like a bowl of light overturned on the flat black land.

The song ended. No one moved or spoke. Laura and Mary were quiet, Pa and Ma sat motionless. Only the wind stirred and the grasses sighed. Then Pa lifted the fiddle to his shoulder and softly touched the bow to the strings. A few notes fell like clear drops of water into the stillness. A pause, and Pa began to play the nightingale's song. The nightingale answered him. The nightingale began to sing again. It was singing with Pa's fiddle.

When the strings were silent, the nightingale went on singing. The bird and the fiddle were talking to each other in the cool night under the moon.

'The walls are up,' Pa was saying to Ma in the morning. 'We'd better move in and get along as best we can without a floor or other fixings. I must build the stable as fast as I can, so Pet and Patty can be inside walls, too. Last night I could hear wolves howling from every direction, seemed like, and close, too.'

'Well, you have your gun, so I'll not worry,' said Ma.

'Yes, and there's Jack. But I'll feel easier in my mind when you and the girls have good solid walls around you.'

'Why do you suppose we haven't seen any Indians?' Ma asked.

'Oh, I don't know,' Pa replied, carelessly. 'I've seen their camping-places among the bluffs. They're away on a hunting-trip now, I guess.'

Then Ma called: 'Girls! The sun's up!' and Laura and Mary scrambled out of bed and into their clothes.

'Eat your breakfasts quickly,' Ma said, putting the last of the rabbit stew on their tin plates. 'We're moving into the house today, and all the chips must be out.'

So they ate quickly, and hurried to carry all the chips out of the house. They ran back and forth as fast as they could, gathering their skirts full of chips and dumping them in a pile near the fire. But there were still chips on the ground inside the house when Ma began to sweep it with her willow-bough broom.

Ma limped, though her sprained ankle was beginning to get well. But she soon swept the earthen floor, and then Mary and Laura began to help her carry things into the house.

Pa was on top of the walls, stretching the canvas wagon-top over the skeleton roof of saplings. The canvas billowed in the wind, Pa's beard blew wildly and his hair stood up from his head as if it were trying to pull itself out. He held on to the canvas and fought it. Once it jerked so hard that Laura thought he must let go or sail into the air like a bird. But he held tight to the wall with his legs, and tight to the canvas with his hands, and he tied it down.

'There!' he said to it. 'Stay where you are, and be –'

'Charles!' Ma said. She stood with her arms full of quilts and looked up at him reprovingly.

'– and be good,' Pa said to the canvas. 'Why, Caroline, what did you think I was going to say?'

'Oh, Charles!' Ma said. 'You scallywag!'

Pa came right down the corner of the house. The ends of the logs stuck out, and he used them for a ladder. He ran his hand through his hair so that it stood up even more wildly, and Ma burst out laughing. Then he hugged her, quilts and all.

Then they looked at the house and Pa said, 'How's that for a snug house!'

'I'll be thankful to get into it,' said Ma.

There was no door and there were no windows. There was no floor except the ground and no roof except the canvas. But that house had good stout walls, and it would stay where it was. It was not like the wagon, that every morning went on to some other place.

'We're going to do well here, Caroline,' Pa said. 'This is a great country. This is a country I'll be content to stay in the rest of my life.'

'Even when it's settled up?' Ma asked.

'Even when it's settled up. No matter how thick and close the neighbours get, this country'll never feel crowded. Look at that sky!'

Laura knew what he meant. She liked this place, too. She liked the enormous sky and the winds, and the land that you couldn't see to the end of. Everything was so fresh and clean and big and splendid.

By dinner-time the house was in order. The beds were neatly made on the floor. The wagon-seat and two ends of logs were brought in for chairs. Pa's gun lay on its pegs above the doorway. Boxes and bundles were neat against the walls. It was a pleasant house. A soft light came through the canvas roof, wind and sunshine came through the window holes, and every crack in the four walls glowed a little because the sun was overhead.

Only the camp fire stayed where it had been. Pa said he would build a fireplace in the house as soon as he could. He would hew out slabs to make a solid roof, too, before winter came. He would lay a puncheon floor, and make beds and tables and chairs. But all that work must wait until he had helped Mr Edwards and had built a stable for Pet and Patty.

'When that's all done,' said Ma, 'I want a clothes-line.'

Pa laughed, 'Yes, and I want a well.'

After dinner he hitched Pet and Patty to the wagon and he hauled a tubful of water from the creek, so that Ma could do the washing. 'You could wash clothes in the creek,' he told her. 'Indian women do.'

'If we wanted to live like Indians, you could make a hole in the roof to let the smoke out, and we'd have the fire on the floor inside the house,' said Ma. 'Indians do.'

That afternoon she washed the clothes in the tub and spread them on the grass to dry.

After supper they sat for a while by the camp fire. That night they would sleep in the house; they would never sleep beside a camp fire again. Pa and Ma talked about the folks in Wisconsin, and Ma wished she could send them a letter. But Independence was forty miles away, and no letter could go until Pa made the long trip to the post office there.

Back in the Big Woods so far away, Grandpa and Grandma and the aunts and uncles and cousins did not know where Pa and Ma and Laura and Mary and Baby Carrie were. And sitting there by the camp fire, no one knew what might have happened in the Big Woods. There was no way to find out.

'Well, it's bedtime,' Ma said. Baby Carrie was already asleep. Ma carried her into the house and undressed her, while Mary unbuttoned Laura's dress and petticoat waist down the back, and Pa hung a quilt over the door hole. The quilt would be better than no door. Then Pa went out to bring Pet and Patty close to the house.

He called back, softly, 'Come out here, Caroline, and look at the moon.'

Mary and Laura lay in their little bed on the ground inside the new house, and watched the sky through the window hole to the east. The edge of the big, bright moon glittered at the bottom of the window space, and Laura sat up. She looked at the great moon, sailing silently higher in the clear sky.

Its light made silvery lines in all the cracks on that side of the house. The light poured through the window hole and made a square of soft radiance on the floor. It was so bright that Laura saw Ma plainly when she lifted the quilt at the door and came in.

Then Laura very quickly lay down, before Ma saw her naughtily sitting up in bed.

She heard Pet and Patty whinnying softly to Pa. Then the faint thuds of their feet came into her ear from the floor. Pet and Patty and Pa were coming towards the house, and Laura heard Pa singing:

> 'Sail on, silver moon!
> Shed your radiance o'er the sky –'

His voice was like a part of the night and the moonlight and the stillness of the prairie. He came to the doorway, singing,

> 'By the pale, silver light of the moon –'

Softly Ma said, 'Hush, Charles. You'll wake the children.'

So Pa came in without a sound. Jack followed at his heels and lay down across the doorway. Now they were all inside the stout walls of their new home, and they were snug and safe. Drowsily Laura heard a long wolf-howl rising from far away on the prairie, but only a little shiver went up her backbone and she fell asleep.

Flambards

K. M. Peyton

Christina Parsons is an orphan, but also an heiress with a fortune to inherit at the age of twenty-one. When she is twelve her Uncle Russell invites her to live with him and his two sons – Mark and William – at Flambards, his beautiful but neglected country house. As Mr Russell is a violent, bad-tempered man whose only interest in life is fox-hunting, his invitation seems very out of character until Christina realises that he is hoping she will eventually marry Mark and bring her fortune to Flambards. All the money Mr Russell possesses goes on his stables, even though, since a riding accident, he can no longer hunt himself. His son Mark, however, is as fanatically keen on riding as his father. William is not so lucky. His passion is for the new flying machines, which in 1908 when this story opens, were in the very early stages of development. Will hates riding so much that he is thankful when a bad fall puts him in bed. K. M. Peyton's absorbing trilogy follows Christina's and her cousins' fortunes through the years. This particular extract opens as Christina inadvertently betrays Will's interest in flying machines to his father.

'MR William Russell live here, miss?'
'Yes.'

The man handed her a parcel. 'With the regards of Mr Dermot,' he said and, touching his cap, walked away down the drive.

Christina took the parcel back into the library and handed it to her uncle. 'A man delivered this, with the regards of Mr Dermot.'

'Who the devil's Mr Dermot?' Russell said, with a glare at the parcel.

'He didn't say.'

'Open it, girl.'

Christina did as she was told, and was shocked by her own stupidity. For the parcel was a book called *A Scientific Statement of the Progress of Aeronautical Science up to the Present Time*, and on the fly-leaf a small hand had written, 'To help while away the time.' It was for William upstairs, not his father.

She said, 'It's for William.'

'Show me,' said Russell.

Christina handed it over reluctantly. She had a feeling that William would have preferred to keep his reading-matter private. Russell stared at the title.

'Good God, what's this stuff?'

Mark leaned over the back of the chair to read the cover, and laughed. 'That's Will's passion. Flying.'

'*Flying!*' Russell was disgusted. He opened the book and read the inscription. 'I'll give him something. Here, Christina, take these out. I'll give him something to while away his time! I've never seen him show any interest in my books, the brainless puppy! Who is this Dermot, filling his head with rubbish? Eh, Mark? You know him?'

'Never heard of him,' said Mark.

'Holy Moses, if he wants to while away his time' – Russell was thumping about, stumbling over to the bookcase, red with anger – 'I'll give him something. Here, Christina, take these out. I'll give him reading-matter. Take this up to him, and this one. Here. And this.'

Christina took the awkward tomes, silent with horror. They were *The Breeding of Foxhounds*, *Baily's Hunting Directory*, *Observations on Fox-hunting*, *Thoughts on Hunting*, *The Essex Foxhounds*, and *Goodall's Practice with Foxhounds*.

'Take him those! Go on! With my compliments. I'll see he gets his reading-matter. And when he's finished those I'll send him some more.' He took the slim volume on flying and threw it on the fire, where it burst into merry flames. Christina could not restrain a gasp of dismay, and even Mark looked disconcerted.

'Oh, I say, Father.'

Russell aimed a great swipe at Mark with his crutch, which Mark avoided with a quick, practised sidestep.

'Get out, both of you! Get upstairs with those, girl, and tell Will to start reading. Get out of my sight before I tan the hides off you!'

He was scarlet with passion, crashing his crutches in the hearth, poking the flying-book deeper into the fire. Christina, clutching her load of books, hurried out, and Mark opened the door for her, grinning.

'Phew! What a paddy!'

Once in the hall, Christina burst into tears. She could not wipe her eyes for the books, and stood gulping uncontrollably. 'It's – it's not fair! The – the – book was for – for Will! It's all – my fault!'

'Oh, Will's used to it,' Mark said. 'Don't upset yourself, we're always like this here. You just have to keep out of the old man's way till he's over it.'

To her amazement, Mark was not the least concerned. Christina was outraged, and horrified by her own part in the matter. It need never have happened at all, if she had not been so dull-witted. Her heart ached for poor helpless William as she lugged the books up the stairs. Mark had already washed his hands of the incident and gone out of the front door with the foxhounds at his heels. Christina's sense of injustice choked her. She fumbled for William's doorknob, and backed into the room with her burden, the sobs still shaking in her throat.

'Whatever's all that?' William asked cheerfully.

'For – for you!'

'What's the matter? What's wrong?'

Christina set the pile of books on the chair beside William's bed, and told him what had happened. As she had expected, William's rage turned itself on her. She buried her head in the bedclothes and sobbed: 'I'm sorry! I didn't know he was so awful!'

'Oh, look, I'm sorry too,' William said, immediately embarrassed by her despair. 'It wasn't your fault. Oh, look, please don't cry, else I shall too.'

He gave her a white, desolate look, biting his lip with disappointment. His glance passed on to the gold-tooled hunting-books, and a look of utter contempt came into his face.

188

'If he thinks I'm going to read that rubbish! I'd – I'd like to tear them into shreds! If only I had the nerve –'

'Oh, William, don't make it worse! Don't be so stupid.'

Christina pulled herself together and wiped her eyes. William lay back, glaring at the ceiling, his lips tight. His face was very pale, and there were dark shadows under his eyes. Christina said nervously, 'Who is Mr Dermot, then?'

'A friend,' said William distantly.

Later that evening Russell sent a message up to William to the effect that when he came downstairs, he was going to answer questions on the hunting-books, and if he could not answer correctly, he would get a flogging, smashed knee or no smashed knee. William picked up *Baily's Hunting Directory* and threw it across the room, where it landed under the washstand, half its leaves bursting out across the floor.

The incident of Mr Dermot's book weighed on Christina. As she went to bed that night she heard, for the first time, William sobbing. His door was open, and a nightlight burned, but she did not go in. She could not face him again, with the knowledge that the whole beastly thing was her fault. She lay in bed, and the winter moon shone coldly on the mottled wallpaper, and whitened the rampaging garden below. In the morning the long grass would be a fretwork of silver webs, and a cold fog would roll across the fields where she was to ride with Mark. She dreaded riding with Mark. She thought of Aunt Grace, and the ordered life she had lived with the dressmaking and lessons at Miss Peasgood's and tea in front of the fire, with the blinds drawn, and nobody to shout and argue and coerce.

'They are all mad here,' she thought, 'in different ways.' Mark, who could be so amiable at times, and yet so rough, was two years older than she was, yet seemed a whole generation older. 'He fits in here,' she reflected. 'But William . . .' William would never fit in. William was doomed, Christina thought, to struggle. She thought he would lose: he was so delicate. He had stopped crying, but from his room came a thump, and then a shuffling noise. 'What is he doing?' she wondered, straining her ears. Silence. William was thirteen, but a child compared to Mark. 'And what am I!' Christina thought, seeing herself as someone who had learned to fit in, wherever she was put, uncomplaining, forced to adapt. Always she had done as she was told, having been threatened more than once (but never by kind Aunt Grace) that if she was a nuisance she would go to the orphanage. Was she really going to stay at Flambards, and marry Mark? Aunt Grace had written, but said nothing about her going back. Christina lay looking at the moon, thinking of the long years ahead of her in the troubled atmosphere of Flambards. 'It's better than an orphanage,' she thought. And Mark would make a very handsome husband. And then, suddenly she remembered Dick, dear, kind Dick who was always nice to her, and she thought, 'What a pity I can't marry Dick.' She fell asleep, and did not hear the thumping and shuffling that went on in William's room, and the muffled, painful sobbing.

Two days later Mark took her out. She rode Sweetbriar and Mark rode Treasure, his favourite, who was nervous and sweating. Dick led the horses out and held Sweetbriar while Christina got into the saddle. He held her stirrup for her, patted the mare's neck and said softly, 'Have a good ride, miss.'

Christina wanted to tell him that she would rather be going with him, but decided it would be out of place. Dick went to Mark, to tighten Treasure's girths, and the horse stood for him, flitching his long, nervous ears. Mark looked down on Dick from the saddle and said, 'Don't be all day.' He wore a black jacket and black cap, and sat very easily, his reins all in one hand. Christina felt worried, and tried to sit her best, and look confident.

'Come on,' Mark said.

Sweetbriar moved off to Christina's heel, and Treasure pranced past her, rattling his bit, a white rim showing round his eyes. Mark turned in his saddle and laughed. 'What a horse, eh? You wouldn't think he galloped ten miles yesterday, would you? I reckon Father's right when he says he'll be winning races in a year or two's time.'

Christina nudged Sweetbriar into a trot to keep up, and Mark watched her critically.

'Sit square, hands still. That's better.'

Unaccountably, Christina felt furious, although she had never minded Dick's instruction. She stared crossly between Sweetbriar's ears and wondered why Mark let Treasure proceed at a crabwise jogging pace, instead of making him walk or trot properly. From Dick, she had learnt that this was a bad habit in a horse, but Mark, allowing bad habits himself, criticized her. Christina raged, her lips tight.

'Not bad,' Mark said. 'Let's see you canter.'

Treasure was off at a bound, fighting his bit, the sweat gathering on his neck. Christina had to admit that Mark sat him beautifully, very strong and yet graceful in the saddle, completely master of the difficult horse. She let Sweetbriar go, dear Sweetbriar whom she could always trust to look after her – and the mare went easily, light on her bit, ignoring the headstrong youngster raking along at her side, fighting for his head.

'Why, you're not bad at all,' Mark shouted, sounding quite surprised, and Christina's anger changed to a hot glow of pride. She did not let her expression change, but thought, 'Nice Dick. You are all right, I've saved you.'

She steadied Sweetbriar as they came to a gate, and Mark brought Treasure to a halt with a cruel pressure on the curb.

'Honestly, he's a mad horse,' Mark said. 'You wait here, and I'll show you what he can do, get the tickle out of his toes. He'll be all right when he's run it off a bit.'

He turned Treasure sharply on his hocks and went off at a fast canter away from Christina across the field. Christina watched him go, glad that Sweetbriar was content to stand, mildly switching her ears to the winter crying of the rooks. Mark made for a low part of the cut and laid fence and Treasure flew it with scarcely a change in his stride, and continued at a gallop across the field beyond.

'Show-off,' Christina thought. She had never been left alone on a horse before. The air was cold and clear, and she felt confident. She looked down at her gloved hands on the reins, quiet and firm, and the frosted neck of the mare shining with her two hours' daily polishing. She thought of the spotless stables, and the great feeds the horses got, and wondered if Dick and the others lived in anything like the same luxury as the horses they cared for. Dick, in spite of his stocky frame, was thinner than he should be, and had been coughing recently. If a horse coughed, it was rested and given stuff out of a bottle and invalid gruel with an egg beaten in it, but when Christina had said to Dick, 'You ought to stay by a fire with a cough like that,' he looked at her in amazement and said, 'But I couldn't stay off work, miss.' 'Why not?' Christina had asked, but Dick had only laughed, rather bitterly. Christina thought, 'I ought to know about the servants. I don't know anything.' She thought that when you lived in a big house in the country, you were supposed to go round and give food and clothes to the poor, but how could she do it when she was the poor herself? Her thoughts had wandered far away from Mark and Treasure by the time they reappeared, still galloping, back over the cut and laid fence and, more soberly, back to Sweetbriar's side. Mark's eyes were sparkling.

'There, that's satisfied him, eh? He'll go easily enough now.'

Treasure certainly looked quieter, breathing easily through his distended nostrils. He was in superb condition, his coat gleaming like the dining-room mahogany.

'Look, you ought to try him,' Mark said. 'You've never ridden a proper horse yet. I don't know what Dick's thinking of.'

'What do you mean, a proper horse?' Christina said indignantly. 'What's wrong with Sweetbriar?'

'You know what I mean,' Mark said. They were walking side by side across the field to the gate in the corner. 'You ought to ride all sorts. You'd feel a difference, I can tell you.'

'I don't want to ride Treasure.'

'Are you afraid?' Mark asked cruelly, smiling.

'No, of course not. But if Dick thought I was up to riding Treasure he would probably have let me by now.'

'Oh, Dick, Dick, Dick! He's only a servant. What does he know? Don't be so stupid. Come on, I'll change the saddles over for you, and you try him. I tell you, it'll be an experience for you – you'll be able to tell Father.'

Christina hesitated. She felt doubtful about riding Treasure, but not afraid. Mark pulled up. 'Come on. You ought to be jolly proud I'll let you.'

Christina had no alternative but to get down. She held the horses while Mark changed the saddles over, then Mark gave her a leg up on to Treasure.

'Oh, all these reins!' Christina said, confused. She felt nervous now, looking at the very different neck in front of her, and the white rim of Treasure's eye.

'Look, you should learn. These are the snaffle reins, and these the curb. You hold them like this.' He showed her. 'There, that's right.'

He mounted Sweetbriar, and looked at her critically. 'Don't jab him with the curb, or he'll show you he doesn't like it.'

Christina did not feel very happy. She was not afraid, she told herself. But Treasure was all spirit. Even as he walked, she could feel it inside him; it quivered in her fingers as he tossed his head, pulling at the reins. He started to dance, moving along at the jog, instead of a walk. Mark laughed. Suddenly a gun went off in the woods behind them and Treasure gave a great leap forward. Christina, carried by the pommel beneath her thighs, was lifted with him, not even losing a stirrup. She heard Mark laugh again, and cry, 'Hold him! Hold him!' But Treasure did not want to be held. He reached out his neck and pulled the reins through her fingers, and then he was galloping, and Christina knew that she was on her own.

194

She was not afraid, immediately. The sheer exhilaration of the horse's speed thrilled her, but his strength was ominous. When she looked down she saw his shoulders moving with the smooth rhythm of steam-pistons; she saw his black, shining hoofs thrown out, thudding the hard turf, and felt the great eagerness coming up through her own body. She knew that she could never stop him, if he decided he did not want to stop. She saw the hedge ahead of them, and the first stab of real fear contracted her stomach. She gathered her reins up tight, and pulled hard. It made no difference at all.

'Don't panic,' she thought, but the panic was in her, whether she wanted it or not.

Treasure's stride lengthened as he approached the hedge. Christina, remembering William, shut her eyes and buried her hands in Treasure's mane, and the horse surged beneath her. There was a cracking noise of breaking twigs. Christina gasped, clutched and gasped again, but to her amazement they were galloping again, the incident behind them, and she still in place. She let go of Treasure's mane and pulled on his mouth again, with all her strength, but he had the bit firmly between his teeth and should could make no impression. A great despair filled her.

'I shall be killed,' she thought.

Treasure was turning right-handed across another large, yellow field. Beyond it was the home paddock where Christina had taken her safe, enjoyable lessons with Dick. It dawned on her that the horse was making for home, but between the field they were in and the home paddock there was a hedge, very much larger than the one they had just jumped, solid and newly layered all along its length, and a good five feet high. Christina knew that Treasure was not the horse to be stopped by such an obstacle; she knew that he was going to jump it, and, by the grace of God, so was she. A great sob of despair broke from her throat.

'Treasure, don't! Don't, don't!' She leaned back on the reins, trying to saw them in the horse's mouth, but she could do nothing.

The creak of leather beneath her, the heavy thrumming of the horse's hoofs, filled her ears, which ached with the cold wind. Her hair flew behind her. The horse, never tiring, galloped on, raking out with his flying hoofs.

Suddenly, in the mist of her watery vision, Christina saw a grey horse come into sight at the top of the field. It was cantering towards her, but circling slightly in such a way that it looked as if it would come round and join her on her own headlong course. Christina thought it was Mark, impossibly flown to save her. She lifted her head, and screamed into the wind, 'Help me! Please help me!' The hedge was getting rapidly closer, and she started to cry out with fear, half-sob, half-entreaty. Treasure's strength grew with every stride.

The grey horse, very much under control, had now circled so that he was on the same course as her, but ahead and to her right. As Treasure galloped on, the grey horse's stride lengthened to match, and quite suddenly Treasure was galloping with his nose close by the grey horse's side. They were both galloping, and Christina heard a voice shout, 'Hold tight, Miss Christina!' The grey was hard against Treasure's shoulder, its rider's legs crushed against the horse's wild movement. Treasure was forced off course, ridden off by the grey, and Dick was leaning over to take the reins, his face puckered with anxiety.

'Hold hard!'

Christina felt the horses sliding, skidding, the great gallop broken up into a series of jolts and crashes, Treasure berserk beneath her. Strips of turf peeled up under his hoofs. Dick was pulled up out of his saddle, and hung for a moment, precariously straddled between the two horses, then at last Treasure dropped his jaw and pulled up and Dick, still holding on, half fell and half jumped from his saddle, staggering and swearing.

'You great ruddy brute! You devil you!' But as Treasure pulled up he was stroking his neck, gentling him and swearing at the same time; then he came round to Christina's side and lifted her down. Christina's legs had no strength in them and she stumbled against him.

'Dick! Oh, Dick!' she wept, and Dick tried to comfort her, with Treasure plunging round in circles on one hand, and Woodpigeon, the grey, sidling about on the other. He was full of indignation.

'Oh, Miss Christina, he shouldn't ever have put you on Treasure. He must be out of his mind. Steady on, my old beauty!' – this to Treasure, who was now beginning to quieten – 'And you riding not a couple of months yet! There, miss, it's all right now.'

Being spoken to as if she were a horse had a soothing effect on Christina, and she found that she was able to stand without her knees shaking. She wiped the mud and tears off her face and looked round dubiously.

'It was very clever of you to stop him, Dick,' she said. The thorn hedge was some thirty yards away, and even nastier than she had supposed. There was a big drainage ditch on the take-off, newly-dug, with the earth thrown out all along its lip. 'What do you think would have happened if –?' Christina's knees started shaking again. 'I don't think I shall like hunting,' she said. She thought of having to report to Uncle Russell that she had funked the big hedges and gone through the gates, and Mark would tell him that she was no good.

'Only a fool would put at a hedge like that, miss, even out hunting. You mustn't get afraid now, because of this. You sat him a treat. There, my old fellow, my old boy. You take it easy now.' He had Treasure quite quiet, lipping at his fingers. 'This horse isn't bad, miss. He's only young. He needs steady riding, not like he gets with Mr Mark.'

'Where is Mark?' Christina said.

'Coming now, miss.'

Christina was furious with Mark, now that her fright was over. Mark cantered slowly up on Sweetbriar, looking very unconcerned. But when he pulled up beside them and looked at them both, Christina could see that he was afraid, and angry, but did not want it to show. He laughed and said to Christina, 'Well, how about that for a gallop? Did you enjoy it?'

'He'd have gone through that hedge if Dick hadn't stopped him,' Christina said coldly. 'Then where would I have been?'

'Home by now,' Mark said flippantly.

'She could have been killed, sir, and you know it,' Dick said suddenly. 'You had no right to put her on this horse.'

'So you're taking credit for saving her life?' Mark said, his face flushing angrily.

'No. But I reckon it was lucky Mr Fowler told me to take Woodpigeon out for an hour, that's all.'

Mark got down from Sweetbriar and said to Dick abruptly, 'Change the saddles back.'

Dick did as he was told, silently. When Sweetbriar was ready he gave Christina a leg up, and Christina settled herself gratefully on the mare, and said, very gravely, 'Thank you very much, Dick.' She loved Dick very much at that moment, and hated Mark with a cold, flat contempt. Dick looked up at her and smiled one of his rare, sweet smiles.

'That's all right, miss.'

Mark said to him, 'Hold Treasure while I mount.'

Dick soothed the bay horse, who sensed Mark's anger and was nervous again. When Mark had gathered up his reins, he paused and looked down at Dick.

'You won't mention what happened, when you get back?'

Dick said nothing. Mark flushed again, his anger rising. 'You heard what I said? No one is to know what happened.'

'If you say so, sir.'

'Look,' said Mark, very evenly, 'I do say so. And I'll say something else. If I find out that anyone in the stables knows what happened this morning, I'll see that you get dismissed.'

Dick's eyes opened very wide. He stroked Treasure's neck, silent, turning away from Christina.

'Well?'

'Yes, sir,' Dick said. 'I understand.'

The Great Gilly Hopkins

Katherine Paterson

Gilly Hopkins has lived in foster homes for most of her life, but no one has been able to put up with her for long. . . Her latest home is with fat, kindly Maime Trotter who is also looking after little William Ernest – W.E. for short. Gilly has no intention of making life easy for Trotter, W.E. or for Mr Randolph – the blind man who comes to supper every night. There is only one person Gilly loves: the mother she never sees. This passage opens with Gilly's first day at her new school.

'I see they call you Gilly,' said Mr Evans, the principal.

'I can't even pronounce the poor child's real name,' said Trotter, chuckling in what she must believe was a friendly manner.

It didn't help Gilly's mood. She was still seething over the hair combing.

'Well, Gilly's a fine name,' said Mr Evans, which confirmed to Gilly that at school, too, she was fated to be surrounded by fools.

The principal was studying records that must have been sent over from Gilly's former school, Hollywood Gardens Elementary. He coughed several times. 'Well,' he said, 'I think this young lady needs to be in a class that will challenge her.'

'She's plenty smart, if that's what you mean.'

Trotter, you dummy. How do you know how smart I am? You never laid eyes on me until yesterday.

'I'm going to put you into Miss Harris's class. We have some departmentalization in the sixth grade, but. . .'

'You got *what* in the sixth grade?'

Oh, Trotter, shut your fool mouth.

But the principal didn't seem to notice what a dope Trotter was. He explained patiently how some of the sixth-grade classes moved around for maths and reading and science, but Miss Harris kept the same group all day. What a blinking bore.

They went up three flights of ancient stairway to Miss Harris's room slowly, so that Trotter would not collapse. The corridors stank of oiled floors and cafeteria soup. Gilly had thought she hated all schools so much that they no longer could pain or disappoint her, but she felt heavier with each step – like a condemned prisoner walking an endless last mile.

They paused before the door marked 'Harris–6'. Mr Evans knocked, and a tall tea-coloured woman, crowned with a bush of black hair, opened the door. She smiled down on the three of them, because she was even taller than the principal.

Gilly shrank back, bumping into Trotter's huge breast, which made her jump forward again quickly. God, on top of everything else, the teacher was black.

No one seemed to take notice of her reaction, unless you counted a flash of brightness in Miss Harris's dark eyes.

Trotter patted Gilly's arm, murmured something that ended in 'honey', and then she and the principal floated backward, closing Gilly into Harris–6. The teacher led her to an empty desk in the middle of the classroom, asked for Gilly's jacket, which she handed over to another girl to hang on the coatrack at the back of the room. She directed Gilly to sit down, and then went up and settled herself at the large teacher's desk to glance through the handful of papers Mr Evans had given her.

In a moment she looked up, a warm smile lighting her face. 'Galadriel Hopkins. What a beautiful name! From Tolkien, of course.'

'No,' muttered Gilly. 'Hollywood Gardens.'

Miss Harris laughed a sort of golden laugh. 'No, I mean your name – Galadriel. It's the name of a great queen in a book by a man named Tolkien. But, of course, you know that.'

Hell. No one had ever told her that her name came from a book. Should she pretend she knew all about it or play dumb?

'I'd like to call you Galadriel, if you don't mind. It's such a lovely name.'

'No!' Everyone was looking at Gilly peculiarly. She must have yelled louder than she intended to. 'I would prefer,' she said tightly, 'to be called Gilly.'

'Yes' – Miss Harris's voice was more steel than gold now – 'Yes. Gilly, it is then. Well' – she turned her smile on the rest of the class – 'Where were we?'

The clamour of their answers clashed in Gilly's brain. She started to put her head down on the desk, but someone was shoving a book into her face.

It wasn't fair – nothing was fair. She had once seen a picture in an old book of a red fox on a high rock surrounded by snarling dogs. It was like that. She was smarter than all of them, but they were too many. They had her surrounded, and in their stupid ways, they were determined to wear her down.

Miss Harris was leaning over her. Gilly pulled away as far as she could.

'Did you do division with fractions at Hollywood Gardens?'

Gilly shook her head. Inside she seethed. It was bad enough having to come to this broken-down old school but to be behind – to seem dumber than the rest of the kids – to have to appear a fool in front of. . . Almost half the class was black. And she would look dumb to *them*. A bunch of—

'Why don't you bring your chair up to my desk, and we'll work on it?'

Gilly snatched up her chair and beat Miss Harris to the front of the room. She'd show them!

At recesstime Monica Bradley, one of the other white girls in the class, was supposed to look after her on the playground. But Monica was more interested in leaning against the building and talking with her friends, which she did, keeping her back toward Gilly as she giggled and gossiped with two other sixth-grade girls, one of whom was black with millions of tiny braids all over her head. Like some African bushwoman. Not that Gilly cared. Why should she? They could giggle their stupid lives away, and she'd never let it bother her. She turned her back on them. That would show them.

Just then a ball jerked loose from the basketball game nearby and rushed toward her. She grabbed it. Balls were friends. She hugged it and ran over to the basket and threw it up, but she had been in too much of a hurry. It kissed the rim but refused to go in for her. Angrily she jumped and caught it before it bounced. She was dimly aware of a protest from the players, but they were boys and mostly shorter than she, so not worthy of notice. She shot again, this time with care. It arched and sank cleanly. She pushed someone out of the way and grabbed it just below the net.

'Hey! Who you think you are?'

One of the boys, a black as tall as she, tried to pull the ball from her hands. She spun round, knocking him to the concrete, and shot again, banking the ball off the backboard neatly into the net. She grabbed it once more.

Now all the boys were after her. She began to run across the playground laughing and clutching the ball to her chest. She could hear the boys screaming behind her, but she was too fast for them. She ran in and out of hopscotch games and right through a jump rope, all the way back to the basketball post where she shot again, missing wildly in her glee.

The boys did not watch for the rebound. They leaped upon her. She was on her back, scratching and kicking for all she was worth. They were yelping like hurt puppies.

'Hey! Hey! What's going on here?'

Miss Harris towered above them. The fighting evaporated under her glare. She marched all seven of them to the principal's office. Gilly noted with satisfaction a long red line down the tall boy's cheek. She'd actually drawn blood in the fracas. The boys looked a lot worse than she felt. Six to one – pretty good odds even for the great Gilly Hopkins.

Mr Evans lectured the boys about fighting on the playground and then sent them back to their homerooms. He kept Gilly longer.

'Gilly.' He said her name as though it were a whole sentence by itself. Then he just sat back in his chair, his fingertips pressed together, and looked at her.

She smoothed her hair and waited, staring him in the eye. People hated that – you staring them down as though they were the ones who had been bad. They didn't know how to deal with it. Sure enough. The principal looked away first.

'Would you like to sit down?'

She jerked her head No.

He coughed. 'I would rather for us to be friends.'

Gilly smirked.

'We're not going to have fighting on the playground.' He looked directly at her. 'Or anywhere else around here. I think you need to understand that, Gilly.'

She tilted her head sassily and kept her eyes right on his.

'You're at a new school now. You have a chance to – uh – make a new start. If you want to.'

So Hollywood Gardens had warned him, eh? Well, so what? The people here would have learned soon enough. Gilly would have made sure of that.

She smiled what she knew to be her most menacing smile.

'If there's anyway I can help you – if you just feel like talking to somebody. . .'

Not one of those understanding adults. Deliver me! She smiled so hard it stretched the muscles around her eyes. 'I'm OK,' she said. 'I don't need any help.'

'If you don't want help, there's no way I can make you accept it.

But, Gilly' – he leaned forward in his chair and spoke very slowly and softly – 'you're not going to be permitted to hurt other people.'

She snuffled loudly. Cute. Very cute.

He leaned back; she thought she heard him sigh. 'Not if I have anything to do with it.'

Gilly wiped her nose on the back of her hand. She saw the principal half reach for his box of tissues and then pull his hand back.

'You may go back to your class now.' She turned to go. 'I hope you'll give yourself – and us – a chance, Gilly.'

She ignored the remark. Nice, she thought, climbing the dark stairs. Only a half day and already the principal was yo-yoing. Give her a week, boy. A week and she'd have the whole cussed place in an uproar. But this afternoon, she'd cool it a little. Let them worry. Then tomorrow or maybe even the next day, *Wham*. She felt her old powers returning. She was no longer tired.

=—◦◀◉◀◀(◉)▶◉▶◦—=

She met Agnes Stokes the next day at recess. Agnes was a shrivelled-up-looking little sixth grader from another class. She had long red hair that fell rather greasily to her waist, and when she sidled up to Gilly on the playground, the first thing Gilly noticed was how dirty her fingernails were.

'I know who you are,' the girl said. For a moment Gilly was reminded of the story of Rumpelstiltskin. Like that little creature, this girl had power over her. She knew who Gilly was, but Gilly didn't know who she was.

'Yeah?' said Gilly to let the evil little dwarf know that she wasn't interested.

'That was great about you beating up six boys yesterday.'

'Yeah?' Gilly couldn't help but be a little interested.

'It's all over the school.'

'So?'

'So.' The girl leaned against the building beside her, as though assuming Gilly would be pleased with her company.

'So?'

The girl twitched her freckled nose. 'I thought me and you should get together.'

'How come?' Rumpelstiltskins were always after something.

'No reason.' The smaller girl had on a jacket the sleeves of which were so long that they came down to her knuckles. She began to roll up first her left sleeve and then her right. She did it slowly and silently, as though it were part of some ceremony. It gave Gilly the creeps.

'What's your name?' Gilly blurted out the question, half expecting the girl to refuse to answer.

'Agnes Stokes' – she lowered her voice conspiratorily – 'You can call me Ag.'

Big deal. She was glad when the bell rang, and she could leave Agnes Stokes behind. But when she left school that afternoon, Agnes slipped out from the corner of the building and fell in step with her.

'Wanta come over?' she asked. 'My grandma won't care.'

'Can't.' Gilly had no intention of going into Agnes Stokes's house until she found out what Agnes Stokes was up to. People like Agnes Stokes didn't try to make friends without a reason.

She walked faster, but Agnes kept up with funny, little skip steps. When they got all the way up the hill to Trotter's house, Agnes actually started up the walk after Gilly.

Gilly turned around fiercely. 'You can't come in today!'

'How come?'

'Because,' said Gilly, 'I live with a terrible ogre that eats up little redheaded girls in one gulp.'

Agnes stepped back, with a startled look on her face. 'Oh,' she said. Then she giggled nervously. 'I get it. You're teasing.'

'*Arum golly goshee labooooooo!*' screamed Gilly, bearing down on the smaller girl like a child-eating giant.

Agnes backed away. 'Wha—?' Good. She had succeeded in unsettling Rumpelstiltskin. 'Maybe tomorrow,' said Gilly calmly and marched into the house without turning around.

'That you, William Ernest, honey?' It made her want to puke the way Trotter carried on over that little weirdo.

Trotter came into the hall. 'Oh, Gilly,' she said. 'You got home so quick today I thought it was William Ernest.'

'Yeah.' Gilly started past her up the stairs.

'Wait a minute, honey. You got some mail.'

Mail! It could only be from – and it was. She snatched it out of Trotter's puffy fingers and raced up the stairs, slamming the door and falling upon the bed in one motion. It was a postcard showing sunset on the ocean. Slowly she turned it over.

> My dearest Galadriel,
> The agency wrote me that you had moved.
> I wish it were to here. I miss you.
>> All my love, Courtney

That was all. Gilly read it again. And then a third time. No. That was not all. Up on the address side, in the left-hand corner. The letters were squeezed together so you could hardly read them. An address. Her mother's address.

She could go there. She could hitchhike across the country to California. She would knock on the door, and her mother would open it. And Courtney would throw her arms around her and kiss her all over her face and never let her go. 'I wish it were to here. I miss you.' See, Courtney wanted her to come. 'All my love.'

Inside her head, Gilly packed the brown suitcase and crept down the stairs. It was the middle of the night. Out into the darkness. No. She shivered a little. She would pick a time when Trotter was fussing over W.E. or Mr Randolph. She'd steal some food. Maybe a little money. People picked up hitchhikers all the time. She'd get to California in a few days. Probably less than a week. People were always picking up hitchhikers. And beating them up. And killing them. And pitching their dead bodies into the woods. All because she didn't have any money to buy a plane ticket or even a bus ticket.

Oh, why did it have to be so hard? Other kids could be with their mothers all the time. Dumb, stupid kids who didn't even like their mothers much. While she—

She put her head down and began to cry. She didn't mean to, but it was so unfair. She hadn't even seen her mother since she was three years old. Her beautiful mother who missed her so much and sent her all her love.

'You all right, honey?' Tap, tap, tap. 'You all right?'

Gilly sat up straight. Couldn't anyone have any privacy around this dump? She stuffed the postcard under her pillow and then smoothed the covers that she'd refused to straighten before school. She stood up at the end of the bed like a soldier on inspection. But the door didn't open.

'Anything I can do for you, honey?'

Yeah. Fry yourself, lard face.

'Can I come in?'

'No!' shrieked Gilly, then snatched open the door. 'Can't you leave me alone for one stupid minute?'

Trotter's eyelids flapped on her face like shutters on a vacant house. 'You OK, honey?' she repeated.

'I will be soon as you get your fat self outta here!'

'OK.' Trotter backed up slowly toward the stairs. 'Call me, if you want anything.' As an afterthought, she said, 'It ain't a shameful thing to need help, you know.'

'I don't need any help' – Gilly slammed the door, then yanked it open – 'from anybody!' She slammed it shut once more.

'I miss you. All my love.' I don't need help from anybody except from you. If I wrote you – if I asked, would you come and get me? You're the only one in the world I need. I'd be good for you. You'd see. I'd change into a whole new person. I'd turn from gruesome Gilly into gorgeous, gracious, good, glorious Galadriel. And grateful. Oh, Courtney – oh, Mother, I'd be so grateful.

'Lord, you are so good to us.' Mr Randolph was saying the supper blessing. 'Yes, Lord, so very good. We have this wonderful food to eat and wonderful friends to enjoy it with. Now, bless us, Lord, and make us truly, truly grateful. Ah-men.'

'Ay-men. My, Mr Randolph, you do ask a proper blessing.'

'Oh, Mrs Trotter, when I sit before the spread of your table, I got so much to be thankful for.'

Good lord, how was a person supposed to eat through this garbage?

'Well, Miss Gilly, how was school for you today?'

Gilly grunted. Trotter gave her a sharp look. 'It was OK, I guess.'

'My, you young people have such a wonderful opportunity today. Back when I was going to school – oh, thank you, Mrs Trotter – what a delicious-smelling plate. My, my. . .'

To Gilly's relief, the blind man's attention was diverted from his tale of childhood schooldays to the organization of the food on his plate and the eating of it, which he did with a constant murmuring of delight, dropping little bits from his mouth to his chin or tie.

Disgusting. Gilly switched her attention to William Ernest, who, as usual, was staring at her bug-eyed. She smiled primly and mouthed, 'How do you do, sweetums?'

Sweetums immediately choked on a carrot. He coughed until tears came.

'What's the matter, William Ernest, honey?'

'I think' – Gilly smiled her old lady principal smile – 'the dear child is choking. It must be something he ate.'

'Are you all right, baby?' asked Trotter.

W.E. nodded through his tears.

'Sure?'

'Maybe he needs a pat on the back,' Mr Randolph offered.

'Yeah!' said Gilly. 'How about it, W.E., old man? Want me to swat you one?'

'*No!* Don't let her hit me.'

'Nobody's gonna hit you, honey. Everybody just wants to help.' Trotter looked hard at Gilly. 'Right, Gilly?'

'Just want to help, little buddy.' Gilly flashed her crooked-politician smile.

'I'm all right,' the boy said in a small strangled voice. He slid his chair a couple of inches toward Trotter's end of the table, so that he was no longer directly across from Gilly.

'Say, W.E.' – Gilly flashed her teeth at him – 'how about you and me doing a little red-hot reading after supper? You know, squeeze the old orange reader?'

W.E. shook his head, his eyes pleading with Trotter to save him.

'My, oh, my, Mrs Trotter. I can tell how old I am when I can't even understand the language of the young people about me,' said Mr Randolph.

Trotter was looking first at W.E. and then at Gilly. 'Don't you fret yourself, Mr Randolph.' She leaned across the corner of the table and patted William Ernest gently, keeping her eyes on Gilly. 'Don't you fret, now. Sometimes these kids'll tease the buttons off a teddy bear. Ain't nothing to do with age.'

'Hell, I was just trying to help the kid,' muttered Gilly.

'He don't always know that,' Trotter said, but her eyes were saying 'like heck you were'. 'I got a real good idea,' she went on. 'They tell me, Gilly, that you are some kind of a great reader yourself. I know Mr Randolph would like to hear you read something.'

The little wrinkled face brightened. 'My, my! Would you do that, Miss Gilly? It would be such a pleasure to me.'

Trotter, you rat. 'I don't have anything to read,' Gilly said.

'OK, that ain't a problem. Mr Randolph's got enough books to start a public library, haven't you, Mr Randolph?'

'Well, I do have a few,' he chuckled. 'Course you've got the Good Book right here.'

'What good book?' demanded Gilly, interested in spite of herself. She did like a good book.

'I believe Mr Randolph is referring to the Holy Bible.'

'The *Bible*?' Gilly didn't know whether to laugh or cry. She had a vision of herself trapped forever in the dusty brown parlour reading the Bible to Trotter and Mr Randolph. She would read on and on forever, while the two of them nodded piously at each other. She jumped up from her chair. 'I'll get a book,' she said. 'I'll run over to Mr Randolph's and choose something.'

She was afraid they would try to stop her, force her to read the Bible, but they both seemed pleased and let her go.

Mr Randolph's front door was unlocked. The house was pitch-black and mustier than Trotter's. Quickly, Gilly pushed a light switch. Nothing happened. Of course. Why should Mr Randolph care if a bulb burned out? She stumbled from the hall to where she thought the living room should be, fumbling along the wall with her fingers until she found another switch. To her relief this one worked – only 40 watts' worth, maybe – but still there was light.

Leaning against two walls of the crowded little room were huge antique bookcases that reached the ceiling. And stacked or lying upside down, even put in backward, were books – hundreds of them. They looked old and thick with dust. It was hard to think of funny little Mr Randolph actually reading them. She wondered how long he had been blind. She wished she could push her mind past those blank white eyes into whatever of Mr Randolph all these books must represent.

She went toward the larger shelf to the right of the door, but she felt strangely shy about actually touching the books. It was almost as though she were meddling in another person's brain. Wait. Maybe they were all for show. Maybe Mr Randolph collected books, trying to act like some big-shot genius, even though he himself couldn't read a word. No one would ever catch on. They'd think he didn't read because he couldn't see. That was it, of course. She felt better. Now she was free to look at the books themselves.

Without thinking, she began to straighten out the shelves as she read the titles. She saw several volumes of an encyclopedia set: 'Antarctica to Balfe', then 'Jerez to Liberty'. She looked around for other volumes. It bothered her to have everything in a muddle. High on the top shelf was 'Sarsaparilla to Sorcery'. She dragged a heavy stuffed chair backward to the shelf and climbed up on the very top of its back. On tiptoe, leaning against the rickety lower shelves to keep from toppling, she could barely reach the book. She pulled at it with the tip of her fingers, catching it as it fell. Something fluttered to the floor as she did so.

Money. She half fell, half jumped off the chair, and snatched it up. Two five-dollar bills had fallen out from behind 'Sarsaparilla to Sorcery'. She put the encyclopedia down and studied the old, wrinkled bills. Just when she was needing money so badly. Here they'd come floating down. Like magic. Ten dollars wouldn't get her very far, but there might be more where these came from. She climbed up again, stretching almost to the point of falling, but it was no good. Although she could just about reach the top shelf with her fingertips, she was very unsteady, and the lower shelves were much too wobbly to risk climbing.

Heavy footsteps thudded across the front porch. The front door opened. 'You all right, Gilly, honey?'

Gilly nearly tripped over herself, leaping down and grabbing up 'Sarsaparilla to Sorcery' from the chair seat, stretching her guts out to tip the book into its place on the shelf. And just in time. She got down on the chair seat, as Trotter appeared at the door.

'You was taking so long,' she said. 'Then Mr Randolph remembered that maybe the bulbs was all burned out. He tends to forget since they really don't help him much.'

'There's a light here,' Gilly snapped. 'If there hadn't been, I'd have come back. I'm not retarded.'

'I believe you mentioned that before,' said Trotter dryly. 'Well, you find anything you wanted to read to Mr Randolph?'

'It's a bunch of junk.'

'One man's trash is another man's treasure,' Trotter said in a maddeningly calm voice, wandering over to a lower shelf as she did so. She pulled out a squat leather-bound volume and blew the dust off the top. 'He's got a yen for poetry, Mr Randolph does.' She handed the book up to Gilly, who was still perched on the chair. 'This is one I used to try to read to him last year, but' – her voice sounded almost shy – 'I ain't too hot a reader myself, as you can probably guess.'

Gilly stepped down. She was still angry with Trotter for bursting in on her, but she was curious to know just what sort of poetry old man Randolph fancied. *The Oxford Book of English Verse*. She flipped it open, but it was too dark to see the words properly.

'Ready to come along?'

'Yeah, yeah,' she replied impatiently. Holding her neck straight to keep from looking up at 'Sarsaparilla', she followed Trotter's bulk back to her house.

'What did you bring?' Mr Randolph's face looked like a child's before a wrapped-up present. He was sitting right at the edge of the big brown chair.

'*The Oxford Book of English Verse*,' Gilly mumbled.

He cocked his head. 'I beg your pardon?'

'The poems we was reading last year, Mr Randolph.'

Trotter had raised her voice as she always did speaking to the old man.

'Oh, good, good,' he said, sliding back into the chair until his short legs no longer touched the worn rug.

Gilly opened the book. She flipped through the junk at the beginning and came to the first poem. 'Cuckoo Song,' she read the title loudly. It was rather pleasant being able to do something well that none of the rest of them could. Then she glanced at the body of the poem.

> Sumer is icumen in,
>   Lhude sing cuccu!
> Groweth sed, and bloweth med,
>   And springth the wude nu –
>   Sing cuccu!

Cuckoo was right. 'Wait a minute,' she muttered, turning the page.

> Bytuene Mershe ant Averil. . .

She looked quickly at the next.

> Lenten ys come with love to toune. . .

And the next –

> Ichot a burde in boure bryht,
>   That fully semly is on syht. . .

She slammed the book shut. They were obviously trying to play a trick on her. Make her seem stupid. See, there was Mr Randolph giggling to himself. 'It's not in English!' she yelled. 'You're just trying to make a fool of me.'

'No, no, Miss Gilly. Nobody's trying to make a fool of you. The real old English is at the front. Try over a way.'

'You want the Wordsworth one, Mr Randolph?' asked Trotter. 'Or do you have that by heart?'

'Both,' he said happily.

Trotter came over and leaned across Gilly, who was sitting on the piano bench. 'I can find it,' said Gilly, pulling the book out of her reach. 'Just tell me the name of it.'

'William Wordsworth,' said Mr Randolph. 'There was a time when meadow, grove, and stream . . .' He folded his small hands across his chest, his voice no longer pinched and polite, but soft and warm.

Gilly found the page and began to read:

> 'There was a time when meadow, grove, and stream,
> The earth, and every common sight,
>   To me did seem
>   Apparell'd in celestial light,
> The glory and the freshness of a dream.'

Midnight is a Place

Joan Aiken

Lucas Bell's parents are dead and he lives with his unfriendly, bad-tempered guardian Sir Randolph in Midnight Court. The huge grim house has few inhabitants and Lucas is lonely and bored until, on the eve of his thirteenth birthday, he is suddenly told to go with Mr Oakapple (his tutor) to the Mill. The Mill is really called 'Murgatroyd's Carpet, Rug and Matting Manufactory' and Lucas is to learn how the business is run and eventually take his father's place as Sir Randolph's partner. Lucas has never visited the Mill before and he is shocked and amazed at what he sees and hears. And there is another surprise awaiting him on his return to Midnight Court.

Joan Aiken's enthralling story is an extraordinary mixture of fact and fantasy. In this extract we see the first of many changes in the fortunes of Lucas Bell and Anna-Marie Murgatroyd – the little girl who becomes his friend.

THEY set off in silence. Mr Oakapple driving.
  'Why are we going to the Mill?' Lucas finally summoned up courage to ask. He always felt ill at ease with Mr Oakapple whose manner was invariably short, preoccupied, as if the centre of his thoughts were a very long way off. Although the two of them spent hours together every day doing French, arithmetic, geography, Lucas did not have the least knowledge of what went on inside Mr Oakapple's head.
  'Oh.' Mr Oakapple turned slightly at the question, then concentrated once more on the dark road. 'I thought Sir Randolph had told you. We are going because it is your birthday tomorrow.'
  'I don't understand.'

Lucas knew that he ought to have been pleased at his birthday's being remembered, but he could only feel cold, wet, and anxious. They jolted on through the rainy dark. By now the lodge gates had been left behind; they were descending the broad main hill that led into Blastburn. Gas lamps flared at intervals; the mare's feet slipped and rang on granite cobbles.

'Well.' Mr Oakapple drew a sharp, impatient sigh. 'You know that your father was Sir Randolph's partner.'

'Yes.'

'And after he died it was found that he had left a will appointing Sir Randolph as your guardian.'

'Yes,' Lucas answered despondently, remembering his journey back from India to England last year, after the death of his parents from smallpox, and the miserable arrival at Midnight Court.

'It was also laid down in your father's will that from the age of thirteen you should be permitted to learn the business, in order that, when you were of age, you could take your father's place as partner. Your father stipulated that some part of each day should be spent in the Mill, studying how it was run. And I have to go with you.'

Mr Oakapple's tone indicated that he did not in the least relish this programme, but Lucas did not notice the tutor's shortness for once.

His great relief at learning that he was not immediately to be put to work as a stripper or fluff-picker was mixed with another anxiety. How, he wondered, did one set about running a carpet factory? He found it quite hard enough to perform the tasks in geometry or history prepared for him by Mr Oakapple, who often called him a slowtop; he was unhappily certain that learning how to look after a whole factory would be completely beyond him.

They had reached the town. There were very few shops, taverns, or dwelling-houses. The buildings for the most part were factories, workshops where articles were made — nail-foundries where clanging lengths of iron were cut into strips, gasworks where coal was baked in huge ovens, papermills where wood-pulp and clay were boiled into a porridge that was the raw material for books and magazines — jute mills, cotton mills, potteries, collieries. None of these places looked as if they were built by human beings or used by them. Huge, dark, irregular shapes rose up all around; they were like pinnacles in a rocky desert, like ruined prehistoric remains, or like the broken toys of some giant's baby. The potteries were enormous funnels, the gasworks huge flowerpots, the collieries monstrous pyramids, with skeleton wheels the size of whole church-fronts which stood above them against the fiery sky.

Every now and then the roadway was cut by sets of iron rails, and sometimes a clanking train of waggons would run slowly across in front of the governess-cart, and the mare would sweat and whinny and shudder her coat at the sudden loud noise, and the smell of hot metal, and the spark-filled smoke.

'Why do we have to go to the factory at this time?' said Lucas nervously in one of these pauses, while they waited for a train to cross. 'Won't it be shut for the night?'

'Factories never shut.' The tutor glanced at him briefly. 'Didn't you know about shift-work? When the day-workers leave, the night-workers come on, so that the machines, which cost a great deal of money, need never stand idle. We shall get there just as the night shift come on duty. It makes no difference when we arrive, people are always at work.'

Somehow this idea filled Lucas with dismay. He thought of the machinery always running by night and day, the great fires always burning, the huge buildings always filled with little black people dashing to and fro; never any darkness, or silence, or rest; he felt a kind of terror at the thought of wheels turning on and on, without ever stopping.

'Don't the machines ever stop at all?'

'Oh, perhaps for one week in the year, so that they can clean the boilers and put a new lining on the main press. Here we are,' said Mr Oakapple with gloom, turning the mare's head in at a pair of huge gates through a wall even higher than that around Midnight Park. Tram rails ran right through the gates and across a wide cobbled area beyond, which was lit by gas flares.

Mr Oakapple brought the mare to a halt, and found a place to tether her in a line of stable-sheds at one side of the factory yard. As he did this, they were passed by a dismal little procession going in the opposite direction. Two or three women with checked shawls over their heads accompanied a pair of men who were carrying something, a small shape, on a plank, covered by a blanket.

A short distance behind them walked another shawled woman. Her arms were folded, her head bent. She walked draggingly, as if she had been dead tired for more weeks than she could remember.

As she passed near Lucas and Mr Oakapple, a black-frock-coated man came out of a small brightly lit office and spoke to her.

'Mrs Braithwaite – ah, Mrs Braithwaite! Mr Gammel said to tell you that the compensation will be sent up tomorrow morning – you may be sure of that – ten shillings and a free doormat. The very best quality!'

'Ten shillings?' The woman flung back her shawl and stared at him for a moment, in silence. Her face was very pale. Then she said, 'What do I care about your ten shillings? That won't bring my Jinny back, that had the sweetest voice in our lane and could make a bacon pudding to equal mine, though she was only eight.'

The frock-coated man shrugged. 'Say what you please, there's not many turns up their noses at ten shillings and a free mat – why, you could sell *that* again, if you already have one, for double the factory price.'

'Have one?' she said bitterly, her voice rising. 'Why, we have *three*, already. Three fine free doormats. What do you say to that, Mr Bertram Smallside?' Then she drew the shawl over her face again and followed the plank-bearers out through the gate into the rainy night.

'What did she mean?' whispered Lucas uneasily, as he and Mr Oakapple left the cart and walked towards the frock-coated man, who had turned back in the direction of his office.

'Oh –' the tutor's voice was low, and dry; he spoke hurriedly. 'I suppose her child may have been injured by the great press – she was one of the fluff-pickers, maybe; it does happen from time to time, I have heard –'

He entered the office. Lucas remained outside, looking towards the gateway, which was empty now. He remembered the words of Bob the groom – 'Nineteen or twenty a year, regular – specially fluff-pickers – even more than falls into the soap-plodders at Lathers and Smothers –'

Inside the office he heard his tutor saying, 'Mr Smallside? Good evening. I believe Sir Randolph has already sent word. I come from the Court; I have brought down young master Lucas Bell, as arranged, to be shown the work.'

Mr Smallside's manner changed completely. He had been looking irritably at the visitors as if he had little time for them; now he smiled. And the brisk, matter-of-fact tone he had used with Mrs Braithwaite was replaced by obsequious, hand-rubbing civility, as he emerged.

'Young Master Bell? Yes indeed, yes *indeed*, Sir Randolph did graciously think to mention it. He sent a note. Delighted to meet you, Master Bell, delighted indeed! What a pleasure, what a pleasure! How well I remember your dear father, at least I almost remember him, for in fact he left to look after our Indian supply-office just the year before I became manager here but I've heard his name spoken so often that it's much the same. Such a sad loss when he passed away. And so you're his son! Young Master Bell! Well, well, well, young Master Bell, what can we do for you?'

'I – I don't exactly know,' stammered Lucas, quite taken aback by all this politeness, so extremely different from his usual treatment. In spite of it – or even because of it – he was not sure that he liked Mr Smallside, who was a lean, pallid man with a balding head and a face the colour and shape of a bar of carpet soap; his hand, also, with which he grasped that of Lucas and shook it up and down very many times, had a kind of damp, soapy feel to it. Lucas withdrew his own as soon as possible, and, when he could manage it without being observed, rubbed his palm vigorously against the skirts of his rough frieze jacket.

'Now,' said Mr Smallside, leading them into the office, which was a kind of little hut in the middle of the yard, cramped, hot, piled high with dusty papers, and lit by hissing gas globes. 'Now, what can we offer young Master Bell? A bit of parkin? A drop of prune wine? A caraway biscuit? Young gentlemen usually have a sweet tooth, *I* know!'

'Nothing, thank you,' Mr Oakapple replied for Lucas. His tone was brusque. 'I think we should commence our tour straight away. The boy still has his school work to do as well.'

'Dear, dear, dear!' Mr Smallside shook his head sorrowfully. 'Don't stretch the young shoot too far, though, Mr Oakapple? All work and no play won't make the best hay, we used to say when I was a young lad –' Putting his head on one side he smiled at Lucas so much that the smile seemed likely to run round and meet at the back of his head. Lucas felt more than ever that he could not possibly be at ease in the company of Mr Smallside, and hoped that they would not have him as escort while they went over the Mill.

He soon discovered that he need have had no anxieties on this score. It was suddenly plain that Mr Smallside felt he had kept his smile on long enough; it dropped from his face like melted butter and he went to the door of his hut and bawled across the yard:

'Scatcherd! Scatcherd! Where are you? Hey, one of you trimmers – Barth, Stewkley, Danby, Bloggs – send Scatcherd to me directly. Make haste, there.'

His tone was quite different again – bullying, loud, sharp, as if he enjoyed showing off his power.

A man left the rest and ran across the yard.

'There you are, then,' Mr Smallside addressed him disagreeably. 'Took your time, didn't you? You're to show young Master Bell here over the works, anything he wants to see.'

'What about the new load o'wool?' said the man who had come into the hut. His tone was not quite insolent, but it was by no means humble; he stood in the doorway, panting a little, and looked squarely at Smallside. He was a thin, white-faced, muscular, youngish man, with sharp features and black hair, a lock of which had fallen across his forehead, partly obscuring but not concealing the fact that he had one eye covered by a black patch. It might have been the reflection from the red flares outside, shining through the unglazed window, but Lucas thought that Scatcherd's other eye held a spark of something bright, fierce, and dangerous; he looked like a circus animal that had not been very well tamed.

'Bloggs can handle the wool,' Smallside answered shortly. 'Show the young gentleman round, anywhere he asks you to take him.'

'Where shall I start?' said Scatcherd in a sulky tone.

'At the beginning. Show him the wool intake. And then the cutters. And then the looms. And the glueing. And the trimming. And so on – good heavens, I don't have to wet-nurse you, do I?'

'Shall I show him the press?' Scatcherd inquired. There was nothing out of the way about his manner but the question somehow fell oddly.

Smallside's answer took a moment in coming.

'Later – that can come later. After the rest. If there's time. Get on, man! I have all these orders to countersign.'

Mr Smallside turned with a preoccupied busy air to the papers on his desk and Scatcherd, by means of a sideways jerk of his head, indicated that Oakapple and Lucas were to follow him. They hurried after him across the cobbled yard. Lucas, glancing back, felt sorry for poor Noddy the mare, left alone in the dark, noisy, dreary place, and highly apprehensive for himself as to what lay ahead.

He was to dream, that night and for many nights to come, of what he saw during the next couple of hours.

It was not so much that the sights were frightening, though some were that; but they were so strange, so totally unfamiliar compared with anything that he had ever seen before; the shapes and movements of the machines were so black, quick, ugly, or sudden; the noises were so atrociously loud, the heat was so blistering, the smells so sickly, acid, or stifling.

'This here's the melder – or the grabber – or the sorting-press – or the tub-thumper –' Scatcherd kept saying, as he dodged nimbly under great metal arms, round swiftly spinning enormous screws, by wheels that were almost invisible from speed, and ever-whirling belts, through arches of pistons that rose and fell like the legs of some giant insect whose body was hidden in the forest of machinery above them. Scatcherd never bothered to turn his head or to raise his voice while he imparted information about the work. Often Lucas could see his lips move but could catch less than a tenth of what he said. Could those be the right names for the machines, or could Scatcherd be deliberately misleading them? In either case, Lucas felt that at the end of the two hours he would be no wiser than at the start; he was totally bewildered by all he saw.

The wool intake was the only part of the process that he could really grasp: raw wool, as taken from the sheep's backs, came clanking into the works on the trains of trucks that ran through the forecourt. The wool was in huge bales, corded up like outsize parcels. Men slashed through the cords and the bales immediately exploded apart into masses of springy fluff which was sent sliding down a great chute into a kind of hopper where it was washed and graded; then it was teased, to have the knots and lumps and prickles taken out; then, according to the grade, some wool was dyed, some was bleached; the men in charge of the dye vats were a strange sight for they were splashed all over in brilliant colours; their hair was coloured, their arms were green or blue or crimson to the elbows.

Some of the carpets were woven with shuttles on looms. The looms, with their high and complicated machinery, occupied several of the large central buildings. But other carpets, the more inexpensive ones, were made in a new way, invented, Scatcherd told them, by Sir Quincy Murgatroyd, the original founder of the factory. He had devised a means of sticking short lengths of wool on to canvas, which was both faster and cheaper than the weaving process; and if the carpets tended to come unstuck after a few years, what did that matter? They were not the kind of carpets that were bought by rich folks. Imparting this information, Scatcherd gave his audience a malicious sidelong glance.

'T'glue's not t'best grade, you see,' he remarked, pausing beside a huge vat which contained a frothy brown vile-smelling brew that was just coming to the boil, 'very poor glue that is, and joost as well, for when chaps falls into it, which happens from time to time, they stand a better chance o' coming out alive. Which they never did, mind you, in owd Sir Quincy's day; the glue he used would ha' stuck Blastburn Town Hall oopside down on top o' Kilnpit Crags till the week after Joodgement Day.'

'People fall in *there*?' said Lucas faintly.

'Ah, it's slippery roond the edge, you see; you don't want to step too close, young master, or you'll get those nice nankeen britches splashed,' Scatcherd told him with a mocking smile.

Oakapple opened his mouth as if he would have liked to put in some remark, but Scatcherd led them on, talking all the time, past wide rollers, which spread the glue on the canvas backing, and complicated mechanical arms which, working back and forth on hinges, sprinkled the chopped-up wool over the gluey surface. Then there were implements like rakes, or combs, which straightened the pile, teasers to remove any clots of glue, sponges to mop away loose hairs, and a sucker-fan to draw the wool up so that it stood on end, while the carpet was whirled round on a platform called a swiveller.

'Had enow, happen?' Scatcherd inquired drily, as they stood by the swiveller which spun and rocked so giddily that it made Lucas feel dizzy just to watch it. 'Reckon you've looked at as mooch as you can take for one shift?'

Lucas did feel so, but his pride was pricked by Scatcherd's tone.

'What was that thing you spoke of to Mr Smallside — the press? We haven't seen that yet, have we?'

'Oh, I think we've looked at quite enough for one evening —' Oakapple was beginning, but Scatcherd, again without appearing to hear the tutor, said, seeming to find this a most unexpected request, 'The press? You want to see the press? Eh — very well,' and he turned on his heel. 'Down this way then — pressing's the end o' the manufacturing process. After that, the carpet's ready for sale. This here's the pressing room — careful down t'steps. They're slippery — t'glue gets all over.'

The pressing room was a huge place like the crypt of a church. Steps led down to it on all four sides.

'Where *is* the press?' Lucas began, and then, looking up, he saw that the whole ceiling was in fact a great metal slab which could be raised or lowered by hydraulic machinery.

A carpet was being unrolled and spread at feverish speed in the square central part of the room. The very instant it was laid out flat the men who had done so bounded up the steps, not a moment too soon, for the press came thudding down with a tremendous clap of dull sound.

'Toss a cob-nut in there, you'll get it cracked free gratis,' Scatcherd said briefly.

Lucas could well believe him. If anybody slipped and fell under the press they would be done for. It rose up again much more slowly than it had come down, and the carpet was snatched away by a mechanical grab; then half a dozen overall-clad children with brooms, who had been ready waiting on the steps, darted out on to the floor and swept it with frantic speed and assiduity before the next piece of carpet was unrolled.

'Why can't the floor by swept by machinery?' Lucas asked.

'Childer's cheaper,' Scatcherd answered laconically, with another of his sidelong glances. 'Machines has to be kept cleaned and oiled, but there's always a new supply o' kids.'

A question trembled in Lucas's mind but he couldn't bring himself to voice it.

'Isn't that job very dangerous?' he wanted to ask, but Scatcherd, as if hearing the unspoken words, went on, 'That bit's not *so* risky, but what does come up chancy is when there's a bit o' fluff or dirt discovered on the carpet when it's spread out – ah! Like there, see?'

A new carpet had been spread out, brown and gold; in the middle, clearly visible on a circle of gold, was a clot of black oily wool, seemingly left from one of the previous processes.

'The chaps on the swiveller work too fast, you see; it often happens,' Scatcherd said. 'Now someone has to go get it off, o' course, before it's ground in by t'press. The quickest one on the shift has to do it – the one they call the Snatcher. Watch now –'

A barefoot girl dashed out on to the carpet, snatched up the bit of wool with a pair of metal tongs, and leapt back to safety on the steps just before the great press thudded down again. She slipped a little on the steps, but recovered by throwing herself forward on to hands and knees, while two mates grabbed her arms.

Lucas took off his hat and rubbed his forehead with the back of his sleeve.

'O' course they gets paid a bit extry for snatching,' Scatcherd
said. 'Ha'penny an hour danger money. Most of us has been
snatchers at one time or another when we was yoonger, but not for
long – you can't keep on long at it, you gets nervous. You begin to
dream at night, then your legs begins to shake and you can't run so
fast.'

Lucas could imagine it. Just having seen the snatcher at work
made him sick with fear. Mr Oakapple evidently shared this
feeling.

'We have to go back,' he said abruptly. 'We have seen enough for
this evening. Thank you.'

Scatcherd nodded; with a shrug that showed he perceived how
they felt, he began moving away towards a pile of unopened bales of
wool.

At that moment a man in a wheelchair spun past Oakapple and
Lucas with almost uncanny speed. Veering his chair towards
Scatcherd, he called, 'Ey, David! Coom to t'sing-song at t'Mason's
Arms tonight?'

Scatcherd turned. Without replying to the invitation he said,
'Two o' thy lazy, feckless cackhanded swivel-hands left clots on this
afternoon. Has tha heard aboot t'Braithwaite kid?'

The man in the wheelchair made no reply; the silence between
him and Scatcherd seemed condensed, like the air before thunder.
Then the wheelchair turned and shot away. Oakapple walked into
the forecourt and Lucas followed.

'There will be no need to say good night to Mr Smallside. He's
busy,' Mr Oakapple said, and untied the mare. They climbed
silently into the trap. The mare was eager to be off and broke into a
trot, jolting the wheels over the cobbles and the tram-tracks. They
rattled briskly through the open gates and then slowed down for the
long climb out of Blastburn.

228

Halfway up, on the other side, stood the Blastburn Municipal Infirmary, which, Lucas knew, had been built at the expense of Sir Quincy Murgatroyd. As they passed the gates he wondered if the Braithwaite child was in there.

But near the top of the hill he was surprised to perceive ahead of them what seemed to be still the same sad little procession of men and women, still slowly carrying the hurt child.

'Where can they be going?' he demanded of Mr Oakapple. 'No one lives up here, so far out of town – do they?' he added, as his tutor remained silent.

'No – nobody lives up here,' Mr Oakapple said reluctantly, after another pause. 'I suppose they are going to the cemetery.'

The cemetery gates, guarded by large granite pillars, each topped with a stone angel, stood to the right, just over the brow of the hill.

By the time the governess-cart had reached the gates, the group of mourners had passed through, but the shawled woman whom Mr Smallside had addressed as Mrs Braithwaite remained outside. She was sitting on a milestone by the roadside, rocking herself back and forth, repeating the same words over and over.

'They got my Jean, they got my Nance, they got my Jinny. But they shan't get Sue, they shan't get Betsy – I'd sooner see them starve. I'd sooner see them starve.'

One of the men returned from the graveyard.

'Coom along, then, missus?' he said awkwardly. 'Doesn't tha want to be there?'

'Coom on, Bess lass,' said another woman, putting a hand on her friend's shoulder. But Mrs Braithwaite shook her head.

'I seen it three times. I know what happens,' she said. 'I said my good-bye to Jinny the day she went through the Mill gates.' And she returned to her rocking and murmuring.

Mr Oakapple whirled the reins sharply and slapped them against the mare's withers. She had been going slowly, but broke into a trot, and soon the cemetery gates were left behind.

Neither of the passengers in the cart said anything more until they were back in the stable yard where Garridge, the head groom, was waiting to take the mare and rub her down.

'Sir Randolph wants Mester Lucas in t'stoody,' he said briefly.

Lucas felt his spirits, already lowered by the evening's happenings, decline still further. Would Sir Randolph be waiting for an account, a report of all they had seen? Would Lucas now be obliged to answer a whole series of questions on the carpet-manufacturing process? He tried in vain to assemble his thoughts, and recall the sequence of actions that turned wool into carpets. All he could think of was the snatcher, dashing out from under the murderous weight of the press, and Mrs Braithwaite, sitting huddled in her shawl by the graveyard gates.

'Well, bustle along, then, boy,' Mr Oakapple snapped, with a sudden return to his usual impatient manner, which had not been evident during their visit to the Mill. 'You know Sir Randolph can't abide being kept waiting. Here – I'll take your hat and coat. You may go up the front stairs, it's quicker.'

Lucas nodded, with a dry mouth, and made his way to the main hall. His heart had begun to thud uncomfortably in his chest, with almost as much impact, he felt, as the press itself. Slowly climbing the marble stair he was weighed down by the whole burden of the day, which seemed to have been going on for about twenty hours already. For a moment he stood outside the study door, reluctant to knock. He had not entered this room above three times during the year he had spent at Midnight Court, and on none of these occasions had his guardian appeared at all friendly or pleased to see him. There seemed little chance of any difference on the present occasion.

It must be very late – nearly midnight. But Sir Randolph kept late hours, everybody knew – he was a poor sleeper; often throughout the hours of dark his lamp could be seen shining out over the blackened grass of Midnight Park.

No sound came from behind the door and Lucas tapped softly, with a stifled hope that perhaps his guardian had dozed off since issuing the summons, but the high irascible voice called, 'Come in – come in – don't dawdle on the threshold, curse you!'

Lucas quickly opened the door and walked in.

The study – a room almost as bare and shabby as the schoolroom – was lit by only one candle, which had burned down to a stub. A couple of red coals glowed faintly on the hearth. An almost empty decanter and tumbler stood on the desk by the guttering candle. There was a powerful smell of brandy in the room.

Sir Randolph, with all his face and body in shadow, sat half curled, half crouched, in the big leather chair by the desk, with the folds of a plaid rug wrapped round his shoulders and spread over his knees; his two knobbed canes leaned against the arm of the chair.

'Well – don't just stand there – come forward, boy!' he ordered sharply, in his high voice that was like the croak of some angry bird.

'Shan't I put some more coal on the fire, sir?'

'No, rot you! Coal costs money – perhaps you hadn't heard? Leave it alone! Stay – you may light another candle. Then come here.'

Lucas found a candle, set it in place of the stub, and lit new from old. As the yellow flame grew taller he noticed with part of his mind that the carpet on Sir Randolph's study floor was of the very same brown and gold pattern as the one he had seen an hour ago on the floor of the pressing room.

'Well – have you been down there? Have you been over the Mill?' Sir Randolph demanded, as the light was placed in front of him. The strength of his voice seemed to rise and fall with a variability like that of wind or the sea; he leaned forward abruptly and drank, splashing some of the contents of his tumbler on to the leather top of the desk.

'Yes, sir.'

'Understand it?'

'Not – not altogether, sir –' Lucas began.

'Be quiet, then! I don't want to hear about it. Don't – want – hear 'bout it,' he repeated, in a kind of snarling sing-song, though Lucas had not ventured to speak. 'Jus' learn 'bout it, that's all – you are to go there every day until you do understan' 'bout it – every day – that's what you have t'do.'

'May – may I go now, sir?' Lucas was confused and alarmed by his guardian's manner, which seemed half angry, half absent, as if his attention were directed to matters far away in the distant past.

Seeking for some resemblance to this behaviour which had struck him recently, Lucas thought of his tutor, Mr Oakapple. How strange! And yet there seemed no real point of similarity between the two men.

Sir Randolph was gazing at the new candle dreamily; in the dim light little could be seen of his deeply lined face but the outline of the hooked nose, heavy eyelids, and thin mouth, of which the lower lip was set somewhat behind the upper one, making his profile even more like that of a bird of prey. Although not much above sixty, Sir Randolph could have been taken for a man ten or fifteen years older than that. Troubles, and his own nature, had aged him early.

'Go? No! Who said you could go? Stand still – don't fidget.' Sir Randolph's head lifted sharply. He took off his worn black velvet smoking-cap and looked into it as if he hoped to find a memorandum written inside. '*I'll* tell you when you may go and it isn't yet. Was something else I had to say t'you.'

He fell into a brown study again.

Lucas waited nervously.

'Ah – know what it was – yes.' Sir Randolph roused himself again. 'Fellow said you'd been complaining of loneliness. Wanted comp'ny – something of th'sort –' His next words sank into a mutter but 'puling milksop' seemed to be detectable among them.

'Loneliness? Sir – I never –' Lucas began, very much startled. Whom could Sir Randolph have meant by that 'fellow' – surely not Mr Oakapple, to whom Lucas had never spoken of his longing for a friend or companion of his own age.

'Quiet, boy! I don't fesh – fetch you here t'entertain me, do I? Deuce knows you don't do that. Where was I? Yes, comp'ny. Well, now you've got comp'ny, due t'that fellow's int'ference. Company you have got. So don' let me hear word'f any *more* complaints, d'unnerstan'?'

'I have company? What company, sir?' Lucas was completely puzzled.

'Turned up today – 's evening. Old Gourd been seeing t'arrangements. Oak Chamber. So no more moaning, no more grouching, hear? Now, *go* – d'think I want you staring at me with that cheese-faced look all evening? You put me in mind – can't stand it. – No matter. But *she* was beautiful,' he muttered to himself, then looked up at Lucas and said, 'Get out of my sight.'

'May I – may I go to the Oak Chamber?'

'Oh, certainly – go an' play billiards t'll cockcrow if you wish, don' let me detain you,' snarled Sir Randolph, dragging savagely at his crimson wool bellpull. 'Skate, play marbles, ride the farmhorses, break the windows, pull the whole *house* down – only clear out of here!'

Lucas waited no longer. Leaving his guardian muttering, cursing, and hauling on the crimson rope, he slipped out of the room and sped along the passage in the direction of the Oak Chamber, from which he had seen Mrs Gourd emerging earlier that evening.

It did briefly cross his mind that the hour might be somewhat late to disturb the newcomer, but his eagerness and his loneliness were too great to bear any delay. A companion! A friend with whom he could share lessons and exercises, a friend to talk to, read with, accompany on scrambles up Grimside, the great black hill to the north of the town – perhaps even farther. If the other boy was older, and sensible, they might, at holiday time, be allowed to take the governess-cart out by themselves with food for the day; they could go fishing, or crag-climbing, things Lucas had never done but dreamed of doing. They might even get as far as the sea. They could play tennis and battledore in the old tumbledown court, they could climb the sooty chestnuts and explore the old ice-house in the park – there seemed no end to the possibilities that might be achieved, with a real companion.

In the most secret corner of his mind, Lucas already had such a companion, an invented one. When he went out for his solitary trudge across Midnight Park to the town moor, when he munched his lonely meals, when he lay sleepless at night with the silence of the house around him, words inside his head automatically flowed into an accustomed pattern:

Once upon a time, Lucas and Greg started out for a walk. They had left their horses behind for once, because they were going to cross the dangerous quagmire known as Scroop Moss; in their knapsacks they carried a scanty but sufficient repast of bread, dried meat, and a handful of dates; their quest was to locate the huge and dreadful monster said to lurk at the bottom of Grydale Water . . .

The features of Greg were as clear to Lucas, in his mind's eye, as those of Sir Randolph or Mr Oakapple. Greg was tall, with dark hair and blue eyes, he was fifteen or sixteen, quick-minded, with a ready smile, fond of riding, reading, and swimming, better at some things than Lucas, algebra, knew more about wild birds and music, but didn't know so much French and couldn't draw so well . . .

Of course it would be stupid to hope that the exact image of Greg would be waiting in the Oak Chamber, Lucas knew better than that, but still – And whatever he was like, almost certainly the poor fellow would want cheering up, Lucas thought, knocking gently on the door, remembering his own solitary and uncomforted days when he had first arrived at Midnight Court, the period of utter misery before even Mr Oakapple had been brought in to instruct him.

I'll just go and introduce myself, he thought, simply say a friendly word or two, and then I'll leave him to sleep. He's possibly come a long way – I wonder where from?

He knocked at the Chamber door. To his great surprise he heard Mrs Gourd's voice rather tartly bidding whoever it was come in and not make too much noise about it.

Lucas turned the handle and entered. The Oak Chamber was one of the few bedrooms which had any furniture left now; what remained was somewhat stiff and old-fashioned, a fourposter bed with thick dark hangings, an iron-bound chest, a carved oak grandfather-clock, a high chair, a large clothes-press; the walls were covered by aged worn tapestries which Lucas had occasionally exercised his mind over, if Pinhorn chanced to be in a good mood and let him in while she cleaned the room; he had never decided to his own satisfaction if the embroidered scenes depicted Hannibal crossing the Alps or the Israelites crossing the Red Sea.

The Oak Chamber was looking slightly more cheerful than usual due to the fact that a bright fire blazed on the hearth. In other respects the somewhat sombre furnishings were unchanged. But an air of gay disorder was given by the quantity of clothes and belongings which were strewn about the room. Several boxes, uncorded, spilled their contents on to the carpet; travelling-wraps hung over chairs; hairbrushes and shoes lay scattered at random; a bottle of rose-water, set down by the fireside, sparkled in the light of the flames; a canary in a half-covered cage let out a sudden loud sweet snatch of song.

'My gracious, Mester Lucas, what in the plague's name are *you* doing here at this time of night?' demanded Mrs Gourd in a tone not much above a whisper. 'I thought you were the maid with the warm milk or I'd never have bidden you come in –'

'It's all right, I have leave from Sir Randolph –' Lucas put in quickly. 'Where is –'

'However now you *aye* here I daresay it's for the best,' Mrs Gourd pursued without heeding him. 'You can stay a moment while I go below stairs, for I forgot to ask Fanny to put a pinch of spice in the milk. Any road, you study the French lingo, don't you, wi' that tutor of yours?' she added cryptically as she made for the doorway and passed through it. She put her head back to say, 'Bide till I come again, I'll not be long –' and then vanished from view.

Lucas moved towards the fireplace, mystified by this reception, looking about him for the newcomer. At first he thought that no one else was in the room, then he perceived a shadowy shape on the bed, huddled among cast-off capes, shawls, and pelisses.

Who lay there? Was the person asleep? He waited silently by the fire, unwilling to disturb whoever it was, but also itching with the wish to speak, to start the new friendship. His problem was solved by a half-burnt log, which broke in the middle and fell on to the hearth-stone with a sudden crackle and blaze. Lucas heard a movement from the bed, and a yawn that was half a sob, followed by a low cry:

'Papa?'

Wholly taken aback by the sound of this voice, so completely different from what he had in his mind, Lucas nevertheless started a step or two in the direction of the bed. There, illumined by the blaze, he saw a child, a tiny girl, who looked – to his inexpert guess – not more than five or six years old, staring at him with huge black eyes. Her dark hair was cut in a straight line across her forehead, and dangled on either side of her small face in two untidy plaits; the traces of recent tears showed on her pale cheeks, and as she saw him she began to cry again.

'Oh,' she wept, '*you* aren't my Papa. Go away, I hate you! My Papa is dead, he is dead! And Sidi fell off the boat, and I wish I was dead too. Go away, hateful boy!'

Though he was not aware of the fact, Lucas had turned almost as white as the child on the bed; the shock of this reality, after his hopeful imaginings, had been very great. Who was this strange ghostly little creature? Where could she have come from? He stared down at her with a feeling of something like rage – wretched, useless little midget – who wanted her here? Could she really have been the company Sir Randolph had promised him? Was the whole thing a kind of hateful joke on his guardian's part?

But the little girl had thrown herself down on the floor and was crying so wildly, in such frantic hiccuping sobs, that Lucas felt a twinge of compunction mingled with his shock of disappointment. If Mrs Gourd were to come back now, she would be sure to think that he had said something unkind to her and been the cause of this outburst.

'Come,' he said curtly, 'you can't lie there, get up! Stop crying so and get back on the bed. I'll move some of these things –'

He did so, and tried to lift her up, but she shook her shoulder out of his grasp and flung herself away from him with more abandonment, crying, 'Papa – Papa! I don't want you – I don't want anybody but my Papa!'

Only then did Lucas realize with utter stupefaction that she was speaking in French. But what amazed him even more was that, although she had spoken in French, he had understood her. True, for the past ten months he had studied French for two hours every day with Mr Oakapple, but the lessons had not seemed to add up to anything or make sense to him; now, suddenly, he realized that French was a *real* language, in which people spoke, and thought, and understood one another. – And it also suddenly struck him that perhaps Mr Oakapple might be quite a good teacher. But all this passed through his mind with great speed; meanwhile he was leaning over the child, and saying, in a tone that sounded more reasonable than he felt, 'Don't lie there, you will get cold and make yourself ill. It is stupid to lie on the floor, it does no good. It is useless. C'est inutile,' he repeated, listening to himself with astonishment. He was speaking French, and much more fluently than he ever had when conversing with Mr Oakapple. Then it had seemed like a silly game, since they could understand each other so much better in English.

What was even more remarkable, the little girl evidently understood him. She looked at him with dislike, indeed she put out her tongue at him, and said, 'Why should I do what *you* say? You are only a great ugly boy!' But she allowed him at length to pick her up and put her back on the bed. There she sat and stared at him with hostility through her tears.

He looked longingly towards the door and wished that Mrs Gourd would reappear; he was dying to get away, back to his own room. But the silence drew on, and he could hear no footstep in the corridor.

'What is your name? And where do you come from?' he asked the child presently.

At first she looked as if she did not intend to answer. But at length she said, 'Je m'appelle Anna-Marie Eulalie Murgatroyd.' This last she pronounced very slowly and carefully, Mur-ga-troyd. 'Et je suis venue de Calais aujourd'hui.'

'Is that where you have been living – Calais?'

She nodded. 'I and Papa at the house of old Madame Granchot. But,' her little face crumpled again in desolation, 'Papa is dead and Madame is too old to look after me and a lady brought me from Calais to here and Sidi fell off the boat and the man would not stop it to go back, oh-oh-oh-oh-oh –'

'Who is Sidi?' Lucas asked, hoping somehow to stem this new outburst.

'My cat – he is my cat. The boat frightened him and he was strong – he got away from me –'

With a sudden pang Lucas remembered his dog Turk, left behind in Amritsar last year.

'Have you come to live here? I daresay Sir Randolph would let you keep a cat –'

He was not at all sure about this, but in any case the comfort failed to work.

'I do not want another cat, I want my Sidi!'

'Oh, don't be so silly,' Lucas snapped, his patience evaporating. There is nothing so tiring as a person who cannot be comforted, and Lucas already found himself much more tired than usual.

Luckily at this moment Mrs Gourd reappeared with a mug of hot milk. She clicked her tongue in disapproval at the sight of the child's tears.

'It's not my fault –' Lucas began rather defensively.

'Oh, I daresay not. She's been going on like this all the time about her Papa and some *Seedy* she keeps calling for, I don't know who Seedy is –'

'Her cat.'

'Oh, is that it? *I* can't make head or tail of what she says. We'll have to get Mr Oakapple to teach her English right off, she won't get far with that lingo living at Midnight Court. And not a bite of food have I been able to get down her since she set foot in the house. – Come, miss, drink up your milk like a good girl. *Milk*,' she repeated loudly and slowly, holding out the cup.

The child, who was evidently hungry after her nap, did finally begin to drink the milk, holding the cup in both hands, looking first at Mrs Gourd, then suspiciously at Lucas over the rim.

'I'll be going then. Good night. Bonne nuit,' said Lucas, seizing his chance to escape. Mrs Gourd looked as if she had half a mind to ask him to stay on and interpret Anna-Marie's talk, but he had had quite enough; he slipped out and closed the door behind him.

Not until he was halfway to his own bedroom did the full blow of his loss and disappointment strike home.

A portrait hung at the head of the back stairs which led up to the room where he slept. It was a picture of some bygone son of the house, a faded representation of a boy in Cavalier dress who stood smiling, holding up a falcon on his wrist. This boy, with his dark hair and laughing eyes, had, though Lucas hardly realized it, formed the model on which he had built his imaginary friend. Passing it now he was suddenly stabbed by a sense of loss, a feeling that he had been cheated. The pain was so sharp that he involuntarily pressed his hand to his chest, with a kind of sigh that was almost a groan. Hardly aware of what he did, instead of proceeding to his own room, he turned in the other direction, passed along a complicated series of landings, galleries, and corridors, and came at length to Mr Oakapple's door.

A light showed underneath, and he knocked.

'Come in?' called the tutor's voice. He sounded surprised.

Lucas, pushing open the door, stopped short in almost equal surprise, forgetting the urgency of the impulse that had drawn him there.

The tutor lay half reclined in an armchair, facing the door, with his feet up on a stool; a violin rested on his left arm and shoulder, in the position for playing, and his right hand held the bow. But Lucas was certain that he had not been playing. No sound of music had been audible as Lucas approached the door.

'I – I didn't know you played the fiddle, sir?' Lucas blurted.

'I don't,' Mr Oakapple replied shortly, putting the instrument on a table with a somewhat hasty action, covering it with a velvet cloth.

'Are – are you learning?' Confusion made Lucas want to fill the silence.

'Don't be a fool,' said the tutor, with great ill-humour. 'How could I possibly play with two fingers missing?'

Only then, far too late, did Lucas recall the injured fingers which Mr Oakapple invariably kept concealed by a leather glove. The tutor himself never alluded to his disability, but Bob the groom had told Lucas of a household rumour that it was the result of a duel, fought long ago when Mr Oakapple was younger; now, he was quite old, at least thirty-five.

'I – I ask your pardon, sir – I didn't think,' he stammered, hot-faced.

'You never do think about other people, do you? Always shut up in your own world.'

The tutor's tone was depressed, weary, not angry. To Lucas, staring abashed at his own feet, a novel thought came pricking through his depression: was the somewhat chilly relationship between them his own fault, rather than Mr Oakapple's? Would the tutor really prefer it if he, Lucas, tried to be more friendly?

'Anyway, it's of no importance,' the tutor added drily. 'I used to play – once – that's all. – But what brings you here? Why aren't you in bed?' – with a return to his usual severe manner. 'Did you not see Sir Randolph?'

'Yes, sir, I saw him.' A recollection of his grievances rushed back over Lucas and momentarily forgetting this new light on his tutor, he exclaimed, 'Was it you, sir, who told Sir Randolph I'd been complaining about being lonely?'

'Not exactly,' Mr Oakapple said coolly. 'I have certainly said to him that it might benefit your studies if you had a companion.'

'Then was it your idea to bring that – that girl – that *child* who has just come? To be a companion for me?'

'Oh, Anna-Marie?' Mr Oakapple began to laugh. 'No, no, I am not quite such an optimist as to hope that *she* might encourage you in your work. Was that what Sir Randolph suggested? He likes his little joke.'

'Who is she? Why has she come here?' Lucas demanded.

'Well, as you have begun learning the business at the Mill, I don't imagine there is any reason why you shouldn't hear the whole story,' Mr Oakapple replied, looking at Lucas thoughtfully. 'And it might give you something to think about, besides your own fancies. She is little Anna Murgatroyd, grand-daughter of the Mill's original owner, Sir Quincy. But I suppose I had better make sure that Sir Randolph has no objection before I tell you about all that – he might prefer you to hear the history from him.'

'Oh I'm sure he wouldn't,' Lucas said hastily. 'At least, I would much rather hear it from you.'

'Well – you may be right. But at any rate I had better obtain his permission. And tonight is too late. Look at the time! Nearly one. Go to bed, and if Sir Randolph agrees I'll tell you about it tomorrow. Run along – you must be tired after the visit to the Mill. And hungry. You missed your supper. Do you want a piece of pork pie?'

'Why – thank you, sir.' Surprised, awkward, mumbling his thanks, Lucas took the solid heavy hunk of meat wrapped in pastry.

'I get them in the town – old Gourd's cooking doesn't tempt me above half. – Good night then.'

With a nod, dismissing his stammered thanks, Mr Oakapple almost pushed Lucas from the room.

Deep in thought, absently biting off chunks of meat as he walked, Lucas wandered back through the long bare stretches of passage until he reached the schoolroom.

So many things had happened to him since that afternoon – since he wrote his name and the words 'I'm lonely' on the window – that he felt as if half a year had gone by, as if he were six months older than the boy who had looked out so hopelessly at the driving rain. He was still lonely, true, but his thoughts had taken a different turn, they were now reaching out in all directions: like the tendrils of Jack's beanstalk they had found things to grasp and grow on.

He pulled his leatherbound book towards him, righted the fallen bottle of ink, found with relief that it still contained enough to write with, picked up his quill, and began:

Dear Greg, So many things have happened since I last wrote to you yesterday that I hardly know what to tell you first. But perhaps I'll start with the Mill. This afternoon Mr Oakapple suddenly came into the schoolroom . . .

He wrote on for almost an hour, until his hand was numb with cramp, and the last of the ink was gone.

Then, closing the book, he went upstairs to his bedroom, undressed, splashed his face and hands with cold water, climbed into his lumpy bed, and blew out the last of his candle-stubs.

Faces, faces, faces, swam before his mind's eye – smiling Mr Smallside, the mocking Scatcherd with his sidelong look – the haggard, tear-streaked face of Mrs Braithwaite, rocking herself on the milestone. And the little girl, the snatcher, who had darted out so intrepidly as the press descended. And Sir Randolph peering with brandy-reddened eyes into his smoking-cap. And that other sad waif, little Anna-Marie, with her pale cheeks and her great black eyes.

But all the time, behind all these faces, were the never-ceasing wheels, the relentless hammers and pistons of the Mill, and those were what he saw last, for a long, long time, before he finally slept.

Gumble's Yard

John Rowe Townsend

This is a story about children who live in the poorer part of a city in the north of England. Deserted by the adults in their lives, the children decide to set up a home of their own in a disused warehouse. They are afraid of being split up and sent away from the streets they know, so they try and keep out of sight, living on the earnings from Kevin's paper round and what food their friend Dick can bring them. But strange happenings in the warehouse force them out from their hiding place. Here are the opening chapters of this lively and fast-moving story.

IT was a fine spring day, not warm but with a sort of hazy sunshine, and I was walking through the Jungle with my sister Sandra and my friend Dick. The Jungle isn't a real jungle, it's a district off the Wigan Road in the city of Cobchester. We call it the Jungle because all the streets are named after tropical flowers – like Orchid Grove, where we live. That may sound gay and colourful, but there's nothing colourful about the Jungle. It's a dirty old place, and one of these days the Corporation are going to pull it all down – if it doesn't fall down of its own accord first.

But on this sunny Saturday morning, as we walked home to dinner, even the Jungle seemed a cheerful place. Summer was coming, the blades of grass were showing between the stone setts, and soon the weeds would blossom on the empty sites. The days were getting longer. Next week perhaps we would be playing cricket after school. There was a dog in Mimosa Row that I was getting very friendly with. I was going to make a soap-box car for my cousin Harold. Life was full of interesting things to do.

We walked three abreast, with Sandra in the middle. And as we turned into Orchid Grove I felt happy and burst out singing.

'Hark at him!' said Sandra. 'Not a care in the world.'

'Poor old Kevin!' said Dick, with mock sympathy. 'He's got a pain. Where does it hurt, Kevin?'

'I'll hurt *you* in a minute!' I said.

'Oh yes? You and who else?'

'Do you think I couldn't?'

'Yes, I do think you couldn't.'

'Well, I'll show you.' And we started a friendly scuffle, the kind that happens a dozen times a day.

I generally get the worse of any fight with Dick. He's fourteen, a year older than I am, and quite a bit bigger. He's a cheerful red-headed boy, very good-looking, and the only thing wrong with him

is that he's bossy. He thinks he's a born leader (which he may be) and he thinks he's always right (which he isn't). And now he held me off with one hand, grinning in a way that he knew would annoy me.

'Break it up, you two!' said Sandra. Small and thin, with sharp determined face, she stepped between us. 'Fight when you're on your own, not when you're with me. Kevin, what did you start it for? It was all your fault.'

Sandra always blames me – partly because I'm her brother and partly because in her eyes Dick can do no wrong.

'Just wait a minute, Sandra,' said Dick. 'Give me time to bash his brains out. Oh no, I was forgetting, he hasn't any. . . .'

'Oh, leave off!' said Sandra again; and then, as something caught her eye, she added, 'Just look what's happening over there!'

Dick and I broke it up, and looked the way she was pointing.

Along the other side of the street came the two grown-ups from our house. First, Doris, in her best coat and headscarf, stalking ahead as fast as she could walk. Then Walter, with a battered suitcase, scurrying after her.

Walter is our uncle. When our parents died Sandra and I went to live with Walter and his two young children, Harold and Jean. Walter's wife had left him, and Sandra had to act as mother to the younger ones. It was hard work for her. She's only twelve herself.

When Doris, a friend of Walter's, came to live with us, it looked as though things might get better. But not for long. Doris was a blonde, bulky woman with a round, puddingy face. She was always padding about the house in slippers, a cigarette in her mouth, grousing and not getting anything done. She didn't like us children, and she tried to take it out on Walter. Every few days they'd have a row and she'd threaten to go away.

'I'm leaving you,' she'd say. 'I'm not staying in this house another minute.'

'All right, then,' Walter would say. 'Hop it, and good riddance.'

He knew she wouldn't hop it, because she'd nowhere else to go.

'You'll say that once too often, Walter Thompson,' she'd tell him, and then she'd go on grumbling: 'What with you and them brats, it's enough to drive me barmy. . . .' But it would all die down. By evening they'd be round at the George, the pub in the next street, just as if nothing had happened. Sandra would put Harold and Jean to bed, and then she and I would sit up and do what we liked for a bit, until Walter and Doris came back.

But now, this Saturday midday, the two of them were hurrying along Orchid Grove in a very strange manner. Doris strode ahead, looking neither left nor right. Walter caught up with her and tried to say something, but she ignored him. Neither of them took any notice of us.

I was mildly puzzled. 'What's up with them?' I said. 'I've never seen them go off like this before. And at dinner-time, too.'

Sandra looked quite alarmed. She ran across the street and caught Doris by the arm.

'Will you be out for dinner?' she asked.

Doris shook herself free. 'I will that!' she said fiercely.

'What shall we have?'

'You can fend for yourself, can't you?'

'When will you be back?' asked Sandra.

But Walter had now caught up. 'Ask no questions and you'll be told no lies!' he snapped. 'Now get o' t'road!'

And the two of them – Doris with her head in the air, and Walter hurring alongside, still trying to make her listen to him – turned out of Orchid Grove into Hibiscus Street.

As they disappeared round the corner, three or four heads poked out of doorways, and puzzled or knowing looks were exchanged. I shrugged my shoulders.

'They might keep their quarrels to themselves, instead of putting on a show for the neighbours,' I said.

But Sandra still looked anxious.

'There's something behind all this,' she said. 'I've felt for a few days there was real trouble coming. And this has got me worried.'

'Cheer up, love,' said Dick. 'Look on the bright side. They're out of the way for a bit. Enjoy the peace while you've got it.'

'I wish I felt sure it was only a bit,' said Sandra.

'Well, they wouldn't walk out on you, would they?'

'I don't know,' said Sandra thoughtfully, 'I don't know. . . . Anyway, come on, Kevin, we'd better get something to eat.'

'And I'd better get home,' said Dick. He lives just the other side of Hibiscus Street. 'Don't worry, they'll turn up like a pair of bad pennies. See you later.' And off he went whistling.

We went into the house. The younger children, Harold and Jean, had appeared from nowhere and were squabbling mildly in the kitchen.

'Give us a butty, Sandra!' urged Jean. She danced around us, twirling her skirt, a roly-poly, round-faced, cheeky child of six.

'A butty, a butty, a red jam butty!' she chanted. I aimed a clout at her, but missed.

Harold slouched off into a chair and said nothing. At eight he was almost the image of his father Walter: small, slightly built, with wispy fair hair and blue eyes. He seemed to have gone off into his private dream world; but after a minute he got up again and went to the cupboard. He took out a big loaf and put it on the table between Sandra and Jean as if to quieten the row once and for all.

Sandra took the breadknife, and in a minute had sent the two children out with a thick slice of bread and jam in each hand. Then, putting the kettle on, she turned to me.

'I bet they've hooked it!' she said savagely. 'I bet they've hooked it!'

'I don't think Walter would walk out on us,' I said. 'In fact I don't really think Doris would. You know what she is. All talk. She's always planning to do this and that, but nothing ever comes of it. I don't know what they're up to, but I bet they'll be at the George tonight as usual.'

But I didn't feel quite as confident as I tried to sound. I remembered that Doris had been particularly cross and shrill for the last few days. It had begun when Walter came home one evening and said he'd been offered a job in Yorkshire but he'd turned it down because there wouldn't be anywhere for us to live. Doris was furious and had been taking it out of everybody ever since. She'd kept saying she was sick of this house and sick of this town and sick of him and sick of us. What if she'd really gone? And if so, had Walter gone too?

I comforted myself with what Dick had said. Surely they'd be coming back. It was common sense after all. And by the time I'd eaten a few slices of bread and jam and drunk a mug of tea I felt much better.

Afterwards I went to the football match with Dick and his father, while Sandra saw to some mending and the youngsters played out in the street. It was a splendid match, the last day of the league championship, and United won 3–1. They were top of the table already, and this last performance capped it all. I came home full of the afternoon's play and hoarse with shouting, and I'd quite forgotten we had any worries.

Saturday tea time was usually the high point of the week at 40 Orchid Grove. Walter generally went to the match too – though he never took me with him – and Doris went to see a friend, and they both used to come home for a hot tea before going round to the George to spend the evening. It would be a good tea with sausages or beans or tomatoes, and there'd be a big fire, and if United had won Walter would be in a happy mood. He'd even been known to hand out sixpences and shillings (which we spent at once in case he tried to take them back next day).

But today was a chilly contrast. There was no fire in the hearth, no meal on the table. As I stood in the doorway, my spirits sinking, Sandra came in from the street with a child on each hand. She looked grim but calm.

'Light a fire, Kevin, if there's some coal,' she said. 'We're on our own this evening.'

Everybody was hungry. After having only a bread-and-jam dinner, Harold and Jean were whimpering a bit and wiping their faces with grubby hands. So we had a good look round to see what there was to eat, and we found quite a lot of things. There was some bacon that was probably a bit off, but not bad. There were potatoes. There was a whole jar of jam. There were several milk bottles with varying amounts of milk in the bottom, all gone sour. But there was a tin of condensed milk and there was plenty of tea. In fact the cupboard was better stocked than usual. And we had one surprising bit of luck. We found a ten-shilling note under the tea-jar that Doris must have forgotten. Sandra pocketed that. 'You never know when we'll need it,' she said.

We had coal and candles too, so really we were much better off than we might have been. There was no electricity in the house, and we'd no shillings for the gas, but I soon made a good fire and we had a fine fry-up of bacon and potatoes. There was enough for us all to feel full. Then we stoked the fire up again and sat round it.

'Tell us a story, Kevin,' said Sandra. So I made up a story, all about children cast away on a desert island. And we imagined it was us, and that we could hear the waves beating all round us. And we pretended to be alone and in peril, instead of warm and comfortable in our home at Cobchester. I went on with the story for quite a while, because once I get started it's no trouble to make up stories. They just come to me. But after a while we noticed that Jean was nodding, and Harold was getting tired too. So Sandra told them both to go to bed. Then there was a lot of arguing, and Jean cheeked both of us, and Sandra belted her, not hard, but she squawked as if she was being murdered. And Harold did a go-slow and took twenty minutes to get his shoes and socks off, and every time we looked the other way he stopped getting undressed and did something else. And even when they were in bed in a corner of the room they kept grousing and cheeking us and pinching each other and bawling, and it was a long time before we got any peace.

In the end they both went to sleep. We didn't know the time, but it was getting dark. By now I had persuaded myself that Walter and Doris would be in the pub as usual, and I told Sandra so.

'Well, if they are, they won't come out before closing-time,' said Sandra.

'Dick was right, it's peaceful without them,' I said. I'd quite enjoyed my evening. 'It won't be peaceful when they come in, though.'

We both grimaced, for this was the one drawback to Saturday. Not that Walter and Doris were violent when they came home on Saturday night, like a couple we knew in the next street, but there was often a lot of shouting and quarrelling, and Sandra and I would get cuffed if we put a foot wrong, or even sometimes if we didn't.

So we decided we would go to bed, to be out of the way.

Our house, like all the others in Orchid Grove, had a living-room and a scullery and two bedrooms. Our back bedroom was in a bad state because the roof needed repairing, so we four children all slept downstairs in the living-room. We had a big iron bedstead, and Harold and I slept with our heads at one end and Sandra and Jean at the other. There was room for all of us, and we had some blankets and old coats to keep us warm, and it was a very good arrangement. Sandra and I were awake for quite a time, listening to footsteps going past and people singing and shouting, and wondering whether Walter and Doris were coming. Then Sandra fell asleep, but I lay quietly watching the red embers in the grate and thinking how well we'd managed. And eventually I dozed off too, and I didn't know anything more until next morning.

Sandra was shaking me. 'They haven't come!' she said. 'They haven't come!'

The younger children were awake and were racketing round the house. They didn't seem to have noticed anything amiss. Sandra and I looked at each other in dismay.

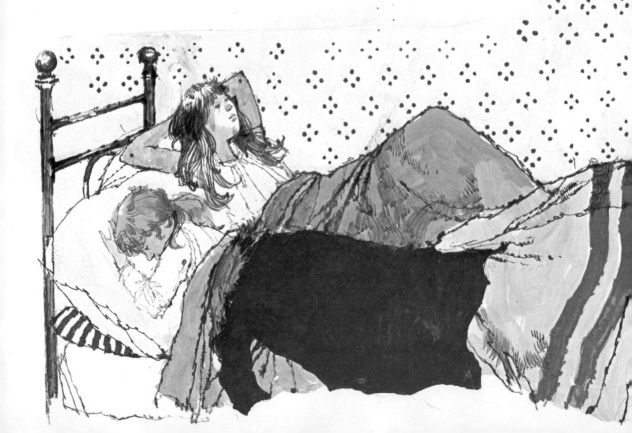

'What if they've been in an accident?' said Sandra. 'Or got into trouble?'

'I don't think so,' I said. 'We should have had the police round. I expect they've had a heavy night. They'll be sleeping it off somewhere. They're sure to be home some time today.'

But even as I said it I felt they wouldn't. I remembered once again the things Doris had said. I knew how unreliable Walter was. I had a picture in my mind that was all too convincing, of Walter and Doris hitching a lift into Yorkshire and planning to make a fresh start without us.

'If they're not back tonight,' I said, 'we'll have to go to the police, or the Cruelty.'

'Mmm,' said Sandra. She didn't sound at all certain. We were both thinking hard as we got tea and bread-and-jam ready for breakfast.

'If we did that, what would happen?' asked Sandra after a while.

I didn't know what would happen. I supposed we would be 'taken into care', as the phrase went, but I'd only the cloudiest idea of what this meant. I imagined us being questioned by police and officials and welfare workers. I pictured us in some chilly institution or being farmed out upon foster-parents we didn't like. Worst of all, I imagined us being split up and sent to different places.

'Oh, let's look after ourselves,' I said, 'for the time being, anyway. Walter and Doris may still come back. If they're not here in a few days' time we can think again.'

I realize now that this decision was wrong. We ought to have sought help that very day. But it didn't seem right at the time. To tell the truth, we were really rather afraid of police and officials, because all we had ever had to do with them was being told off for some mischief or other. Then, we were used to fending for ourselves a good deal already, and it did not seem as difficult as it might have done to children who were used to being looked after more than we were. And, finally, the thought had already crossed my mind that if the worst came to the worst I would try to find my Uncle Bob. But I will come back to that later.

Anyway, Sandra and I decided we would try to keep the home together. It was surprising at first how little the younger ones were worried. At breakfast Harold hardly spoke. He was in his private dream-world again – halfway to the moon this time. Harold had invented a special kind of moon rocket that worked by magnetic repulsion. This got it off the earth, and also prevented it from crashing on to the moon when it arrived there. Harold spent most of his days shooting back and forth in space, with suitable noises and gestures. In his day-dreams he was Sir Harold Thompson, the great scientist-explorer, continually reporting new discoveries to the Queen (he hadn't time to bother with underlings like the Prime Minister). In real life it was another matter, and he would be glad enough of the push-cart I was going to make him.

Jean, on the other hand, had a certain amount to say.

'Where's Auntie Doris?' she demanded, as she walked round the room with her bread in one hand and her mug of tea in the other.

'Gone visiting,' said Sandra. 'Sit down.'

'Who's she visiting? I never heard of anybody going visiting at Sunday breakfast-time. Has she gone for good? I bet she's gone for good.'

'We don't know,' said Sandra. 'I expect she'll be back.'

'I bet she won't,' said Jean, taking a huge bite of bread-and-jam. 'And I don't care if she doesn't. My dad can come back, but I don't want her.'

'Jean!' said Sandra, shocked. 'Don't say such naughty things!'

'Don't care, don't care, don't care!' sang Jean, with her mouth full. I aimed another clout at her, and this time I connected, but it didn't have any effect. 'Don't care, so there! So there, don't care,' she chanted, dancing out of range.

'It's all right for *her*!' said Sandra grimly.

'Will you be our auntie now?' asked Jean with interest. 'You'd be good at it, I bet. I'd rather have you than her.'

'Shut up!' said Sandra. 'I told you, we don't know that she's gone. And don't tell anyone we're on our own, or I'll scrag you.'

After breakfast Jean and Harold went out: Jean to play with a pal of hers from up the street and Harold on a trip to the planet Neptune, for which the point of departure was a launching-pad he'd built with planks in a warehouse yard in Hibiscus Street. Sandra and I stayed in the house for a while talking about our problem but not really getting anywhere.

'Let's go and see Dick,' Sandra suggested after a while.

This seemed the best idea. We always went to Dick with our problems anyway. He'd always know what to do, and he'd be ready to take charge. In fact there'd be no stopping him. At one time when there was a feud between boys from our district and those of St Jude's, at the other side of Camellia Hill, Dick took charge of the Jungle Army. We generally won, too, but the feud had now almost petered out because a new curate came to St Jude's Church and got everybody there busy with organized games and youth clubs and dramatics.

We knocked at the door of Dick's house. His mother came, and didn't look any too pleased. We heard her shouting something to her husband about 'them Thompson children'. We were never very popular with respectable people in the district, because ours was a very poor home, and Walter and Doris were not much liked. But Dick's father was kind and asked us in, and patted Sandra on the cheek and said, 'How do, love?' And he asked us if we had had any breakfast, at which Dick's mother pursed her lips a little.

'Y'd have me feeding all t'lame ducks in t'neighbourhood, you would,' she said to her husband. But then she turned to us and said, 'Well, have you?' and we knew she would have given us something.

I said firmly that we'd had our breakfast. Mrs Hedley began muttering something uncomplimentary about Walter and Doris, but we didn't catch what it was. Just then Dick appeared, so we all got out of the house rather quickly, and Dick came round to Orchid Grove with us. We told him what had happened. Dick whistled.

'Left you high and dry after all, eh?' he said. 'I thought they would.' (This wasn't what he'd thought at all, but we didn't remind him.) And his first reaction was pretty well what I'd expected. 'You'd better go to the police. Or, if you like, I'll ask my dad to go.'

So we explained why we didn't want that. There was a good deal of argument, from which it was clear that Dick had no more idea than we had of what would happen if we reported our difficulties. In the end he seemed to come round to our point of view.

'But you've got a lot of problems, haven't you?' he said. 'Food, money, school, the neighbours . . . To begin with, what are you going to live on?'

We told him we still had some tea and bread-and-jam, but only enough for the midday meal.

'But we've got ten shillings,' Sandra said. 'We can go to the Jewish shop, that's open on Sundays, and get something for tea.'

'You want to save your money,' said Dick. 'I'll tell you what we'll do. You two can come to tea with me, and we'll put food in our pockets for the others while nobody's looking.'

Sandra and I were both doubtful, but Dick went straight on.

'Ten shillings won't go far, anyway,' he said. 'You need an income. You'll have to get a job, Kevin. And the only kind of job you can get is a paper round.'

'That's not so easily got,' I said. 'Not in this district, anyway.'

'You can have my job at Mould's,' said Dick. 'I'll take you there in the morning. I'll say I'm giving up and you can have my round.'

This was generous of Dick, because we knew he was saving up for a bicycle. But he didn't stop to be thanked.

'You'll need more than that,' he went on. 'I'll think of something soon. Now, what about the rent tomorrow?'

'The rent's up to date,' said Sandra, 'and they'll let it run for a week or two.'

'You can't stay long, anyway,' Dick pointed out. 'Somebody will soon notice that you're on your own.'

Now this of course was quite true. Not that ours was one of the houses where people are dropping in all the time. Our neighbours generally felt that the less they saw of Walter and Doris the better they liked them. But Orchid Grove is a great place for curiosity. And just at that moment, as if it had been arranged to prove the point, there was a rat-tat at the door and old Mrs Grimshaw from across the street put her head in.

'All on yer own, eh?' she said. 'All on yer own?'

'Yes,' I said coldly.

There was a moment's pause. Then:

'Where are they?'

Now there was a time when I might have been cheeky and said, 'Mind your own business.' But I had been thinking hard as she spoke, and I had decided I would have to tell a lie in the most matter-of-fact way I could.

'Gone to my Uncle Bob's in Ledford,' I said.

'Gone to Ledford, eh? Left you on your own, eh? All four of you, eh? Little uns an' all?' She spoke in a disapproving tone, but not an unbelieving one. 'And when will they be back?'

I was just going to say I didn't exactly know when Sandra chipped in and said in a very confident voice, 'They'll be back tonight.'

'Oh,' said Mrs Grimshaw. 'Just a nice little week-end jaunt. Well, there's some that can take their responsibilities lightly, I must say.' She looked more disapproving than ever. But she spoke quite kindly. 'Well, if y' want aught you can just come across t'street,' she said, and withdrew.

'Why did you say that?' I asked crossly.

'She'd have been round to the Cruelty right away,' said Sandra. 'I could see it in her eye. I wouldn't be surprised if she went even now.'

We looked out of the window and saw Mrs Grimshaw disappearing into her own house.

'Well, she's not gone straight there,' I said. 'But it'll be all round the district pretty soon.'

'The fact is,' said Dick, 'that you'll have to move tonight.'

'Tonight!' I echoed, but Sandra, who was sharper on the uptake, was merely nodding. 'Tonight!' I repeated. 'But where can we go?'

'I was just thinking about that,' said Dick. 'There's only one place for you. Gumble's Yard.'

'Gumble's Yard!' we both gasped. I was sure that Sandra went white. 'Gumble's Yard!'

Gumble's Yard had been empty for at least a year. It was right down at the bottom end of the Jungle, in the bend of the old North-West Junction Canal. You got to it by way of Canal Street, and it was the farthest point from the main road – a complete dead end. It was just a row of four cottages, with one or two outbuildings, which at one time belonged to a warehouse. In the days when the canal was in use the whole place was called Gumble's Wharf. During the war some bombs fell near by, and the warehouse was badly shaken and had to be pulled down, but the cottages were left because there were people living in them. But now all the people had gone.

We were dismayed when Dick suggested that we should move down there.

'Oh, Dick!' said Sandra. 'We couldn't. Not with the young ones. Why, it's in an awful state – nearly falling down, I should think. And there wouldn't be any light or water. Besides, it's a long way from the nearest houses that are lived in. We wouldn't feel safe.'

'Wait a minute, wait a minute,' said Dick. 'I know it's a long way from the nearest houses, but that's all to the good, because you're less likely to be seen. Nobody goes down there, and there's no reason why anybody should. As for the other objections, well, there's something I'd like to show you. A secret. Let's go there now.'

So we did. We walked down the length of Hibiscus Street and turned into Canal Street, which is just about the deadest street I know, because since the canal went out of use there isn't really any reason for it to exist. At the side away from the canal there are still a few old buildings – warehouses and stabling and so on – but all disused and crumbling away. At the other side, there is just open space between the street and the canal. To get to Gumble's Yard you go right along Canal Street, almost to where it's cut off by the railway viaduct, and then you cross an open site about two hundred yards wide.

It took us about ten minutes to get there. And although it was another fine morning the place certainly looked pretty dismal.

The actual structure still seemed fairly solid, but the four cottages had not a door between them, and all the downstairs windows were broken. Inside was a good deal of rubbish but not much else. It seemed as if everything that could possibly be looted had been taken away. There was a nasty dank smell. We looked round for a minute or two, and then Sandra turned to Dick and I could see that she was just going to tell him the whole idea was impossible. But Dick was all smiles.

'Don't say it!' he told her. 'I'm going to show you my secret. This will surprise you.'

He led us outside, and round to the far end of the row of cottages. Here the gable end faced on to the supports of the railway viaduct. It was a dark, isolated corner, and not overlooked – not even from the railway, as the angle was too sharp.

'Look up,' said Dick. So we looked up at the end wall of the cottages, and high in the gable end we saw a door, an ordinary closed door, but very odd-looking because there was nothing in front of it except a twenty-foot drop to the ground. Beside it was a grime-encrusted window.

'That door,' said Dick, 'belongs to an attic that runs over the tops of all four cottages. At one time it must have had something to do with the wharf, but the earliest thing I can remember was that old man Kite lived there. He was a bit queer in the head, and never spoke to anybody. In his day you got to that door by a sort of iron staircase, like a fire escape, but after he died they pulled that down.'

'Can you get in now?' I asked.

'Watch,' said Dick. He shinned up the drainpipe at the corner of the block. Then, sidestepping where a missing brick gave him a toehold, he reached with one hand for a bracket which must formerly have held a lamp. Transferring the other hand to the bracket, he was able to reach the window-frame. To our surprise the window moved easily, and in a moment Dick was wriggling through. Seconds later the door opened and Dick stood in the doorway looking down at us.

'How's that?' he asked.

'Terrific,' said Sandra sardonically. 'You ought to get a job in a circus. But do you expect us all to do that?'

'Certainly not,' said Dick. He disappeared from view, and the next thing to emerge was the end of a decorator's ladder, which Dick proceeded to lower to the ground.

Sandra stared. I burst into laughter.

264

'How on earth did you get that?' I demanded.

'Come up here and I'll tell you,' said Dick. So we went up, and Dick drew the ladder up behind us and closed the door.

The attic was long and narrow, and you could only stand upright in the middle of it. It had three windows, but they were all thick with dirt and it was pretty dark inside. It smelt much drier than down below, though, and the floor seemed sound. Inside were a camp bed, two or three old chairs, some packing-cases, and a couple of rugs. There was also a paraffin stove. Our astonishment grew.

'Bill Berry and I found this place,' Dick said. 'Bill's in the Army now, but I used to go around with him quite a bit before he joined up. We weren't going to tell anyone about it, but I know Bill wouldn't mind, seeing you're in such a fix.'

'Did you bring all these things in?'

'Not all of them,' said Dick. 'It was a bit strange. The camp bed and a chair and one or two cases were here when we first came, and the ladder too. Somebody must have used the place before us. But it must have been quite a while ago, because everything was covered with dust. And we've not seen any signs of anybody coming here since. So I shouldn't worry about that.'

'Was there anything to show who it might have been?'

'There was practically nothing,' said Dick. 'Cigarette packets, a page of a letter addressed to somebody called – now, what was it? – Flick. And a piece cut from a newspaper of nearly a year ago, something about a Lady Westley. Well, I don't know who Flick is, but he doesn't come here now. If you could have seen that dust . . . Bill and I brought a broom and a scrubbing-brush and bucket – they're still here, in that corner – and we got it really cleaned up. We brought the other chairs and the stove, too. We were going to make it a private den, but there isn't really anything much to do down here, you know – it's so quiet, and nobody goes past.'

'When were you last here?'

'Oh, two or three weeks ago, when Bill was on leave.'

Sandra had been looking round thoughtfully while I asked the questions. 'It's not a bad place,' she admitted. 'But what about water? And how are we all going to get in and out? Maybe Kevin can climb up the way you did, but I can't and I'm sure the younger ones can't. And the ladder isn't much good if it's up above and we're down below.'

But Dick had an answer for everything. Although at the start he had seemed doubtful about our idea of fending for ourselves, he was now getting enthusiastic.

'You can get water from a standpipe in one of the outhouses,' he said. 'I'll show you later how to do it. There's a lot of lumber in there, too, and I think I know how we can make use of that. As for getting in and out, well, look at this.'

He led us to a corner of the room and, with a conjurer's gesture, lifted one of the rugs. We saw that it covered a trapdoor. 'Here's your future route,' he said. 'Bill and I found this when we scrubbed the floor. You couldn't see it before for dust and grime. At the moment you can get down but not up, but we'll soon cure that.'

Dick lowered himself through the trapdoor, hung on with his hands for a moment, and dropped to the floor below. I followed, bending my knees as I landed. We were now in the bedroom of the end cottage. The trapdoor was in a dark corner of the cracked and dirty ceiling, and nobody would notice it when closed.

As Dick had said, you could get down but not up. But halfway up the adjoining wall was a heavy old-fashioned mantelpiece. 'You see,' said Dick, 'all we want is a really strong bracket, right up in the corner, to serve the same purpose as that lamp-bracket outside. Then you'll be able to stand on the mantelpiece, reach over to the bracket, and hang on to it while you push the trapdoor up. It won't be difficult because we'll get an old wooden box that can be the first step to the mantelpiece. Harold can do it quite easily. Jean might need a bit of help.'

'Where will we get the bracket?' I asked.

'I can pick up just the thing in Fred Appleby's yard,' said Dick. 'I'll have a word with him at dinner-time. And, come to think of it, it must be getting on for dinner-time now.'

We helped Sandra to come down through the trap. She was grousing a bit, and muttering something about having to be a family of Tarzans. But I could see that really she was quite impressed.

'You'll have a front door *and* a back,' said Dick cheerfully. 'Might be useful some time.' And he didn't know how right he was, for later on it was to be more useful than we could have guessed.

Sandra and I went back to Orchid Grove. We still half expected to find Walter and Doris there. But there was no sign of them. Harold had returned from his trip to Neptune and was lying on the bedstead reading a battered science-fiction magazine. Sandra hauled Jean in from the street, and we ate what dinner we could find. We finished up all the bits and pieces, including the stale ends of two or three loaves, and all that remained was some tea and half a jar of jam. But of course we still had the ten shillings.

After dinner, Sandra told the younger children what we were doing. She said it was only for a day or two, and then either Walter and Doris would come back or somebody else would look after us. To our surprise Harold took it rather badly. He suddenly came back to earth from all his space dreams, and blubbered a bit about wanting his dad. But Jean was not at all worried.

'I told you, I told you,' she cried. 'Sandra's the auntie now. We'll have a lovely time, Harold, you're a cry-baby. Poor little boy, wants his daddy. . . .'

Harold lashed out at her through his tears. I felt sorry for him. Unlike Jean, he was old enough to feel the full weight of being abandoned, and unlike Sandra and myself he wasn't big enough to stand on his own feet. I didn't really feel too confident myself that we could manage. But a few minutes later Dick came in, full of confidence, and then I felt better. He had a bracket and a big hammer and some sand and cement as well. All five of us went down to Gumble's yard.

There was still nobody about, either there or in Canal Street. The silence, in fact, seemed almost uncanny. Once again, Dick climbed into the attic from outside, but this time he reached down through the trapdoor and helped Sandra and the children up from the cottage bedroom. Then he came down through the trap himself, and he and I made a really good job of fixing the bracket.

Harold had whimpered a bit on the way down from Orchid Grove, but now the novelty of our proceedings took his mind off his troubles for a while. There was some discussion about what we should call our attic. Dick and Bill Berry had merely called it their den, but we didn't feel that was dignified enough. Jean wanted to call it Fairmead, a name she had seen over a house, but nobody else thought that was suitable either. Harold suggested the Spaceship – a part that no doubt the attic could play quite well in his imagination. But in the end we settled on Sandra's choice, which was the Homestead.

When the bracket was fixed, Harold and Jean wanted to practise getting up and down, but Dick insisted that it would have to be left to dry out. Sandra had decided that the attic was still not clean enough, so she and Dick got busy scrubbing it.

'You'll have to do a moonlight flit tonight,' said Dick, 'and bring whatever you need from the other house down here. The sooner you get clear of Orchid Grove the safer you'll be. I'll sneak out at midnight and help you. What is there to bring?'

'Well, we'll have to bring the bedstead,' said Sandra, 'and the table, and we could do with another couple of chairs. Then there's that chest of drawers, and pots and pans and clothes and blankets. . . .'

'H'm. Quite an order,' said Dick. 'How are we going to carry all those things?'

'We've an old pram,' I said, 'that Jean used to sleep in until she got too big.'

'Just the job for the small stuff,' said Dick. 'I don't know about furniture, though. I'll talk to Fred Appleby again and see if I can borrow his hand-cart. Kevin, could you take Harold and Jean and bring some of the smaller things along now?'

'Fair enough,' I said. So the three of us went back to Orchid Grove and filled the old pram with clothes and blankets and anything else that could be packed in tightly and tidily. We didn't worry about anyone suspecting anything, because in the Jungle people are always pushing things about in old prams, and it's such a commonplace sight it's hardly noticed. Of course, if we were making several journeys with tables and chairs and pieces of bedstead it might be another matter. We couldn't do that in broad daylight.

We wheeled our load down Hibiscus Street and turned into Canal Street. And there we had a surprise. Coming towards us from the direction of Gumble's Yard was a light van. We hadn't seen it down there before, and in fact it was the first sign of human activity in the neighbourhood. The driver slowed his vehicle to allow us to get the pram out of the roadway, and I had a good look at him. He had a lean, quite handsome face, and a very tiny moustache. He looked at us with some curiosity, and after we'd passed him we dawdled a little, so that he wouldn't see us crossing the open site to the Homestead. However, in a minute he had turned the corner into Hibiscus Street without showing any further interest in us, so we completed our journey.

'Did you see that fellow with the van?' I asked Dick as soon as we arrived.

'Yes, we saw him, but he didn't see us,' said Dick. 'He drove along here the way you've just come, got out of his van, and had a look in each cottage – only the ground floors, though – and then he went away again. I don't know what he was doing. Nothing at all, probably, just looking round out of curiosity, the way people do. I'm sure he didn't know about the Homestead.'

'I thought you said nobody ever came down here.'

'He's the first person I've seen,' said Dick. 'But don't look so serious. I dare say people will wander round from time to time and I wouldn't be surprised if children came here to play. It doesn't matter, so long as you keep a good lookout and make sure nobody sees you getting in and out of the Homestead.'

All the same, we decided it would be as well if we didn't hang around the place any more than we could help. So when Sandra and I went to Dick's house for tea (he had got his parents to invite us, just as he promised) we took Harold and Jean with us as far as Hibiscus Street and left them playing there, with instructions not to go back to the Homestead until we came for them.

We had already planned that we would slip part of our meal into our pockets to take away for the younger ones. There were ham sandwiches and cheese sandwiches for tea, which was very convenient. But I was surprised that we were not caught. Dick was the cheekiest about it. He would take a sandwich and only pretend to bite it, and then when nobody was looking it would go straight into his pocket. Mr Hedley was never likely to notice, because he was busy telling us anecdotes beginning with 'Aye, when I were a lad . . .' and laughing heartily at the recollection. But Mrs Hedley is a thin, shrewd person who doesn't miss much.

'Y'd think they hadn't et for a month,' she said, with a meaning look at her husband. I knew just what was in her mind. She thought Sandra and I were half starved, which in fact we weren't.

'Are your uncle and auntie in?' she asked later.

I told the same lie that I'd told before to Mrs Grimshaw. I didn't know how to avoid it. 'No,' I said, 'they've gone visiting, over at Ledford.'

'Oh,' said Mrs Hedley. 'Oh, they have, have they?' And she said no more. But when we were leaving she put a newspaper packet into Sandra's hands. And, looking quite thin-lipped and mean, as if she didn't like being caught in a kind action, she said, 'There, that's for t'little ones.' It was more food.

Well, Sandra and I felt dreadful, and Sandra said afterwards it was all she could do to avoid confessing our theft on the spot. But Dick was quite unmoved. 'That'll be breakfast for you,' he said.

'Oh, Dick,' protested Sandra, 'it doesn't feel right at all.'

'Don't worry,' said Dick. 'We'll own up to everything when it's all over. Nobody will mind then.'

'When it's all over,' said Sandra wistfully. 'Why, it's only just beginning.'

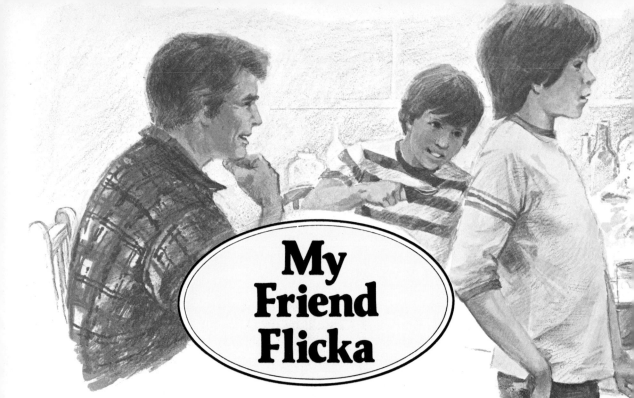

My Friend Flicka

Mary O'Hara

This exciting story about a boy and his horse is set on a ranch in Wyoming, U.S.A. Rob and Nell McLaughlin own the ranch and the story begins one summer when their two sons, Howard and Ken, are home from school. Howard already has a horse of his own and Ken has been told that this summer he may choose one of the foals for himself. In this extract we see how eventful life can be working with unbroken horses and we also hear about Ken's extraordinary choice.

'FOR once you're back to breakfast on time,' said Rob, as Ken took his seat at the table.

Nell filled Ken's bowl with oatmeal and passed it to him.

Ever since she had read in the Government bulletins that all prize stock was raised on elaborate formulas of mixed grains – *or ground oats* – and had noticed that the dogs, when they were hungry, squirmed through the wire fence into the calves' corral and ate the ground oats from the feed boxes, oatmeal had a place on her breakfast table. If you can raise good calves and colts on it, I guess you can raise boys, she reasoned. And McLaughlin, with a long line of oat-eating Scottish ancestors behind his brawn and toughness, agreed.

With the oatmeal there was always a big pitcher of yellow Guernsey cream and a bowl of brown sugar. Nell, smiling, pushed them towards Ken, noticing the unusual colour in his face. The boy flashed a glance at his mother; his eyes were dark with excitement. His whole face was lit up – transfigured really – and she felt a slight sense of shock. What had happened? He had been different all week, more sure of himself, more alert and happy, but this –

Rob McLaughlin was looking at Ken too, not missing a thing. Something had happened that morning on the range –

'What horse did you ride?' he asked.

'Lady.'

'And where is she now? On her way to the border?' jocularly.

'I put her in the Home Pasture. She's out there at the fountain now.'

'Was she hot?'

'No, sir, I cooled her off coming home.' There was a little smile of pride on Ken's face, and Nell thought, all the right answers, so far.

The examination went on. 'Did you give her a good workout?'

'Yes, sir.'

'Then don't ride her again today. Take Baldy if you want a horse.'

'Yes, sir.'

'Break anything? Lose anything?'

'No, sir.'

Rob laughed. He leaned over and patted Ken on the head. 'Good work, young man – coming along!'

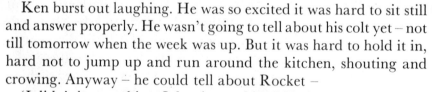

Ken burst out laughing. He was so excited it was hard to sit still and answer properly. He wasn't going to tell about his colt yet – not till tomorrow when the week was up. But it was hard to hold it in, hard not to jump up and run around the kitchen, shouting and crowing. Anyway – he could tell about Rocket –

'I didn't *lose* anything, I *found* something!' He boasted, shovelling in big spoonfuls of oatmeal. 'I found Rocket. She's back.'

'Where?' demanded Rob and Nell and Howard all together.

'With the brood mares.'

'Good,' said McLaughlin. 'Let's see – what day would this be after her colt, Nell?'

'If the colt was less than a week old when she lost it,' calculated Nell.

'Yes – and then this past week – yes, somewhere between the ninth and fourteenth day. That's about it,' McLaughlin grinned. 'So the wild woman came back of herself.'

'She came up from the South, and Banner went out to get her. She's bred already.'

'I'll say she is,' said McLaughlin.

Nell went to the stove, lifted the bacon out of the hot fat and laid it on a platter. 'Orders, please,' she cried.

'*Two on a raft and wreck'em!*' shouted Rob jovially, with his big, white-toothed smile.

'*One, looking at you!*' shouted Ken hilariously.

Howard jumped up. 'I'll do yours *over and easy*, Mother –' No one could do Nell's egg to suit her like Howard. She liked it lightly fried on one side, then lightly on the other, not broken. It had to be flipped. Rob could flip them but he made a big to-do about it and tossed them high and many a one landed on the stove or the edge of the skillet. Howard poured a little of the hot bacon grease into a one-egg skillet and broke an egg in. While it crackled and spat, he salted it carefully, and in a moment loosened the curling brown edges, then with a smooth motion of his wrist, gave the pan a lift and a thrust, and the egg rose a few inches into the air, turned a slow somersault, and slid back into the fat.

Carrying the hot plates with holders, Nell distributed the eggs, and set the bacon on the table. She was still thinking about Ken, and kept looking at him. Every time he caught her eye, he smiled blissfully. He was all excited – there was something he was not telling – something he had seen out on the range that morning – the colt, of course, the colt –

'Nell,' said Rob, 'are you very busy this morning?'

'Nothing special – no baking or cleaning – why?'

'How'd you like to break a bronc for me?'

Nell looked up quickly. 'One of the four? That little mare, Rumba?'

'Yes.'

'I'd love to!'

'Why doesn't Ross do it?' asked Howard.

'Ross is too tough.' Rob's face looked grim. 'I'm not going to let him monkey with her. I've stood all I can with the other three – I wouldn't be surprised if Don's knees are damaged.'

'Not permanently?' cried Nell.

'Well, it'll take a long time for the swelling to go down. He threw himself about so. And, all tied up the way Ross had him he kept falling on his knees. I had to walk away – couldn't look at it. Don't like to interfere with a man when he's been hired to do a job and is doing it his own way, but I couldn't stick it. The little mare – why her feet would fit in a tea cup. And her forelegs –' he picked up Ken's arm, 'about as big round as Ken's wrist.'

'She's a very funny, special little mare,' said Nell. 'I remember her last summer when you brought her in to halter-break her. She fell in the water trough on her back and wouldn't get up.'

Ken remembered too, laughing, 'Yes – she stayed there all afternoon with her feet sticking straight up.'

Howard persisted, 'Then why don't you do it, Dad?'

'I'm far too heavy, Howard. I've been on her and taught her a bit, and she's used to the saddle all right but she needs a light rider; and she's afraid of Ross – even if I didn't let him tie her up. She shakes every time she sees him.'

'Could I ride her?' asked Howard.

'You're light enough, but it isn't only the actual weight. There's something a bit heavy handed about you, Howard. I saw you give Calico's head a bad jerk the other day.'

Howard scowled. 'He was swinging his head up and down. I hate that.'

'So you punished him?'

Howard nodded. McLaughlin said quietly, 'Sometimes one has to punish a horse. Calico's got a bad habit with his head, but you gave him more than he needed. Little Rumba couldn't take anything like that at this stage of her training. It might start her bucking, and I don't want her ever to buck. She needs to be reassured and just held nicely, and sort of coaxed.'

'What about me?' demanded Ken.

McLaughlin laughed. 'Why you'd go off into a dream and the horse could run away with you and you wouldn't know it until ten miles later you'd wake up and wonder where you were. What you've got, Ken, is fine hands, but no control. Rumba needs someone with authority. Your mother's got that, and hands like yours, and she's lighter in the saddle than any of you – not pounds, but balance; seat. I want you both in the corral when your mother rides Rumba. You'll learn something.'

When Nell walked up to the stables she was dressed in well-cut jodhpurs made of carefully softened and faded blue-jean denim. Suitable clothes for her ranch life had been hard to find. She hated to be untidy – hated to be constrained; boots and breeches she found too heavy and binding, so she had her white linen jodhpurs (from Abercrombie and Fitch) copied by a local tailor in blue-jean material. She had half a dozen pairs of these; they were nearly indestructible, light enough to be cool, washed perfectly, and were very becoming to her slender, free-moving body. A darker blue jersey polo shirt with very short sleeves left her brown arms bare; she wore pigskin gloves, a round blue linen hat with a narrow brim to pull down over her eyes and stick on against the Wyoming winds – (it was said by the local wits that, in Wyoming, you can tell a stranger from a native because the stranger, if his hat blows off, will pursue it) – and on her feet, under the straps of her trousers, soft tan jodhpur shoes with small chainless spurs set into the leather of the heel. Even so, long before the day was done she was weary of the denim and leather, and was glad to get back into light cotton dresses.

Rumba, saddled and bridled, was waiting, tied to the post. Ross came riding into the corral on Gangway, and dismounted.

'Mornin', Missus,' he said to Nell, managing to convey both gallantry and deference in his slow drawling voice; and Nell again thought, with a little glow of pleasure, that *Missus* was a royal title in the West. Ross, by the very tilt of his small body as he faced her, put himself at her service.

'How's the pony this morning?' asked McLaughlin.

'A bit spooky and a little stiff – but travellin' all right.'

'Mother's going to ride Rumba,' said Ken.

Ross's eyes moved quickly to Rumba, then to McLaughlin. He busied himself loosening the cinch on Gangway, and said quietly, 'She ain't ready to ride yet. She ain't been sacked out with her feet tied, like I done with Gangway and the others.'

McLaughlin said quietly, 'Rumba's feet are too small and her legs too delicate to tie up.'

'I wouldn't ride her myself,' insisted Ross, 'lessen I was in a Rodeo and paid to. Them hot-bloods is worse than broncs if once they git to buckin'.'

'I think she'll be all right,' said McLaughlin. 'Mrs McLaughlin's about the right weight; she's a little timid, but she won't have any trouble.'

'Timid!' marvelled Ross. 'I put my wife on a ole plug once that was broke pretty fair, and it got to runnin' a little, and she busted out cryin' and came back bawlin'. Did I get it!'

'You don't look old enough to have a wife, Ross,' said Nell.

'I got a wife and two kids 'bout half as big as Howard and Ken,' said Ross grinning. 'I'm twenty-five. My brother's twenty-six.'

Ross rolled himself a cigarette and sat down against the corral fence. Howard and Ken climbed up and sat on the top railing. Nell walked over to Rumba, and Rob stood beside Ross talking to him, and pretending not to watch.

Rumba became taut, her ears forward, looking at Nell, her head up as if she was on the point of rearing, and her hind legs crouching. Nell held out a hand and talked to her reassuringly, but when the hand touched her head, Rumba jerked up. Nell kept stroking her and talking to her until at last the mare was quiet and her trembling and crouching stopped. Nell turned her back to her, leaning against the post, and stood there talking to Rob and Ross, to give the mare a chance to get used to her body and her voice. Under the eye of a human being an unbroken horse is in terror.

'Is your brother a bronco-buster too, Ross?'

'No, Ma'am, he ain't got the heart. You just gotta have the heart fur it.'

'Do you do a lot of it, Ross?'

'Sure do, Ma'am – all summer long. All over the country, wherever there's a show. One summer I made a thousand dollars. As soon as one Rodeo's over, I'm itchin' to git to the next. Everyone says I'll git killed, but, hell, what's the difference? Better than work at that –'

Rumba, feeling more free now because no eye was upon her, reached out her nose and Nell felt the soft muzzle against her back between the shoulders. She paid no attention, but Rumba, as if alarmed by the smell of her, jumped back.

Ross was talking about the Rodeo Riders' Union, called COWBOYS' TURTLE ASSOCIATION, to which he belonged. At a Texas Rodeo, they struck for a share of the gate receipts in addition to the prize money. This held up the show for a couple of hours, but they won out.

Rumba tried again. This time she was bolder and took a long breath, drawing in the very essence of the human being who, she knew in advance, was going to mount her. Nell knew that if a horse hates the smell of a person it is hardly possible to make friends. On the other hand, if he likes it, friendship is only a matter of time and patience.

Obviously Nell passed the test, for Rumba rested then, with her nose touching Nell's arm, her eyes and ears directed to the men who were talking, indulging her natural curiosity. Rob did not want the little mare to feel she was the centre of attention. He said horses were like people – no one liked to feel all eyes upon them except show-offs, like Gangway, who always expected to be watched.

'Don't you ever get hurt, bronco bustin'?' asked Howard, his feet dangling over Ross's head from where he sat on the fence rail above him.

'I'll say,' was the laconic answer. 'Last summer I hurt myself in every show I was in –'

'Break anything?'

'Ribs, collar bone – back hurt – knee wrenched. Spent most of my time in hospital. When I went in fur the third trip last summer, I was broke. They waan't goin' to let me out till I'd paid my bill. I says, You might as well let me out for I ain't got no way to make money layin' here in hospital, I got to git ridin' before I kin pay you off. Well, they wouldn't. An' they was arguin' with me, and I says, You call up the Rodeo Committee here, and tell 'em about me not bein' able to pay my bill. Well, I guess they did, for they let me out, and I never heard nuthin' more about the bill, neither.'

Nell turned around to Rumba and saw that the mare had accepted her. She no longer shivered, but kept her eyes on Nell without fear. Nell gathered up the reins, still stroking her and talking to her. She went to the side, put both arms on top of the saddle and leaned there, now and then lifting her knee up under the mare's belly as if she was going to mount.

Rumba showed no alarm. Her head was turned a little, one eye back watching Nell.

Now Rob joined her and held Rumba's head. Nell put her foot in the stirrup, mounted very slowly, swung her leg over the haunch, got her seat, and Rob untied the halter rope from the post and adjusted the stirrups.

A little pressure of the legs, a little urging with voice and hands, and Rumba started off slowly. Nell was careful to hold the reins fairly short so that, in case the mare took a sudden notion to buck, she could not get her head down. They made the round of the corral several times, then Rob opened the gate, he and Ross mounted Don and Gangway, and all three rode down to the practice field for a morning's work.

─=◦◄◎◄◎►◎►◦=─

When Ken went to bed that night, he kissed his mother, and then threw his arms around her and held her fiercely for a moment.

Smiling, she put her hand on his head. 'Well, Kennie –' her violet eyes were soft and understanding.

He went upstairs, smiling back at her over his shoulder, having a secret with her. He knew that she knew.

He lit the candle in his room and stood staring at the flickering light. This was like a last day. The last day before school is out, or before Christmas, or before his mother came back after a visit in the East. Tomorrow was the day when, really, his life would begin. He would get his colt.

He had been thinking about the filly all day. He could still see her streaking past him, the wild terrified eyes turned to him in appeal – the hair blown back from her face like a girl's – and the long, slim legs moving so fast they were a blur, like the spokes of a wheel.

He couldn't quite remember the colour of her. Orange – pink – tangerine colour – tail and mane white, like the hair of an Albino boy at school. *Albino* – of course, her grandsire *was* the Albino – the famous Albino stud. He felt a little uneasiness at this; Albino blood wasn't safe blood for a filly to have. But perhaps she hadn't much of it. Perhaps the cream tail and mane came from Banner, her sire. Banner had a cream tail and mane too when he was a colt; lots of sorrel colts had. He hoped she would be docile and good – not like Rocket. Which would she take after? Rocket? Or Banner? He hadn't had time to get a good look into her eyes. Rocket's eyes had that wild, wicked, white ring around them –

Ken began to undress. Walking around his room, his eyes caught sight of the pictures on the wall – they didn't interest him.

The speed of her! *She had run away from Banner*. He kept thinking about that. It hardly seemed possible. His father always said Rocket was the fastest horse on the ranch, and now Rocket's filly had run away from Banner.

He had gone up to look at her again that afternoon, hadn't been able to keep away. He had ridden up on Baldy and found the yearlings all grazing together on the far side of the Saddle Back. And when they saw him and Baldy, they all took off across the mountain.

Ken had galloped along the crest above them watching the filly. Footing made no difference to her. She floated across the ravines, always two lengths ahead of the others. Her pinkish cream mane and tail whipped in the wind. Her long delicate legs had only to aim, it seemed, at a particular spot, for her to reach it and sail on. She seemed to Ken a fairy horse. She was simply nothing like any of the others.

Riding down the mountain again Ken had traced back all his recollections of her. The summer before, when he and Howard had seen the spring colts, he hadn't especially noticed her. He remembered that he had seen her even before that, soon after she was born. He had been out with Gus, one day, in the meadow, during the spring holiday. They were clearing some driftwood out of the irrigation ditch, and they had seen Rocket standing in a gully on the hillside, quiet for once, and eyeing them cautiously.

'Ay bet she got a colt,' said Gus; and they walked carefully up the draw. Rocket gave a wild snort, thrust her feet out, shook her head wickedly, then fled away. And as they reached the spot, they saw standing there the wavering, pinkish colt, barely able to keep its feet. It gave a little squeak and started after its mother on crooked, wobbling legs.

'Yeewhiz! Look at de little *flicka!*' said Gus.

'What does *flicka* mean, Gus?'

'Swedish for little gurl, Ken –'

He had seen the filly again late in the fall. She was half pink, half yellow – with streaked untidy looking hair. She was awkward and ungainly, with legs too long, haunches a little too high.

And then he had gone away to school and hadn't seen her again until now – *she ran away from Banner*. Her eyes – they had looked like balls of fire this morning. What colour were they? Banner's were brown with flecks of gold, or gold with flecks of brown – Her speed and her delicate curving lines made him think of a greyhound he had seen running once, but really she was more like just a little girl than anything – the way her face looked, the way her blonde hair blew – a little girl –

Ken blew out the light and got into bed, and before the smile had faded from his face, he was asleep –

'I'll take that sorrel filly of Rocket's; the one with the cream tail and mane.'
Ken made his announcement at the breakfast table.

After he spoke there was a moment's astonished silence. Nell groped for recollection, and said, 'A sorrel filly? I can't seem to remember that one at all – what's her name?'

But Rob remembered. The smile faded from his face as he looked at Ken. *'Rocket's filly, Ken?'*

'Yes, sir.' Ken's face changed too. There was no mistaking his father's displeasure.

286

'I was hoping you'd make a wise choice. You know what I think of Rocket – that whole line of horses –'

Ken looked down; the colour ebbed from his cheeks. 'She's fast, Dad, and Rocket's fast –'

'It's the worst line of horses I've got. There's never one amongst them with real sense. The mares are hellions and the stallions outlaws; they're untamable.'

'I'll tame her.'

Rob guffawed. 'Not I, nor anyone, has ever been able to really tame any one of them.'

Kennie's chest heaved.

'Better change your mind, Ken. You want a horse that'll be a real friend to you, don't you?'

'Yes –' Kennie's voice was unsteady.

'Well, you'll never make a friend of that filly. Last fall after all the colts had been weaned and separated from their dams, she and Rocket got back together – no fence'll hold 'em – she's all out and scarred up already from tearing through barbed wire after that bitch of a mother of hers.'

Kennie looked stubbornly at his plate.

'Change your mind?' asked Howard briskly.

'No.'

'I don't remember seeing her this year,' said Nell.

'No,' said Rob. 'When I drove you up a couple of months ago to look them over and name them and write down their descriptions, there was a bunch missing, don't you remember?'

'Oh, yes – then she's never been named –'

'I've named her,' said Ken. 'Her name is Flicka.'

'Flicka,' said Nell cheerfully. 'That's a pretty name.'

But McLaughlin made no comment, and there was a painful silence.

Ken felt he ought to look at his father, but he was afraid to. Everything was changed again, they weren't friends any more. He forced himself to look up, met his father's angry eyes for a moment, then quickly looked down again.

'Well,' McLaughlin barked. 'It's your funeral – or hers. Remember one thing. I'm not going to be out of pocket on account of this – every time you turn around you cost me money –'

Ken looked up, wonderingly, and shook his head.

'Time's money, remember,' said his father. 'I had planned to give you a reasonable amount of help in breaking and taming your colt. Just enough. But there's no such thing as enough with those horses.'

Gus appeared at the door and said, 'What's today, Boss?'

McLaughlin shouted, 'We're going out on the range to bring in the yearlings. Saddle Taggert, Lady and Shorty.'

Gus disappeared, and McLaughlin pushed his chair back. 'First thing to do is get her in. Do you know where the yearlings are?'

'They were on the far side of the Saddle Back late yesterday afternoon – the west end, down by Dale's ranch.'

'Well, you're the Boss on this round-up – you can ride Shorty.'

McLaughlin and Gus and Ken went out to bring the yearlings in. Howard stood at the County gate to open and close it.

They found the yearlings easily. When they saw that they were being pursued, they took to their heels. Ken was entranced to watch Flicka – the speed of her, the power, the wildness – she led the band.

He sat motionless, just watching and holding Shorty in when his father thundered past on Taggert and shouted, 'Well, what's the matter? Why didn't you turn 'em?'

Ken woke up and galloped after them.

Shorty brought in the whole band. The corral gates were closed, and an hour was spent shunting the ponies in and out and through the chutes until Flicka was left alone in the small round branding corral. Gus mounted Shorty and drove the others away, through the gate, and up the Saddle Back.

But Flicka did not intend to be left. She hurled herself against the poles which walled the corral. She tried to jump them. They were seven feet high. She caught her front feet over the top rung, clung, scrambled, while Kennie held his breath for fear the slender legs would be caught between the bars and snapped. Her hold broke, she fell over backwards, rolled, screamed, tore around the corral.

One of the bars broke. She hurled herself again. Another went. She saw the opening, and as neatly as a dog crawls through a fence, inserted her head and forefeet, scrambled through and fled away, bleeding in a dozen places.

As Gus was coming back, just about to close the gate to the County Road, the sorrel whipped through it, sailed across the road and ditch with her inimitable floating leap, and went up the side of the Saddle Back like a jack rabbit.

From way up the mountain, Gus heard excited whinnies, as she joined the band he had just driven up, and the last he saw of them they were strung out along the crest running like deer.

'Yee whiz!' said Gus, and stood motionless and staring until the ponies had disappeared over the ridge.

Then he closed the gate, remounted Shorty, and rode back to the corrals.

Walking down from the corrals, Rob McLaughlin gave Kennie one more chance to change his mind. 'Better pick a horse that you have some hope of riding one day. I'd have got rid of this whole line of stock if they weren't so damned fast that I've had the fool idea that someday there might turn out one gentle one in the lot, and I'd have a race horse. But there's never been one so far, and it's not going to be Flicka.'

'It's not going to be Flicka,' chanted Howard.

'Maybe she *might* be gentled,' said Ken; and although his lips trembled, there was fanatical determination in his eye.

'Ken,' said McLaughlin, 'it's up to you. If you say you want her, we'll get her. But she wouldn't be the first of that line to die rather than give in. They're beautiful and they're fast, but let me tell you this, young man, they're *loco*!'

Ken flinched under his father's direct glance.

'If I go after her again, I'll not give up *whatever comes*, understand what I mean by that?'

'Yes.'

'What do you say?'

'I want her.'

'That's settled then,' and suddenly Rob seemed calm and indifferent. 'We'll bring her in again tomorrow or next day – I've got other work for this afternoon.'

Playing Beatie Bow

Ruth Park

Abigail Kirk is a moody 14-year-old growing up in Sydney, Australia. Her mother runs a 'trendy trivia' shop called Magpies, but wants to move to Norway to rejoin Abigail's father who left them four years previously. It is Abigail's young neighbour Natalie who first notices the strange 'little furry girl' watching the children playing the scary game 'Beatie Bow'. Upset after a violent argument with her mother, Abigail sees the girl again and follows her, into another world.

When she thought about it, weeks afterwards, Abigail felt that surely, surely she must have believed herself dreaming for longer than she did. Why didn't I think I'd got into some street where the television people were shooting a film or something? But she knew she hadn't. From the first minute, as she lay dazed on the cobbles, she knew that she was real and the place was real, and so were the people in it.

The furry little girl tried to lose her, ducking up dog-leg courts where the houses pressed close to the earth like lichen. They had shingled roofs covered with moss, and heaps of foul debris around their walls. Sometimes the child glanced over her shoulder as she jumped black gullies of water, or dodged urchins with hair like stiffened mop-heads. Her face was distorted with panic.

The houses were like wasps' nests, or Tibetan houses as Abigail had seen them in films, piled on top of each other, roosting on narrow sandstone ledges, sometimes with a lighted candle stuck in half a turnip on the doorstep, as if to show the way. The dark was coming down, and in those mazy alleys it came quicker. The lamplight that streamed through broken grimy windows was sickly yellow.

The little girl darted past the tall stone cliff of a warehouse, its huge door studded with nail-heads as if against invaders. There Abigail almost caught up with her, but a beggar with a wooden stump reared up and waved his crutch at her, shouting something out of a black toothless mouth. And she saw that she had almost trampled on something she thought was a deformed child, until it leapt snarling to its master's crooked shoulder. It was a monkey in a hussar's uniform.

And now she had gained on the little girl, who was beginning to falter.

They had turned into what Abigail did not immediately recognise as Argyle Street, though she had walked up that street a hundred times. The enormous stone arch of The Cut, the cutting quarried through the sandstone backbone of The Rocks, was different. It was narrower, she thought, though so many shops and stalls and barrows clustered along Argyle Street it was hard to see. Where the Bradfield Highway had roared across the top of The Cut there were now two rickety wooden bridges. Stone steps ran up one side, and on the other two tottering stairways curled upon themselves, overhung with vines and dishevelled trees, and running amongst and even across the roofs of indescribable shanties like broken-down farm sheds. These dwellings were propped up with tree trunks and railway sleepers; goats grazed on their roofs; and over all was the smell of rotting seaweed, ships, wood smoke, human ordure, and horses and harness.

She wondered afterwards why people had stared at her, and realised that it was not because she looked strange – for with her long dress and shawl she was dressed much as they were – but because she was running.

Once a youth with a silly face and a fanciful soldier's uniform, or so she thought, stood in her path, stroking his side whiskers and smirking, but she shoved past him.

Picking out the fugitive child's figure she ran onwards, almost to the edge of The Cut, where the child dived into a doorway of a corner house or shop, with a lighted window and a smell of burnt sugar that for a moment made her hesitate, for she had smelt it before.

And while she stood there, hesitating, there was a fearful noise within – a feminine protest, the clatter of metal, and a man's angry roar.

Out of the doorway bounded a grotesquely tall figure in a long white apron, brandishing what she thought was a rusty scimitar above his head. He was bellowing something like 'Charge the heathen devils!' as he rushed past her, knocking her down as he went. She hit her head hard on the edge of the doorstep.

The pain was so sharp she was quite blinded. Other people burst from the doorway, there were cries of consternation, and she was lifted to her feet. The pain seemed to move to her ankle, she could see nothing but darkness and lights gone fuzzy and dim.

'I'm awfully sorry,' she whispered. 'I think I'm going to faint.'

When she came to herself, she kept her eyes shut, for she knew very well that she was in neither a hospital nor her own home. The air was warm and stuffy; she thought there was an open fire in the room, and it was burning coal. She knew the smell, for Grandmother had an open fireplace in her house, and burnt coal in winter. Someone was holding her hand. It was a woman's hand, not a child's, though the palm was as hard as a man's. The hand was placed on her forehead for a moment, and a voice, with the accent of the little furry girl's, said softly, 'Aye, she's no' so burning. Change the bandage, Dovey, pet, and we'll see how the dint is.'

Gentle hands touched a tender spot on her head. She managed to keep still, with her eyes shut, partly because she was filled with apprehension at what or whom she might see, and partly because she still felt confused and ill. A distant throb in her ankle grew into a savage pain.

Still she did not believe she was dreaming. She thought, 'I've gone out of my mind in some way; this can't be real, even though it is.'

A girl's voice said, ''Tis clean, Granny, but I'll put a touch of the comfrey paste on it, shall I?'

'Do that, lass, and then you'd best see if your Uncle Samuel is himself again.'

'He's greeting, Beatie said, heartsick at what he did.'

'Poor man, poor man, 'tis an evil I dunna ken the cure for.'

As with the little furry girl, Abigail at first thought these unknown women were speaking some foreign tongue. Then she realised it was an English she had never heard before. She thought, 'Perhaps it's Scots.' After those first bewildered moments, she found that if she listened closely the words began to make sense. She was so desperate to find out where she was, and who these people were, that she concentrated as well as she could on all they said; and after a little, as though she had become accustomed to their speech, their words seemed to turn into understandable English.

The voices, especially that of the girl, were placid and lilting.

'She's a lady, Granny, no doubt.'

'Aye.'

Abigail felt her hand lifted. Fingers ran over her palm.

'Soft as plush, and will you see the nails? Pink and clean as the Queen's own.'

Abigail's astonishment at this was submerged in a sickening wave of pain from her ankle. Out of her burst a puppy-like yelp of which she was immediately ashamed. But the pain was too much and she began to sob, 'My foot, my foot!' She opened her eyes and gazed wildly about.

Bending over her was one of the sweetest faces she had ever seen, a young girl's, with a soft, baby's complexion. A horsetail of dull fair hair hung over one shoulder.

'Poor bairnie, poor bairnie. Take a sup of Granny's posset, 'tis so good for pain. There now, all's well, Dovey's here, and Granny, and we'll no' leave you, I promise.'

Granny's posset tasted like parsley, with a bitter aftertaste; but although Abigail thought she would instantly be sick she was not. She drifted drowsily away, lulled by the warmth of the fire and the warm hand holding her own.

When she awakened she seemed to be alone. Her clothes had been taken off, and she was wearing a long nightdress of thick hairy material. It had a linen collar that rubbed her neck and chin. She cautiously felt this collar. It had been starched to a papery stiffness. One foot, the painful one, was raised on a pillow. The other was against something hard but comfortingly warm. She felt cautiously around it with her toes.

Then a child's voice said, ''Tis a hot pig you're poking at.'

Abigail snapped open her eyes. Natalie's furry girl sat on a stool beside her, so close that Abigail could see the freckles on her face. Her eyes were excited.

Seeing the child so close was strange but comforting, for she knew this child belonged in her own world; she had seen her and Natalie Crown had seen her. And yet, viewed at close hand, she did not seem like an ordinary little girl at all. There was something headstrong and fierce and resolute in her face. Her little hands were marked with scars and burns.

A wave of intense fright ran over Abigail. The very hairs on her arms prickled. Her breathing became fast. Deep inside her, in her secret place, she began to repeat to herself, 'I mustn't lose hold. I must pretend I haven't noticed anything ... anything strange.'

Now that her head was no longer whirling, though it was still paining, she was able to collect her thoughts. She didn't like the fact that her clothes had been taken away. She remembered all the stories at school, about girls who were drugged and taken away to South America and Uganda and Algeria to be slaves in terrible places there. Nicole Price absolutely swore on the snippet of Elvis's silk bandanna (which was the most sacred thing in the world to her) that her own cousin had been standing in Castlereagh Street waiting for a bus in broad daylight and was never seen again.

After a while she whispered, 'What's a hot pig?'

'Daftie,' said the girl. ''Tis a stone bottle filled with hot water. Dunna ye ken anything?'

'Why does my foot hurt?' asked Abigail.

'Why wouldn't it? You sprained your ankle terrible bad when you fell.'

Abigail felt a feeble spark of anger. 'I didn't fall. Some great ox knocked me over.' She thought for a while. 'He didn't really ... really have a sword, did he?'

'Aye, he did. That's me faither. He has spells.'

Abigail thought this over but could make nothing of it. Briefly she thought that if she went to sleep again she might wake up in her own room. But the strong smell of the tallow candle that burnt on the table beside her, the crash of cartwheels and hoofs on the cobbles outside the window, the blast of a ship's whistle from somewhere near, the anxious look of the little girl, denied this.

'What's your name?'

'Beatie Bow.'

Abigail scowled. 'Quit having me on, whoever you are. That's the name of a kids' game.'

'I ken that well enough. But it's my name. Beatrice May Bow, and I'm eleven years of age, though small for it, I know, because of the fever.'

Suddenly she gripped Abigail's arm. 'Dunna tell, I'm asking you. Dunna tell Granny where you come from, or I'm for it. She'll say I've the Gift and I havena, and don't want it, God knows, because I'm afeared of what it does.'

Abigail thought muzzily, 'There's some sense in this somewhere, and sooner or later there'll be a clue and I'll understand it.' Aloud she said, 'What *is* this place?'

'It's the best bedroom, and it's in faither's house, behind the confectionery shop.'

'I mean, what country is it?'

The other girl looked flabbergasted. 'Have ye lost your wits? It's the colony of New South Wales.'

Abigail turned her head into the pillow, which was lumpy and smelled puzzlingly of chicken-coops, and sobbed weakly. She understood nothing except that she was hurt, and was afraid to her very toes, and wanted her mother or even her father.

Beatie said urgently, 'Promise you won't tell where you come from. From *there*. I shouldna ha' done it; I were wicked, I know. But when I heard the bairns calling my name, my heart gave a jump like a spring lamb. But I didna mean to bring you here, I didna know it could be done, heaven's truth.'

She was talking riddles. Abigail was frozen with terror. Was she amongst mad people? The memory of some of those terrible hag faces that had confronted her while she was running returned to her – the caved-in mouths, the skin puckered with old blue scars – of what? The fearsome beggar and his wooden leg, a thing shaped like a peg, like Long John Silver's in *Treasure Island*. She gave a loud snuffle of terror.

Beatie shook her, so that her head and her ankle shot forth pangs of agony.

'Promise me or I'll punch ye yeller and green!'

'Leave me alone,' cried Abigail. 'I don't know where this place is, I can't understand anything.'

'You've lost your memory then,' said the little girl with satisfaction. 'Aye, that'll do bonny.'

Abigail trembled. 'Have I? But I remember lots of things: my name, and how old I am, and I live in George Street North, and my mother's name is Kathy, and she's angry with me because . . .' At the thought of her mother, coming home and finding her missing, ringing the police, Dad, being frantic, she lost her head and began to scream. She saw the elder girl limp into the room. Why did she limp? And Beatie Bow looking frightened and defiant.

Then she became aware that a tall old woman stood beside her, holding her hand. She wore a long black dress and white apron, and on her head was a huge pleated white cap with streamers. Afterwards Abigail realised she looked exactly like a fairy god-mother, but at the time she thought nothing. She said wonderingly, 'Granny!'

'She's no' your granny, she's ours!' snapped Beatie. Dovey hushed her, smiling.

The old woman put her arms round Abigail, and rocked her against a bosom corseted as hard as a board. Terrified as she was, she was at once aware of the goodness that dwelt in this old woman.

She stole a look upwards, saw the brown skin creased like old silk, a sculptured smile on the sunken mouth. It was a composed, private face, with the lines of hardship and grief written on it.

'There, there, lassie, dinna take on so. Granny's here.'

Abigail pressed her face into the black tucked cloth, and held on tight. Something strong and calm radiated from the old woman.

Never in your whole life could you imagine her addressing snide remarks to her bonnet, or the grey silky hair that showed beneath it. She was a real grandmother.

Above her head she heard the grandmother murmur, 'Fetch Judah, Beatie, pet. I think I heard his step. He's that good with bairns.'

'I want my mother,' moaned Abigail.

'Rest sure, my bonnie, that you'll have your mother as soon as we know where she lives, and what you're called.'

A tall young man entered the room. She had a glimpse of fair hair, cut strangely, a square-cut jacket of black or dark blue, with metal buttons, crumpled white trousers.

'Faither's in a state, fair adrift with fright and sorrow. You'd best sit with him, Dovey, till he comes out of it.'

'I'm frightened, I'm frightened,' Abigail whispered.

The young man sat beside her. She could not see his face because the light was in her eyes. Instead she saw a big brown hand, on the outstretched forefinger of which perched a bird as big as a thimble, its feathers a tinsel green.

'Would you know what that is, Eliza?'

'My name isn't Eliza,' whispered Abigail, 'it's Abigail. And that's a humming-bird. But it isn't alive, it's stuffed.'

The young man stroked the tiny glittering head with one finger.

'She came from the Orinoco. I got her for a florin from a deepwater man. Did ye ever see aught as fine?'

He turned the finger this way and that, and the little bird shone like an emerald.

'Will you listen to the way she speaks,' murmured the old woman to Beatie. 'I fear your dada will be in desperate trouble if he's injured her, for she's a lady.'

'I'm not a lady,' muttered Abigail. 'I'm just a girl. *You're* a lady.'

'Not me, child,' said the old woman. 'Why, we Talliskers have been fisherfolk since the Earls of Stewart.'

Abigail could make no sense of any of it. She buried her face in the chickeny pillow. Maybe when she opened her eyes again she would be in her own bed, her own bedroom. But clearly she heard the young man blowing up the fire. It was with a bellows. She knew the rhythmic wheeze, for bellows were a popular item at Magpies. There! She remembered Magpies, even where things were put; Mum's crazy sixty-year-old cash register with all the beautiful bronze-work, the green plush tablecloth draped over the delicate rattan whatnot.

She forced her eyes open. The room was now much brighter. The firelight leapt up, reflecting pinkly on a sloping ceiling. On the table was now a tall oil lamp, and Dovey was carefully turning down the wick.

There was a marble wash-stand in the corner, with a blue flowered thick china wash-basin set into a recess. Underneath stood a tall fluted water jug, and a similarly patterned chamber-pot. The fireplace had an iron hob and on it was a jug of what Abigail thought, from the delicious smell, was hot cocoa. The jug was large and white, and in an oval of leaves was imprinted the face of a youngish man with long dark silky whiskers. She had seen him before in Magpies, too.

'That's Prince Albert, isn't it?' she asked.

'Yes, God rest him. He was taken too soon,' replied the old woman.

Judah brought something out of his pocket and proffered it to her on the palm of his brown hand. It was a pink sugar mouse.

'Our faither makes them. Do you fancy a nibble?'

Abigail did not even see it. She sat shakily up in bed. She saw over the mantel a picture of a middle-aged woman in black, with a small coronet over a white lace veil.

How many times had Abigail seen that sulky, solemn face – on china, miniatures, christening mugs?

'Why ever have you a picture of old Victoria on the wall?' she asked.

'You mustn't speak of our gracious Queen in that way, child!' said Granny severely.

'But our queen is Elizabeth!'

They laughed kindly. 'Why, good Queen Bess died hundreds of years ago, lass. You're still wandering a little; but don't fret: tomorrow you'll be as good as gold.'

Abigail said nothing more. She stared at Queen Victoria in her black widow's weeds and her jet jewellery. Once again, deep inside her, she was saying, 'I must be calm. There's some explanation. I mustn't give myself away.'

Out in the darkness she could hear ships baa-ing on the harbour. 'Is it foggy?' she asked.

'Aye, so maybe I won't be leaving in the morn,' said Judah. 'I'm a seaman, you see, lass.'

Quite near by a bell blommed slow and stately. Abigail jumped.

'It's naught but St Philip's ringing for evensong,' said Dovey softly. 'Ah, she's all of a swither with the shock she got when Uncle Samuel ran into her, poor lamb.'

Abigail tried to still her quaking body. She said to the young man, 'I want to see where I am. Would you help me to the window?'

'Sure as your life, hen,' replied the young fellow heartily. Abigail had expected only to lean on his arm, but he gathered her up, bedclothes and all, and took her to the window. He had the same dark-blue eyes as the old woman.

'What are ye girning about, Beatie?' he chided. 'Open the shutters, lass.'

Sulkily and unwillingly, the little girl unlatched the shutters and threw them wide. Abigail looked out on a gas-lit street, fog forming ghostly rainbows about the lamps. A man pushed a barrow on which glowed a brazier. 'Hot chestnuts, all hot, all hot!' His shout came clearly to Abigail. Women hurried past, all with shawls, some with men's caps pulled over their hair, others with large battered hats with tattered feathers.

But Abigail was looking for something else. She was upstairs, she knew, above the confectionery shop, and she had a wide view of smoking chimneys, hundreds, thousands of smoking chimneys, it seemed, each with a faint pink glow above it.

Mitchell should have been standing there, lit like a Christmas tree at this time of night. The city was still there – she could see dimmish blotches of light, and vehicles that moved very slowly and bumpily.

'The Bridge has gone, too,' she whispered. No broad lighted deck

strode across the little peninsula, no great arch with its winking ruby at the highest point – nothing. The flower-like outline of the Opera House was missing.

She turned her face against Judah's chest and buried it so deeply that she could even hear his heart thumping steadily.

'What is it, Abby? What ails you, child?'

For the first time she looked into his face. It was brown and ruddy, a snubbed, country kind of face.

'What year is it?' she whispered.

He looked dumbfounded. 'Are you codding me?'

'What year is it?' she repeated.

'Why, it's 1873, and most gone already,' he said.

Abigail said no more. He took her back to the bed, and Dovey gently folded the covers over her.

'It's true then,' she said uneasily to the old grandmother. 'She's lost her memory. Dear God, what will we do, Granny? For 'twas Uncle Samuel that caused it, and in all charity we've the responsibility of her.'

The tall old woman murmured something. Abigail caught the word 'stranger ...'

Dovey looked dubious. 'It's my belief she's an immigrant lass, sent to one of the fine houses on the High Rocks to be a parlourmaid, perhaps, for she speaks so bonny. Not like folk hereabouts at all! But where's her traps, do you think, Granny? Stolen or lost? Just what she stood up in, and the Dear knows there was little enough of that!'

Thus they talked in low voices beside the door, while Beatie Bow crept a little closer and stared with thrilled yet terrified eyes at Abigail.

'You!' said Abigail in a fierce whisper. 'You did this to me!'

''Tisn't so,' objected Beatie. 'You chased me up alley and down gully, like a fox after a hare. It wunna my fault!'

Abigail was silent. She kept saying to herself, 'Abigail Kirk, that's who I am. I mustn't forget. I might sink down and get lost in this place – this time, or whatever it is – if I don't keep my mind on it.'

Judah and Granny had gone down the stairs. Dovey limped over and put a hand on Abigail's forehead. 'You've no fever, and the ankle will be a wee bit easier tomorrow. You stay here and talk to Abby, Beatie, seeing that you're getting on so grand, and I'll heat up some broth for your supper.'

Beatie stared at Abigail crossly, defiantly, and yet with anxiety.

'It'd be no skin off your nose if you codded you'd lost your memory because of that dint on the head. I dunna want my granny to know.'

'I want to go back to my own place,' said Abigail in a hard voice.

'I dunna ken where your ain place is,' protested Beatie. 'I didna mean to go there myself. It were the bairnies calling my name. I dunna ken how I did it, honest. I never did it afore I had the fever.'

As though to herself, in a puzzled, worried voice she said, 'One minute I was in the lane, and the next there was a wall there, and the bairnies skittering about, and all those places like towers and castles and that ... that great road that goes over the water, and strange carriages on it with never a horse amongst them, and I was afeared out of my wits, thinking the fever had turned my brain. And then I heard children calling my name, and they were playing a game we play around the streets here, except that we call it Janey Jo. But they couldna see me, because I tried to speak to one or two. Only you and that wee little one with the yellow coat.'

The child's cocky attitude had vanished. Her face was sallow and the big hollow eyes shone. Abigail remembered that Natalie had wept because she believed that this girl had been unhappy. She had mentioned fever. Perhaps that was why Beatie's hair had been cut so short. Abigail remembered that once it had been the custom to shave the heads of fever patients. She was about to ask about this, when Beatie said in an awed voice, 'Is it Elfland, that place where you come from?'

'Of course it isn't, there isn't any Elfland. Are you crazy?'

Beatie said in a hushed voice. 'Green as a leek, you are. Of course there's Elfland. Isn't that where Granny's great-great-granny got the Gift, the time she was lost so long?'

'You're crazy,' said Abigail. 'You're all crazy.'

She closed her eyes. The fire crackled, the room was full of strange smells, but the smell of burnt sugar was strongest of all. A hand timidly touched hers.

'It's bonny.'

'What is?'

'That place you were. Elfland.'

Abigail opened her eyes and glared into the tawny ones. 'I told you it wasn't Elfland.'

'Where is it then?'

'Guess,' said Abigail snappily.

Beatie Bow was silent. Abigail stared at the ceiling. Then Beatie Bow said, 'How did those children know my name?'

'I wouldn't know, and if I did I wouldn't tell you.'

She wanted to scream like a seagull. With a great effort she kept the sounds of lostness and fright down in her chest. Her head was throbbing again and her ankle felt like a bursting football.

'If it wasna Elfland,' said Beatie slowly and thoughtfully, 'it was some place I dunna ken about. Yet the bairns there don't play Janey Jo any more; they play Beatie Bow.'

Abigail didn't answer.

Suddenly the little girl shouted, 'I will make you tell, I will! I want to know about the castles and palaces, and the lights that went so fast, and the queer old things the bairns were playing on, and how they knew my name. I'll punch ye yeller and green, I swear it, if ye dunna tell!'

'Maybe you've got the Gift,' said Abigail cruelly. Beatie turned so white her freckles seemed twice as numerous. Abigail said, 'You get me back there where I met you, or I'll tell your granny where I come from and who brought me.'

Beatie whipped up a hard little fist as though to clout her.

'I dunna want the Gift. I'm feared of it! I wunna have it!'

Abigail thought hazily, 'When I get back home, or wake up, or whatever I'm going to do, I'll be sorry I didn't ask her what this stupid Gift is. But just now I don't care.'

She turned away from Beatie's anxious, angry face, and pretended to be asleep. Within a moment or two she was.

Ballet Shoes

Noel Streatfeild

*Great-Uncle Matthew (or Gum as he is known) collects fossils. He also,
in the course of his travels during the 1920s and 30s, 'collects' three
orphans and takes them to live in his London house with his great-niece
Sylvia and her old nurse, Nana. The three girls – Pauline, Petrova and
Posy – decide to call themselves 'the Fossils' and they are very happy living
with Sylvia (whom they call Garnie – short for guardian) and Nana. But
Gum goes off travelling and money begins to run short. Sylvia decides to
take in boarders: Theo Dane who teaches dancing at a stage school, Mr
and Mrs Simpson who, much to Petrova's delight, own a car, Dr Jakes
who teaches literature and Dr Smith who teaches mathematics. Theo
suggests that Pauline, Petrova and Posy become pupils at the stage school
where she works, and in this chapter we see their first visit to the Academy.
This marks the beginning of great changes in their lives.*

THE Children's Academy of Dancing and Stage Training was in
Bloomsbury. It was three large houses joined inside by
passages. Across the front was written in large gold letters:
'Children's Acad' on the first house, 'emy of Dancing an' on the
second, and 'd Stage Training' on the third. Theo had arranged
that Nana and Sylvia should take the children round to see the
place and to meet Madame Fidolia on a Wednesday afternoon, and
that they should start their classes on the following Monday. Since
it was a very important occasion, Mr Simpson said he would drive
them all to the Academy in his car. The afternoon started badly.
Pauline wanted to wear a party frock, which she said was the right
thing for a dancing class; Nana, after discussion with Theo, had
ironed and washed their blue-linen smocks and knickers.

'I want to wear our muslins,' said Pauline. 'At Cromwell House
girls who learned dancing wore best frocks.'

'Only for ballroom dancing,' Petrova argued. 'They wore silk tunics for everything else; we haven't got those.'

Nana was firm.

'It's not a matter of what you've got or haven't got; you're putting on the smocks and knickers I've laid on your beds, so get on with changing while I dress Posy.'

'Why can't we wear our muslins?' Pauline growled.

'Because for the exercises and that they're going to see you do Miss Dane said plain cotton frocks and knickers. When you start on Monday you're having rompers, two each, black-patent ankle-strap shoes, and white tarlatan dresses, two each, with white sandal shoes, and white knickers, two pairs, all frills; so don't worry me, because I'm going to have worries enough getting all that lot made by Monday.'

Petrova pulled off her pink check frock and knickers, and got into the clean ones.

'What do we want all those for?'

Nana sighed.

'Ask me, dear! What we've got would do quite well for dancing in, I should say; but there's a printed list come, and there's all that on it, not to mention two rough face-towels for each child, clearly marked, and two special overalls to be bought through the school. Now you know. Come here, Pauline, and let me see to your hair.'

Petrova hurried through her dressing and ran downstairs. She found Mr Simpson sitting in his car.

'Hullo!' he called. 'Come beside me.' She scrambled in. He looked down at her and smiled. 'So they are going to train you as a dancer, are they?'

'Yes.' Petrova sighed. 'And I don't want to be one.'

'Why? Might be fun.'

'Not for me; I'm not any good. At Cromwell House we did dancing games once a week, and I was the worst in the class. Pauline was the best, though.'

'How about Posy?'

'Her mother was a dancer, she became a Fossil bringing ballet shoes with her, so I expect she'll be all right.' She fiddled with the gear lever. 'Do you suppose if you train to be a dancer and to act when you are eight like me, that you can be something else when you grow up?'

'Of course.' He laughed. 'Eight isn't very old. You've at least another ten years before you'll need to worry.'

'Oh, no.' Petrova shook her head. 'Nana says that Miss Dane says that we can start to earn money when we are twelve. I shall be twelve in four years. So if I begin earning then, I shall have been doing it for' – she counted on her fingers – 'five years by the time I'm quite grown-up.'

'Meaning you'd be quite grown-up at seventeen?'

'Yes. Well, would you think then I could be something else?'

'Of course. What do you want to be?'

'I don't know quite. Something to do with driving cars. Can girls be chauffeurs?'

'Lots are.'

She looked pleased.

'Then I think I'll be that.'

When they arrived at the Academy and rang the bell they were shown into a waiting-room. They had to wait in it quite a long time; but the children did not mind because of the pictures on the walls. These were photographs of the pupils of the school. Some were large ones of just one child. These were rather alike – the child wearing a ballet frock and standing on her toes. These were signed: 'To dear Madame Fidolia from Little Doris,' or 'Babsy,' or 'Baby Cora,' or names like that. The children were most impressed by the way the children in the photographs stood on their points, but shocked at the signatures, considering them all too old to have names like 'Little' or 'Babsy' or 'Baby'.

They played a game giving marks for the handwritings; in the end a child signing herself 'Tiny' won. The photographs they liked better were the groups. These were of pantomimes, and though there were lots of Academy pupils in them, the children were not interested. What they liked were the other characters.

'Look,' said Posy, climbing on a seat to see better. 'That's "The Three Bears".'

'It's not.' Pauline got up and joined her. 'It says it's "Puss in Boots".'

Petrova came over to study the picture.

'I think it must have been called wrong. It is "The Three Bears". What are those?'

Pauline put her head to one side hoping to see better.

'More like three cats, I think.'

'But there isn't three cats in "Puss in Boots",' Posy objected, 'There's only one cat.'

Petrova suddenly gave an exclamation.

'Look. Those three cats aren't grown-up people; they are much smaller than that lady in tights.' She turned to Sylvia. 'Would you suppose when I'm twelve and can earn money I could be a cat? I wouldn't mind that.'

'No.' Pauline jumped off the bench. 'I'd love to be a cat, or a dog. A Pekingese would be nice to be – such a furry coat.'

'It's a monkey you'll be in a minute climbing about messing yourself up,' Nana interrupted. 'Come and sit down like little ladies.'

Posy sat next to Sylvia.

'I'd rather be dressed like one of those little girls,' she said thoughtfully. 'I'd like to wear flowers in my hair.'

Pauline and Petrova looked at each other.

'Would you think,' said Pauline, 'that there could be so vain a child?' She turned to Posy. 'And I suppose you'd like to be called "Baby Posy"?'

'I wouldn't mind.' Posy swung her legs happily. 'I'd like to look like one of those children.'

Petrova leant over to her, and spoke in a very shocked voice.

'You wouldn't really like to look like one of those dressed-up misses? You wouldn't, Posy. You'd really much rather be a cat.'

'No.' Posy lolled against Sylvia. 'I'd like to wear flowers in my hair. Cats don't.'

'Very nice, too,' said Nana. 'Cats, indeed; it's the Zoo you two ought to train at, not a dancing school.'

Pauline and Petrova both started to argue when they were interrupted. The door opened, and Madame Fidolia came in. Madame Fidolia had been a great dancer many years before; she had started training at the age of seven in the Russian Imperial Ballet School. She had made a big name for herself before the 1914 war, not only in Russia, but all over the world. When the revolution came she had to leave her country, for she had been a favourite with the Tsar and Tsarina, and so not popular with Soviet Russia. She made London her new home, and for some years danced there, as well as in most of the European capitals and America. Then one morning she had waked up and decided she was too old to dance any more. At the same time she realized she was too energetic a person to lead a lazy life, so she started her academy.

Madame Fidolia had thought, when she opened it, that she would run it as the Old Imperial Ballet School had been run. She soon found that was impossible, as it would cost far more money than pupils would pay. She found, too, that there were very few children who came to her who had real talent. She had discovered none of whom she had made a first-class ballerina. So she gave up trying to do the impossible, and ran an ordinary stage school where the children learnt all kinds of dancing, and actors came to teach them the art of acting. There was only one class through which they did not all pass, and that was Madame Fidolia's own. She watched every pupil who came through the school with care for about three to six months and then perhaps one day she would say: 'My child, you will come to my classes next term.' Going to Madame Fidolia's classes was the highest honour of the Academy.

The children thought her very odd-looking. She had come straight from teaching. She had black hair parted in the middle and drawn down tight into a small bun on her neck. She had on a long practice dress of white tarlatan, and pink tights, and pink ballet shoes. Round her shoulders she had a cerise silk shawl. She stood in the doorway.

'Miss Brown?' She had a very pretty, broken accent.

Sylvia got up.

'I'm Miss Brown.' They shook hands. Madame looked at the children.

'My pupils?'

'Yes. This is Pauline.'

Pauline smiled shyly and held out her hand, but Madame shook her head.

'No. All my children when they see me night and morning, and before and after a class, or any time when we meet say, "Madame" and curtsy. So!' She swept a lovely curtsy down to the floor.

Pauline turned scarlet, but she managed somehow, though it was more a bob than a curtsy, and only 'am' of 'Madame' could be heard.

'And this is Petrova.'

Petrova started her curtsy, but Madame came across to her. She took her face between her hands.

'Are you Russian?'

'Yes.'

'You speak Russian?' Madame's tone was full of hope.

'No.' Petrova looked anxiously at Sylvia, who came to her rescue explaining her history.

Madame kissed her.

'You are the first compatriot of mine to come to my school. I will make a good dancer of you. Yes?'

Petrova scratched at the floor with her toe and said nothing; she daren't look up, for she was sure Pauline would make her laugh.

'And this is Posy,' said Sylvia.

Posy came forward and dropped the most beautiful curtsy.

'Madame,' she said politely.

'Blessed lamb!' Nana murmured proudly.

'Little show-off!' Pauline whispered to Petrova.

Madame sent for Theo and told her to take them to the classroom, and they went into the junior dancing class. Here about twenty small girls in royal-blue rompers and white socks and black patent-leather shoes were learning tap dancing. Theo spoke to the teacher. Madame, she said, wanted to see what classes to put these three children into. Madame sat down, and Sylvia and Nana sat beside her. The twenty little girls settled down cross-legged on the floor. Theo took the children to the middle of the room and told the pianist to play a simple polka, then she began to dance.

'You dance too, dears,' she said.

Pauline turned crimson. She had seen the sort of thing the twenty children in the class were doing, and knew that she could do nothing like that, and that they were all younger than she was.

'Dance, Pauline dear,' Theo called. 'Copy me.'

Pauline gave an agonized look at Sylvia, who smiled sympathy and encouragement, then she held out the skirts of her smock and began to polka.

'Thank goodness we all know how to do this one,' she thought. 'We should have looked fools if it had been a waltz.'

Petrova began to polka straight away, but she did it very badly, stumbling over her feet.

'I won't mind,' she said to herself. 'I know I can't dance like all those children, so it's no good trying.'

She would not look at them, though, for she was sure they were whispering about her.

Posy was delighted to hear the music. Theo had taught her to polka, and she was charmed to show it off. She picked up her feet and held out her skirts, and pointed her toes; she thought it great fun.

'Just look at Posy!' Pauline whispered to Petrova as she passed her.

Petrova looked, and wished she could do it like that.

'Stop,' said Theo. 'Come here, dears.'

She took hold of the children one by one and lifted first their right legs and then their left over their heads. Then she left them and went to Madame Fidolia. She curtsied.

'Elementary, Madame?'

Madame got up; as she did so, all the children rose off the floor.

'Elementary,' she said. She shook first Sylvia and then Nana by the hand. 'Goodbye, children.'

She turned to go, and all the twenty children and the pianist and the instructress and Theo curtsied, saying 'Madame' in reverent voices. Pauline, Petrova, and Posy did it too, but a little late. Sylvia gave rather a deep bow, and Nana a bob.

'Well,' said Nana, as the door closed, 'if you ask me, it's for all the world like taking dancing classes in Buckingham Palace.'

'That's very satisfactory,' Theo explained to Sylvia. 'The elementary classes are from four to five every afternoon. The acting classes are on Saturdays, so that all the children can be brought together. It will be more difficult later on, when they are in different classes.'

They went home on a bus.

'Do you know,' Pauline whispered to Petrova as they sat down together on the front seat on the top, 'that soon it's Posy's birthday, when we have to do our vows again, and we can't.'

'Why not?'

'Well, didn't we vow to make Fossil a name in history books? Whoever heard of people on the stage in history books?'

'We needn't be actresses always, though,' Petrova said comfortingly. 'I asked Mr Simpson, and he said because you were a thing from the time you were twelve till you grew up it didn't mean you had to be it always.'

'It's difficult to see how to be in a history book, anyway,' Pauline said, in a worried sort of voice. 'It's mostly Kings and Queens who are. People like Princess Elizabeth will be; but not us whatever we did – at least, it will be difficult.'

'There's Joan of Arc.' Petrova tried to remember a few more names. 'I know there were a lot, but I didn't get as far as a whole reign, I was only doing "Tales from History" when we left Cromwell House. Then I did that little bit about Alfred the Great with Garnie; and Doctor Jakes hasn't given me a history lesson yet. But there were lots. I know there were. We'll ask Doctor Jakes to tell us about them.'

Sylvia leant over from the seat behind.

'Look, darlings, here is a shilling. I want you all to have cakes for tea to make up for a very hard-working afternoon.'

Wild Lone

'BB'

Rufus the fox, the cunning hero of Wild Lone, *was born in Hieaway Wood. He is a Pytchley fox, which means he lives in the countryside hunted by the Pytchley foxhounds in the English Midlands. 'BB' enables the reader to share the wild existence of Rufus and experience all the sights and scents and sounds of the countryside. This chapter shows Rufus in what proves to be a very dangerous encounter with a band of gipsies.*

To the east of Blueberry Bushes there is a winding, gated lane that leads, after many deviations and with the happy meanderings of a brook, to join up with the main road a mile and a half away. For the first part of its length it is hedged on either hand with tall ragged bullfinches, red now with the hips and haws and glorious riot of deadly nightshade. Wide turf margins open out as the lane proceeds, until finally the fields are reached. Up this lane one evening towards the end of October, there came a ragged cavalcade of gipsies with a hooded caravan.

First came two women, one old and withered, with a crinkled, dark face, the other a young girl of fifteen or thereabouts, a lovely child whose face was as vivid in its beauty as the trailing festoons of autumn berries glowing in the wreckage of the hedges. Over their arms they carried wicker baskets filled with clothes pegs. The girl's slim, honey-coloured legs were bare, and the tattered skirt scarce reached her knees. Behind, came the caravan, drawn by a well-fed, fat, grey horse, and a middle-aged man sat hunched on the shafts, a scarlet neckerchief round his throat, and a short pipe between his teeth. Under the caravan, between the wheels, ran two dogs, as cunning as their lord and master riding up aloft. Tied to the caravan was a small tilt cart with a swinging bucket underneath, and within the cart, in addition to an extraordinary assortment of articles, lay a bicycle, tied on its side by a stout cord passed under the floor of the cart. Bringing up the rear of this picturesque cavalcade, a small, rough-headed boy followed, a stick in his hand, chewing a twig.

They conversed together as they journeyed, these wild and happy folk, in shrill squealing tones, like the yapping of dingoes. Coming to a place where the lane widened somewhat and a little brook ran under the road through a culvert, they stopped, and the horse was taken out of the shafts. After a knotted rag was tied between his forelegs, he was turned out to graze on the green grass. All was bustle and commotion, though they worked with the air of each having a definite job to do. The cart was unhitched from the back of the caravan, and the bicycle untied and set against one wheel of the tilt. The women went along the ditch, collecting firing, and the man walked slowly down the lane with the dogs, his sharp eyes scanning the ditch for a rabbit run in which to set a snare.

315

Soon the lurchers went down into the ditch bottom, among the dead leaves and brambles. A little while after there was a faint suppressed yelp and a rabbit, half-grown, tore across the road, both lurchers hard on its heels, and a moment later a squeal, cut short with a suddenness, told of a kill. The gipsy, after a quick fox-like look up and down the lane, got down into the steep ditch and blackberry bushes, and emerged with a bulge, a warm bulge, under his coat. The two lurchers trotted innocently at his heels as he went back to the encampment. When he turned the corner of the lane he saw the blue smoke of the fire misting through the tawny bushes, and there came to him a lovely reek of burning faggots. The women were busy about the fire already glowing redly in the dusk and flickering on the open door of the caravan.

He walked to the tilt and lifting the corner of a sack, pushed the rabbit's warm body underneath, a needless precaution, for very rarely did anyone come along the lane, and the grass grew where once the stage coaches bowled along to the merry music of the post horn.

As the dusk deepened into the velvet pall of night the fire became more vivid, showing the autumn glow of the trees and bushes, and lighting the interesting faces of these wild people. They differed from the usual country clods one sees in the rural villages, whose faces are as expressionless as cows. It is seldom one sees an uninteresting gipsy face, even in the old people. Soon the fire crackled merrily as they lay about it, and in the dancing light of the ruddy flames, the face of the young gipsy girl seemed of a beauty not of this earth.

Gradually the fire died down, subsiding with rustling clicks, and outside the warm circle the night air struck cold and damp on the gipsies' backs. So with many wranglings and bickerings the family retired within the caravan. As for the lurcher dogs, one went with the family, and the other was tied to the wheel, where it lay nose on paws, eyes fixed on the dying embers of the fire. . . .

Rufus was in mischievous mood, for he was hungry. More rabbit catchers had been at work in the furze of Blueberry and Coldhangar, and the stock was sadly depleted. Moreover, the unreasonable farmers had taken undue precautions with their fowls and poultry, for Rufus was unfortunately beginning to be known to the country people for his daring and cunning. This was an unfortunate state of affairs, because it meant every man's hand was against him, and since the episode of Jackman's farm, he was known by sight to the Hunt and country people. Rufus, the one-eared fox, a criminal of the deepest dye, whom no hound or man could ever catch, or snare. . . .

Rufus came across from Coldhangar in the early dawn. He was on his way to Hieaway, where for the last week or so he had been kennelling. He had had no game, hunting was bad. Therefore, he was in mischievous mood, and so prepared to run risks. Half-way across Penny Plain, where the restless peewits roosted among the ant-hills, his sharp nose caught the smell of fire, and he stopped, deliberating. There were also other smells, of man and dogs and refuse, so he decided to investigate. He slipped through the ragged bullfinch fifty yards above the sleeping encampment, and stopped on the grass verge, trying the air.

He saw the still, rounded hump of the caravan against the hedge, and a few dull red cinders before the door, which threw a faint glow on the spokes of the wheels. Above was the arch of stars, a little pale now because an unearthly greenish tinge suffused the eastern sky, as the light began to filter over the curve of the earth. But what interested him most was a strong smell of rabbit coming from the tilt cart at the back of the caravan, and so, very slowly, he stole forward along the bottom of the hedge, stopping ever and again to listen and sniff. As he drew nearer the scent of fresh-killed rabbit grew stronger, and the smell made him feel very hungry.

Beneath the caravan lay the cur, fast asleep, talking and twitching because subconscious senses told of a strange smell, and the scent became entangled in its dreams. It was that time when all day-hunting animals, man included, sleep most soundly in the open air, and even the cocks were fast a-slumber. The red sparks of the almost dead fire shone like rubies in the darkness, and a faint breeze, coming from beyond the fire to Rufus, sent a little tiny spark into the grass between the wheels of the caravan. Still the cur slept, and in the caravan, the gipsies slept too, snoring like owls. Only the girl lay awake, lying on her back with a moth-eaten fur coat drawn over her slim lovely body, staring through the chink of the half-drawn curtains, at a little wistful star. . . .

Rufus came up to the tilt cart, and stood on his hind legs, resting his forepaws on the shafts, and sniffing the crack between the tail-board and the floor. The scent of rabbit was very strong, and was obviously just under the sacking. He took one more peep at the sleeping cur, then jumped nimbly, with the beautiful grace of a panther, on to the top of the tail-board.

Within the caravan the gipsy father stirred in his sleep muttering plaintively, and the snores of the other inmates died to a soft breathing. The fox heard the muttering of the man and leapt lightly down to the grass again, ready to vanish into the shadows. But all was still, the cur slept on. After waiting a moment, Rufus again leapt on the cart and poked his nose under the sack. He pulled the rabbit out, but put it down for an instant, listening, for the cur was stirring below; a back eddy of breeze had brought the reek of fox to his sleeping senses. Rufus stood on top of the dusky cart, his one erect ear giving him an even more tense appearance. Then he picked up the rabbit and turned round to run down the shaft of the cart. At that moment, the cur was wide awake and sprang to its feet, eyes dilated and ears cocked. Immediately his awake senses told him all was not well, and he went off into a paroxysm of staccato barks that split the silence like a knife.

Inside the caravan, the other cur awoke and bounded to the door. The man awoke, cursing and muttering, still half-dazed with the drugs of slumber, and pushed his head out. . . .

Rufus, with the rabbit in his jaws, leapt off the top of the cart, and at the same moment, the cur jumped out of the caravan and was hard on his heels. Under the caravan the other dog leapt and strangled at his string, his wild yapping choked in his throat. What excitement then to be sure! The man shouting, the women screaming angrily at this sudden disturbance, and the ragged urchin jumped to the ground and stood looking after the departing cur that was hard on the heels of Rufus. The latter had dropped the rabbit when he found the dog gaining on him, and, badly frightened, dived into the culvert. He ran through the shallow water that was not more than two inches deep at the most, to the far end, and there he found his way barred by an iron grating . . . he was trapped! The cur had followed him in and was a plucky scoundrel. He flew at the fox, who turned about and faced him, and in the confined space they bit and worried savagely. Rufus was a match for the light-built dog, and he drove him back yard by yard towards the mouth of the culvert. Meanwhile, the gipsy urchin and his father came up with the other dog, a thicker-set beast with a dash of terrier in his blood, who was afraid of nothing. The bleeding cur backed out, tail between legs and 'ki-wi-ing' plaintively, and the gipsy shouted to the boy to fetch a sack from the tilt cart. . . . A fox's skin might fetch a few shillings. . . .

Telling the terrier to guard the entrance, he ran to the other end of the culvert, stumbling down the bank in the half-darkness of the dawn. He saw the iron grating and realized the fox was unable to get out. Then he felt the grating and found it loose in its socket and he called the boy down the bank to him there. He lifted the grating out and fixed the mouth of the sack in position, laying a stone on the bottom inside edge and holding the top edge against the upper rim of the cement drain.

By now the dawn had greyed sufficiently to reveal the dew-wet hedges and the green-painted van drawn up on the grass, and at the door the women, shading their eyes.

'Goo you to t'other end and send Grip into him, you,' shouted the gipsy. So the boy urged the terrier into the drain, while the whippet stood with trembling hind quarters by the mouth of the hole, not daring to face those teeth again. Rufus in the culvert saw the sudden darkening of the dim light at the grating end, and the dark form of the terrier coming towards him down the tunnel, its hairs on end and growling savagely. . . .

For a moment there was a tense silence, the gipsy waiting crouched over the sack, and his strong brown hands clutching the folds. . . .

A faint subterranean yapping, sounds of a scuffle, and something shot like a bolt into the sack. Like a flash the gipsy raised it, closing the top, and with the struggling animal inside it, climbed triumphantly up the bank.

'I got the b—. Gie I a big stick.'. . . He carried the sack to the top of the bank, and taking the stick from the boy, hit the squirming sack a sickening blow. Within, all movement ceased. The man, with his white teeth showing in a bestial grin, held the sack upside down, and there dropped out on the dewy grass – the body of the terrier cur with its back broken. . . .

Neither had realized that the terrier had not come out of the culvert, and by now Rufus was speeding across the grey fields to Hieaway, his body smarting with two savage bites on his flank. Once he stopped and glanced back, his sly eyes slits, the one ear cocked like a question mark. From over the ragged rust of the hedge a faint, blue smoke was drifting, and the sound of wrangling and screams were borne to him on the breeze. The gipsies were all talking at once, and the sound was as of a lot of jackals on a kill.

Rufus cocked his leg against a dead thistle and went on down into the dewy valley where the early rooks were getting their breakfast. Mushrooms gleamed in the grass like white stones, and on one of them, nibbling the luscious pink flesh, a huge black slug was sprawled. Rufus sniffed it, took it in his teeth and shook it, throwing it away into the grass.

He went into Hieaway under the gate and slunk up to the box bushes. And there he was lulled to sleep by the rush of the wind in the dark firs, for no one came near the wood all day. He slept till a blackbird awoke him, and he found the sun setting behind the grill of trees, now almost bare in the upper branches that showed so blackly against the tender sky.

Knight Crusader

Ronald Welch

The young Knight Crusader Philip d'Aubigny has been captured by the Turks and is being held in Damascus in the house of the Emir Usamah. All his life Philip has lived in Outremer, a tiny Christian kingdom in the Holy Land founded by the Crusaders who remained in the East after the First Crusade. By 1185 Outremer was in great danger. The Turks had found a powerful leader in Saladin and the Crusaders are overwhelmingly defeated at the Battle of Hattin. Philip's life is spared and Usamah treats him well but he loses his father, friends and liberty. In this extract from Ronald Welch's thrilling historical novel we read of Philip's attempt to escape after four long years of captivity.

PHILIP went out riding the next morning with half a dozen of the Emir's servants. They were bound for a spot outside the walls where a falcon trap was set up, for although Usamah had long since flown his last hawk, he still loved to catch and train the birds. By the Beirut Gate they waited while a caravan passed into the city. The streets of Damascus were not very different to those of Jerusalem, Philip was thinking, as he watched the beggars. They were as filthy and repulsive as those Llewellyn had once driven away.

One of them rushed across to Philip. He held out his hands.

'Sheyan-lillah!' he howled. 'Something for the love of God!'

The same cry, too, Philip thought, and fumbled for a coin. The beggar took it, spat on it, and glanced up.

'You are Sir Philip d'Aubigny of Blanche Garde?' he asked quietly.

Philip's horse shied as he jerked roughly at the reins. For this scarecrow of the Damascus slums had spoken in the *langue d'oeil*, the language of France and the Normans, and his accent was that of a nobleman.

'Show no signs of listening!' the beggar hissed. 'Meet me tonight or any night at that tavern by the gate. Ask for Ali the Beggar.'

He was gone, running nimbly away, shrieking out his high-pitched plea for alms. Philip took a deep breath, resisted the impulse to turn and watch, and shook the reins of his horse.

They rode through the circle of cultivated land that surrounded Damascus, through the green orchards and fields, and out into the flat, open country beyond, that stretched away monotonously to the ring of mountains on the horizon.

The falcon trap was a small stone building, about six feet high, covered with dry grass and vegetation, so that the bricks were concealed, and the shed appeared as a harmless mound of turf.

Two men crawled inside, and then their faces appeared at a small opening, where they held out sticks to which pigeons were tied. The procedure for catching wild falcons was simple enough, but demanded patience. The pigeons would flutter helplessly, and their noise and movement would attract falcons, who could not resist such a tempting bait. As they swooped down and grappled with the unfortunate pigeon, the stick would be pulled inside the hut, and the falcon grasped by expert fingers.

Normally, Philip would have followed the trapping with interest, for hawking was one of his passions. But the day passed with infuriating slowness, and he made little attempt to join in the work. He would see this beggar with the nobleman's voice tonight, he decided. There was no difficulty in leaving Usamah's house when he wanted to, and he would not be stopped or molested in the streets if he wore Turkish clothes. His Arabic was faultless now, and no one would take him for a Frankish knight in the dark, for his tell-tale grey eyes would not be seen.

Five hours later he was standing outside the inn, near the Beirut Gate. The single eating-room was more than half full, which reassured him, for there would be less chance of anyone paying him much attention. It was just as well he was wearing shabby clothes and a tattered cloak, he thought, for the inn was a disreputable place.

He pushed his way through the ill-lit room, and sat on a bench

with his back against the wall. A Negro came up, and Philip ordered some food. As he waited, he glanced around the room. But he could see no sign of Ali the Beggar. With some difficulty Philip forced the unappetizing food down his throat. A few years ago he would have burst out with anxious questions about the beggar. But the silent man who bent his head over the bowl of stew was a different person from the young knight who had marched out of Blanche Garde Castle.

Philip pushed away the empty bowl, and beckoned to the Negro.

'Do you know Ali the Beggar?' he asked casually.

The Negro eyed him doubtfully, then shrugged his broad shoulders, and jerked a hand in the direction of a curtained doorway.

'Upstairs,' he said, accepting the few coins that Philip pushed over the table in payment for his meal, and shuffling away.

Nobody seemed to be paying any attention to Philip. Why should they? he thought, as he slipped through the curtain, and climbed the rickety stairs to the landing above. But one hand was under the cloak, and he could feel the hilt of the dagger that Jusuf had once given him.

There were three doors on the landing. One was open. Philip stood motionless, his tall figure throwing a long black shadow against the peeling plaster of the wall.

From below came the buzz of conversation and the clatter of crockery. But it was very quiet up there on the landing. Then from the open room came a cough, and the rustle of someone moving.

Philip went to the door, and raising the knife, he tapped with the hilt on the door. 'Ali the Beggar?' he asked softly.

'Come in,' said a voice in Arabic.

Philip braced himself, and moved his grip on the dagger. There was no particular reason why he should suspect treachery, but he had learnt to trust no man. Then he slid through the door, and pushed it shut behind him.

A single rushlight flickered on a low table in the centre of the room. The furniture was rough and battered; a truckle bed, two stools, and a chest by the window. The beggar was sitting at the table, and looked up as Philip shut the door.

'You will not need that knife, Sir Philip,' he said in his faultless French.

'Who are you?' Philip asked suspiciously. He still could not credit the familiar speech from the lips of this repulsive beggar.

'I am John de Vitry,' the beggar said. 'A knight of the Hospitallers.'

'De Vitry!' Philip suddenly had a vision of the waiting-room in the Palace at Jerusalem, a group of young men with scented handkerchiefs, and a voice, Joscelin's, saying something about a brother in the Hospitallers to young Jacques de Vitry.

'I knew your brother, Sir John,' he said.

'Yes, Jacques. He was killed at Hattin.' De Vitry pushed forward the spare stool.

Philip sat down, and slid the dagger back into its sheath.

'What are you doing in Damascus, de Vitry?' he asked. 'Are you in hiding, after escaping?'

'Oh, no. I came here of my own accord. From Krak des Chevaliers.'

'Of your own accord!'

De Vitry laughed, 'We have a regular connection with Damascus, you see, Sir Philip. I have been here before, because I speak fluent Arabic.'

'But why come here?'

'We like to know what is going on. And we are arranging the escape of prisoners. You are the next on our list.'

Philip shrugged his shoulders helplessly, and laughed. 'I think you had better explain, Sir John,' he said.

'It's quite simple,' de Vitry said. 'We have unlimited money, and

even the most devout Infidel will do a great deal for money. We have succeeded in releasing several barons. Horses are the difficulty, you see. It's fairly simple for you people to get outside the walls, isn't it?' Philip nodded. 'But not so easy to go much farther. And that's where we help. We have a place outside, and a supply of good horses. There is one waiting for you. In two days' hard riding, you will be at Krak.'

'I want two horses,' Philip said instantly.

'Two?'

'Yes, Gilbert d'Assailly is coming with me. He's in Damascus too.'

De Vitry shook his head doubtfully. 'But I only had orders about you, Sir Philip. The Grand Master was most insistent.'

'Who?'

'Sir Garnier de Nablus. He was not killed with the other Hospitallers at Hattin, you know. He mentioned you particularly, Sir Philip. You see, you have some powerful friends. Sir Balian d'Ibelin and Guy of Lusignan asked that you should be helped to escape.'

Philip's eyebrows lifted slightly. Otherwise he gave no sign of surprise or gratification at the information that such important barons were interested in his fate.

Five minutes later he had persuaded de Vitry to allow him the use of another horse. It would have needed a stronger personality than the young Hospitaller to stand against such a forceful person as Philip had become.

De Vitry gave Philip a detailed description of the place where the horses could be found, and the password which would ensure that the man holding the horses would hand them over. More instructions followed about the route to Krak, and the necessity for taking sufficient food and water for the journey.

'What about you, de Vitry?' Philip asked curiously.

'I must stay here. There is a good deal more for me to do.'

Philip seized his hand and shook it warmly. 'You are a brave man, Sir John,' he said. 'One day I will repay you for this.'

'Escape first, and then you can thank me,' de Vitry said.

Philip hurried back to Usamah's house. He would find Gilbert in the morning. They must leave Damascus the next night. There would not be much difficulty about that, for the house Gilbert was living in was on the wall of the city. The drop to the foot of the ditch was not too great for active men, with the help of a rope.

Philip went through the details as he walked through the dark streets, and let himself in by a side door to the courtyard of Usamah's house. Food, fruit, water, a rope, weapons; he went through the list in his mind. Everything must be ready by the next evening.

He met Gilbert in the bazaar early next day. The position of Christian knights in Damascus was a peculiar one. They were prisoners, but were allowed a considerable amount of freedom. As long as they did not attempt to escape, they were left alone. For the Turks were a curious mixture, friendly enough and respectful to enemies of high rank, but ferociously cruel to men who were caught attempting to leave the city.

So Philip was able to meet Gilbert, and talk to him quite openly. Gilbert had changed little in the four years. He was still the grave young man who had arrived at Blanche Garde, slow of speech, lanky, and ungainly in movement, and regarding the world with a pessimistic air.

Like Philip, he was dressed in shabby clothes. In that way they escaped drawing too much attention to themselves in the streets, for an obvious Christian often received a kick or a passing blow, if nothing worse, from any Turk who felt so disposed.

They squatted down in the shadow of a high wall, two humble figures, and talked in low tones.

'We are going to escape tonight,' Philip said. He felt Gilbert stiffen by his side. 'Don't look excited,' he muttered.

'I'm not, Philip. I'm worried. Don't be such a fool. We can't get away from this infernal place. And if we're caught . . . remember what they did to Jacques de la Tort last month.'

Philip tried not to remember. Jacques had been a friend of his.

'This is different, Gilbert,' he said, and told him about de Vitry. 'The only difficulty is climbing down from your window. I can find the rope. But we dare not risk leaving a rope dangling down the wall. The sentries will see it. Is there anyone who can pull it up after we've gone?'

Gilbert was reassured by the story of de Vitry, and he settled down to give the plan his serious consideration.

'There's a Syrian slave in my place,' he said. 'He's a Christian, and he's grateful to me for some kindness. He gets a pretty rough time, you know. They flogged him last week for breaking a bowl in the kitchen, so he's not too fond of the Infidels at the moment.'

Philip did not like the idea much. 'He would be taking a dangerous risk in helping us, Gilbert,' he said doubtfully. 'It won't be a flogging if he's caught.'

'I know. But I think he'll take the chance. If we don't try him, who else is there?'

They decided to meet again that afternoon, when Usamah would be taking his afternoon siesta, and Philip would not be needed for dictation. Gilbert could report then about the Syrian, and, if that was satisfactory, they would escape that night.

Philip went back to Usamah. For one moment he nearly told the old man about his plans. He was fairly certain that Usamah would not stop him. Several times he had hinted at the idea himself. But it might be safer to take no chances. And Usamah might be glad to know nothing. The Eastern idea worked in a peculiar way, Philip had learnt.

He met Gilbert again, this time in Usamah's garden.

'Malik will do it,' Gilbert said, when they were sure that no one could overhear their conversation. 'But he wants some payment.'

'I haven't any money,' Philip said. 'Only the pearls.' He had told Gilbert about Usamah's gift. 'And one of those would be no use to Malik. A slave with a black pearl would be suspect immediately. They're far too valuable.'

'What about that cross around your neck?' Gilbert said.

Philip fingered the thin gold chain from which hung a small gold cross. His father had given it to him. His mother had once worn it. He was not very happy about the prospect of handing over such a gift to an unknown Syrian slave.

'It would make all the difference,' Gilbert said softly, reading Philip's thoughts.

'Very well. He can have the cross.'

The other arrangements were soon made, and they parted once more. Philip went about his preparations methodically, for nothing could be left to chance. There would be risk enough when they started to climb down the walls, and went off in search of the horses, if they got so far in the plan as that.

He pulled on his hauberk, and slipped dark, shabby clothes on top. He still had his chausses, but they would show beneath the cloak. The mail coif of the hauberk would hang down out of sight over his shoulders. His precious sword, polished carefully each day, and well greased, went in a long bundle, together with the chausses, the coil of rope, a supply of waterskins, dates, and figs, and some cold meat.

Philip did not see Usamah again that evening. Perhaps it was for the best. The old man was far too clever not to have noticed something, skilful as Philip now was in concealing his feelings. But Philip was fond of the Emir. He would have liked to bid him farewell.

An hour after the sun was down, Philip slipped through the side door of the garden into the narrow, high-walled street outside. On his shoulder was a long, sausage-shaped bundle. No one would stop to question a humble slave carrying a burden for his master, and Philip had his story all ready.

There were few people about in the ill-lit streets. No one was interested enough to look twice at the wearily hunched-up figure who shambled along with the clumsy package on his back, moving obsequiously aside to the walls to give free passage for any pedestrians coming towards him. Philip paused outside the house of Shuhab-al-Din, where Gilbert lived. Then he crossed the road, pushed open the door with his foot, and stepped inside.

The kitchens were on his right, and he could hear the sound of voices. If he was seen, he would say that he was bringing a present from the Emir Usamah to Shuhab. He had done such a thing before, and the servants knew him by sight.

But no one saw him. He pattered swiftly up the shallow stairs. The clumsy bundle brushed against the wall, and he slowed down. He did not want to make a noise now.

The passage was dark, but a faint yellow strip of light showed under Gilbert's door. Philip tapped lightly with his knuckles. The door creaked open, and Gilbert pulled him inside.

'All well, Philip?'

'So far. What about that Syrian of yours?'

'He'll do it. I told him to come here in half an hour. The sentries will be round this section of the wall in a few minutes. Then you'll hear the muezzin, and they come round again. There's over half an hour in between, and that should be enough.'

'You're sure of that?' Philip asked, though he knew it was unlikely that the methodical Gilbert would make a mistake on such a vital point.

'Quite certain,' Gilbert said. 'I've listened to them often enough in the last four years,' he added bitterly.

'Well, tonight will be the last night,' Philip said.

He was pulling on his chausses. Now he was covered from neck downwards in mail, and he adjusted the coif over his head. But for a helm, he was fully armed. Round his waist he buckled the wide sword belt; it was pleasant to feel once more the heavy drag of the long blade at his side.

'That mail will jingle a bit,' Gilbert said. He had lost all his armour after Hattin, and a knife was the only weapon he could muster.

'If we're seen on the wall it won't matter how much noise we make, or how we're dressed,' Philip said grimly.

For there would be no mercy from the Turks. And there would be none on his side. Philip decided. His mouth closed in a thin line. There would be four years of humiliation to repay. Gilbert saw the expression, and sighed. This was a different Philip from the smiling young squire whom he had first met in Jerusalem at Sir Fulk's house. He had seen the gradual change during the last few years.

There was a faint scratching noise from the direction of the door. Gilbert jumped round nervously.

'Malik, I expect,' he said.

He heard a click from behind him as he opened the door. Philip was against the wall, knife in hand. He was not taking the slightest chance that night.

It was Malik. A slouching figure slipped furtively into the small room, jerking his head in sudden, swift gestures of sheer fright.

'Had all the stuffing whipped out of him,' Gilbert muttered.

Philip nodded. He was not impressed with the Syrian. This was not the man he would have chosen to hold one end of a rope while he slid down the walls of Damascus. But they had no other choice.

'Show him the cross,' Gilbert said.

Malik's claw-like hand closed over the thin gold chain, and he gloated over the cross with a grunt of satisfaction.

'You know what to do, Malik?' Gilbert demanded.

'Yes, my lord.'

'Now, remember, if that rope is seen on the wall after we're gone, we shall all be caught. You, too, Malik. And you know what they will do to you if they catch you?'

It was only too clear that the wretched Syrian did know. His face went grey with fear, and his eyes rolled up until the whites could be seen against the darkness of his swarthy skin.

Philip sighed. He wondered if it had been wise of Gilbert to remind the man of his probable fate. His nerves were jumpy enough already. 'You're too heavy to lower by hand,' Gilbert said, picking up the rope. 'We'll have to make this end fast here.'

Fortunately the framework of the window was solid, and without much difficulty they knotted the end round the centre pillar. Philip put his weight on the loose end of the rope, and tugged. The window frame took the strain without even the faintest creak.

'Right,' he said. There had been no question as to who should go first. Philip was instinctively the leader of this expedition, and Gilbert never suggested anything else.

Philip let himself through the open window feet first. He took a firm grip with his mailed hands, and slid down cautiously into the warm darkness of the night.

He could see nothing. And he had enough sense not to look down at the sheer drop to the ground below. But he would probably have seen nothing if he had looked.

He had no idea of how far he had gone. Steadily he let himself down, taking most of his weight with his feet twining them tightly around the thick rope.

Then his feet were free. He had reached the end of the rope. He must look down now, and he was afraid of what he might see. The drop to the bottom might be too far to take without a risk of breaking a leg.

He held on with his hands, and glanced down. For a moment he could see nothing. But his eyes were more accustomed to the darkness by this time, and he could distinguish the darker blur of the ground below. Not very far, he decided. There was no point in hesitating. He must let go sometime.

He let go. He held his breath, and tried to flex his knee so as to cushion himself against the shock of the fall. But the drop was shorter than he had estimated. His feet hit the hard ground with a jar that sent a painful jolt through his entire body, and he rolled over gasping.

He lay there for a moment, and then leapt to his feet. He was down, and unhurt.

The wall shot up above him, towering up into the night, so high that he could only just pick out the parapet against the lighter blackness of the sky. Coming down the rope was a gigantic spider, or perhaps a moth, Philip decided, seeing the dark grey cloak that Gilbert was wearing.

Gilbert came down quickly. Then he, too, came to an abrupt halt as his feet reached the end of the rope.

'All right!' Philip muttered. 'Only a few feet to come. Let go, Gilbert.'

He heard a grunt, and then Gilbert swooped down. With another grunt he crashed to the ground, and rolled over.

'All right?' Philip asked anxiously. He had been afraid of this. For Gilbert, with his lanky figure, and ungainly legs, might fall awkwardly.

Gilbert stood up, and swayed to one side. A groan of pain came from his lips.

'What is it?' gasped Philip, a sudden cold spasm of fear clutching at the pit of his stomach. If Gilbert had broken his ankle, they were lost.

'Sprained ankle, I think,' Gilbert said.

Philip knelt down, and gently ran his fingers over Gilbert's foot and ankle. 'Try your weight on it,' he said.

'Just do it, I think,' Gilbert said. 'But we'd better wait here for a few minutes now.'

Philip fought down the inclination to run, to get clear of the wall. In a few minutes the patrol would be back.

'The rope!' Gilbert said. 'Why doesn't Malik pull it up?'

They stared up fearfully. The sentries might not see them at the foot of the wall. But they could not cross the gap quickly to the thick cover of the orchards, for Gilbert could only hobble, and he would never reach those blessed trees before the patrol came round. If the rope was still on the wall then, they were certainly lost.

The rope lay still, like some enormous serpent against the wall. Philip stood up, and tried to reach the end with the idea of twitching it frantically as a signal to Malik. Then it moved, paused, and slid upwards.

With a sigh, Philip sank back to the ground. He could feel the chilly sweat on his forehead, and that agonizing cramp of fear in his stomach subsided slowly.

Gilbert moved suddenly. 'The muezzin,' he said.

Through the still night came the voice of the muezzin from his lofty minaret, calling the Faithful to prayer.

'*Hai ala-as-salah! Allahu-akbar! La ilaha illa'lah!*'

Philip smiled grimly. Old Usamah would be kneeling down in obedience to that cry, his bowed face towards Mecca, his thin, reedy voice muttering the prescribed prayer. '*Allahu-akbar*, prayer is better than sleep. There is no God but Allah. He giveth life, and he dieth not. My sins are great; greater is thy mercy. I praise his perfection. *Allahu-akbar!*'

'May it be many years before I hear that cursed cry again,' Gilbert whispered fervently.

The clear, ringing voice fell silent. They both pressed themselves against the wall, crouching down on the dry earth. The patrol would be above their heads at any moment.

How long they waited, Philip had no idea. Probably not for more than a few minutes, but it felt and passed like an hour. Then he heard the clank of armour, and voices far above. They passed, and died away. He breathed out deeply, surprised to find that he had held his breath during that tense minute.

'Right,' Gilbert said. 'Another half hour before they're round again.'

Philip helped him to his feet. They hobbled as quickly as poor Gilbert could move for the direction of the orchards. The night was still very dark, and Philip knew that they could not possibly be seen, for neither was wearing anything white. But the moon would be up soon, and they must be in the trees before that.

A black mass loomed ahead, and with a final rush, Gilbert trying to stifle his groans, they dashed into the trees. Philip turned to look back.

A yellow moon was rising behind the walls of Damascus. In that bright light the spires and minarets shone whitely. It seemed a fairy city of lovely buildings and romantic walls.

But Philip did not waste time admiring the beauty before him. He took his last glance at Damascus, turned and grasped Gilbert by the arm, and led him through the orchards.

The Magician's Nephew

C. S. Lewis

Polly was the first to disappear and so, of course, Digory had to go after her. Polly and Digory live next door to each other and it is Digory's mad Uncle Andrew who tricks them into taking part in one of his experiments. The children become involved in a series of amazing adventures as they disappear out of this world into some very strange places!
C. S. Lewis' The Magician's Nephew *is a very important book because it explains how human beings first visit the enchanted world of Narnia – about which C. S. Lewis has written many other exciting stories. Here we see Polly and Digory meeting each other – and mad Uncle Andrew – for the first time.*

THIS is a story about something that happened long ago when your grandfather was a child. It is a very important story because it shows how all the comings and goings between our own world and the land of Narnia first began.

In those days Mr Sherlock Holmes was still living in Baker Street and the Bastables were looking for treasure in the Lewisham Road. In those days, if you were a boy you had to wear a stiff Eton collar every day, and schools were usually nastier than now. But meals were nicer; and as for sweets, I won't tell you how cheap and good they were, because it would only make your mouth water in vain. And in those days there lived in London a girl called Polly Plummer.

She lived in one of a long row of houses which were all joined together. One morning she was out in the back garden when a boy scrambled up from the garden next door and put his face over the wall. Polly was very surprised because up till now there had never been any children in that house, but only Mr Ketterley and Miss Ketterley, a brother and sister, old bachelor and old maid, living together. So she looked up, full of curiosity. The face of the strange boy was very grubby. It could hardly have been grubbier if he had first rubbed his hands in the earth, and then had a good cry, and then dried his face with his hands. As a matter of fact, this was very nearly what he had been doing.

'Hullo,' said Polly.

'Hullo,' said the boy. 'What's your name?'

'Polly,' said Polly. 'What's yours?'

'Digory,' said the boy.

'I say, what a funny name!' said Polly.

'It isn't half so funny as Polly,' said Digory.

'Yes it is,' said Polly.

'No, it isn't,' said Digory.

'At any rate I *do* wash my face,' said Polly. 'Which is what you need to do; especially after –' and then she stopped. She had been going to say 'After you've been blubbing,' but she thought that wouldn't be polite.

'Alright, I have then,' said Digory in a much louder voice, like a boy who was so miserable that he didn't care who knew he had been crying. 'And so would you,' he went on, 'if you'd lived all your life in the country and had a pony, and a river at the bottom of the garden, and then been brought to live in a beastly Hole like this.'

'London isn't a Hole,' said Polly indignantly. But the boy was too wound up to take any notice of her, and he went on –

'And if your father was away in India – and you had to come and live with an Aunt and an Uncle who's mad (who would like that?) – and if the reason was that they were looking after your Mother – and if your Mother was ill and was going to – going to – die.' Then his face went the wrong sort of shape as it does if you're trying to keep back your tears.

'I didn't know. I'm sorry,' said Polly humbly. And then, because she hardly knew what to say, and also to turn Digory's mind to cheerful subjects, she asked:

'Is Mr Ketterley really mad?'

'Well either he's mad,' said Digory, 'or there's some other mystery. He has a study on the top floor and Aunt Letty says I must never go up there. Well, that looks fishy to begin with. And then there's another thing. Whenever he tries to say anything to me at meal times – he never even tries to talk to *her* – she always shuts him up. She says, "Don't worry the boy, Andrew" or "I'm sure Digory doesn't want to hear about *that*" or else "Now, Digory, wouldn't you like to go out and play in the garden?".'

'What sort of things does he try to say?'

'I don't know. He never gets far enough. But there's more than that. One night – it was last night in fact – as I was going past the foot of the attic-stairs on my way to bed (and I don't much care for going past them either) I'm sure I heard a yell.'

'Perhaps he keeps a mad wife shut up there.'

'Yes, I've thought of that.'

'Or perhaps he's a coiner.'

'Or he might have been a pirate, like the man at the beginning of *Treasure Island*, and be always hiding from his old shipmates.'

'How exciting!' said Polly. 'I never knew your house was so interesting.'

'You may think it interesting,' said Digory. 'But you wouldn't like it if you had to sleep there. How would you like to lie awake listening for Uncle Andrew's step to come creeping along the passage to your room? And he has such awful eyes.'

That was how Polly and Digory got to know one another; and as it was just the beginning of the holidays and neither of them was going away to the sea that year, they met nearly every day.

Their adventures began chiefly because it was one of the wettest and coldest summers there have been for years. That drove them to do indoor things: you might say, indoor exploration. It is wonderful how much exploring you can do with a stump of candle in a big house, or in a row of houses. Polly had discovered long ago that if you opened a certain little door in the box-room attic of her house you would find the cistern and a dark place behind it which you could get into by a little careful climbing. The dark place was like a long tunnel with brick wall on one side and sloping roof on the other. In the roof there were little chinks of light between the slates. There was no floor in this tunnel: you had to step from rafter to rafter, and between them there was only plaster. If you stepped on this you would find yourself falling through the ceiling of the room below. Polly had used the bit of the tunnel just beside the cistern as a smugglers' cave. She had brought up bits of old packing cases and the seats of broken kitchen chairs, and things of that sort, and spread them across from rafter to rafter so as to make a bit of floor. Here she kept a cash-box containing various treasures, and a story she was writing and usually a few apples. She had often drunk a quiet bottle of ginger-beer in there: the old bottles made it look more like a smugglers' cave.

Digory quite liked the cave (she wouldn't let him see the story) but he was more interested in exploring.

'Look here,' he said. 'How long does this tunnel go on for? I mean, does it stop where your house ends?'

'No,' said Polly. 'The walls don't go out to the roof. It goes on. I don't know how far.'

'Then we could get the length of the whole row of houses.'

'So we could,' said Polly. 'And oh, I say!'

'What?'

'We could get *into* the other houses.'

'Yes, and get taken up for burglars! No thanks.'

'Don't be so jolly clever. I was thinking of the house beyond yours.'

'What about it?'

'Why, it's the empty one. Daddy says it's always been empty since we came here.'

'I suppose we ought to have a look at it then,' said Digory. He was a good deal more excited than you'd have thought from the way he spoke. For of course he was thinking, just as you would have been, of all the reasons why the house might have been empty so long. So was Polly. Neither of them said the word 'haunted'. And both felt that once the thing had been suggested, it would be feeble not to do it.

'Shall we go and try it now?' said Digory.

'Alright,' said Polly.

'Don't if you'd rather not,' said Digory.

'I'm game if you are,' said she.

'How are we to know when we're in the next house but one?'

They decided they would have to go out into the box-room and walk across it taking steps as long as the steps from one rafter to the next. That would give them an idea of how many rafters went to a room. Then they would allow about four more for the passage between the two attics in Polly's house, and then the same number for the maid's bedroom as for the box-room. That would give them the length of the house. When they had done that distance twice they would be at the end of Digory's house; any door they came to after that would let them into an attic of the empty house.

'But I don't expect it's really empty at all,' said Digory.

'What do you expect?'

'I expect someone lives there in secret, only coming in and out at night, with a dark lantern. We shall probably discover a gang of desperate criminals and get a reward. It's all rot to say a house would be empty all those years unless there was some mystery.'

'Daddy thought it must be the drains,' said Polly.

'Pooh! Grown-ups are always thinking of uninteresting explanations,' said Digory. Now that they were talking by daylight in the attic instead of by candlelight in the Smugglers' Cave it seemed much less likely that the empty house would be haunted.

When they had measured the attic they had to get a pencil and do a sum. They both got different answers to it at first, and even when they agreed I am not sure they got it right. They were in a hurry to start on the exploration.

'We mustn't make a sound,' said Polly as they climbed in again behind the cistern. Because it was such an important occasion they took a candle each (Polly had a good store of these in her cave).

It was very dark and dusty and draughty and they stepped from rafter to rafter without a word except when they whispered to one another, 'We're opposite *your* attic now' or 'this must be halfway through *our* house'. And neither of them stumbled and the candles didn't go out, and at last they came where they could see a little door in the brick wall on their right. There was no bolt or handle on this side of it, of course, for the door had been made for getting in, not for getting out; but there was a catch (as there often is on the inside of a cupboard door) which they felt sure they would be able to turn.

'Shall I?' said Digory.

'I'm game if you are,' said Polly, just as she had said before. Both felt that it was becoming very serious, but neither would draw back. Digory pushed round the catch with some difficulty. The door swung open and the sudden daylight made them blink. Then, with a great shock, they saw that they were looking, not into a deserted attic, but into a furnished room. But it seemed empty enough. It was dead silent. Polly's curiosity got the better of her. She blew out her candle and stepped out into the strange room, making no more noise than a mouse.

It was shaped, of course, like an attic, but furnished as a sitting-room. Every bit of the walls was lined with shelves and every bit of the shelves was full of books. A fire was burning in the grate (you remember that it was a very cold wet summer that year) and in front of the fireplace with its back towards them was a high-backed armchair. Between the chair and Polly, and filling most of the middle of the room, was a big table piled with all sorts of things – printed books, and books of the sort you write in, and ink bottles and pens and sealing-wax and a microscope. But what she noticed first was a bright red wooden tray with a number of rings on it. They were in pairs – a yellow one and a green one together, then a little space, and then another yellow one and another green one. They were no bigger than ordinary rings, and no one could help noticing them because they were so bright. They were the most beautifully shiny little things you can imagine. If Polly had been a very little younger she would have wanted to put one in her mouth.

The room was so quiet that you noticed the ticking of the clock at once. And yet, as she now found, it was not absolutely quiet either. There was a faint – a very, very faint – humming sound. If Hoovers had been invented in those days Polly would have thought it was the sound of a Hoover being worked a long way off – several rooms away and several floors below. But it was a nicer sound than that, a more musical tone: only so faint that you could hardly hear it.

'It's alright; there's no one here,' said Polly over her shoulder to Digory. She was speaking above a whisper now. And Digory came out, blinking and looking extremely dirty – as indeed Polly was too.

'This is no good,' he said. 'It's not an empty house at all. We'd better bunk before anyone comes.'

'What do you think those are?' said Polly, pointing at the coloured rings.

'Oh come *on*,' said Digory. 'The sooner –'

He never finished what he was going to say for at that moment something happened. The high-backed chair in front of the fire moved suddenly and there rose up out of it – like a pantomime demon coming up out of a trapdoor – the alarming form of Uncle Andrew. They were not in the empty house at all; they were in Digory's house and in the forbidden study! Both children said 'O-o-oh' and realized their terrible mistake. They felt that they ought to have known all along that they hadn't gone nearly far enough.

Uncle Andrew was very tall and very thin. He had a long clean-shaven face with a sharply-pointed nose and extremely bright eyes and a great tousled mop of grey hair.

Digory was quite speechless, for Uncle Andrew looked a thousand times more alarming than he had ever looked before. Polly was not so frightened yet; but she soon was. For the very first thing Uncle Andrew did was to walk across to the door of the room, shut it, and turn the key in the lock. Then he turned round, fixed the children with his bright eyes, and smiled, showing all his teeth.

'There!' he said. 'Now my fool of a sister can't get at you!'

It was dreadfully unlike anything a grown-up would be expected to do. Polly's heart came into her mouth, and she and Digory started backing towards the little door they had come in by. Uncle Andrew was too quick for them. He got behind them and shut that door too and stood in front of it. Then he rubbed his hands and made his knuckles crack. He had very long, beautifully white, fingers.

'I am delighted to see you,' he said. 'Two children are just what I wanted.'

'Please, Mr Ketterley,' said Polly. 'It's nearly my dinner time and I've got to go home. Will you let us out, please?'

'Not just yet,' said Uncle Andrew. 'This is too good an opportunity to miss. I wanted two children. You see, I'm in the middle of a great experiment. I've tried it on a guinea-pig and it seemed to work. But then a guinea-pig can't tell you anything. And you can't explain to it how to come back.'

'Look here, Uncle Andrew,' said Digory, 'it really is dinner time and they'll be looking for us in a moment. You must let us out.'

'Must?' said Uncle Andrew.

Digory and Polly glanced at one another. They dared not say anything, but the glances meant 'Isn't this dreadful?' and 'We must humour him.'

'If you let us go for our dinner now,' said Polly, 'we could come back after dinner.'

'Ah, but how do I know that you would?' said Uncle Andrew with a cunning smile. Then he seemed to change his mind.

'Well, well,' he said, 'if you really must go, I suppose you must. I can't expect two youngsters like you to find it much fun talking to an old buffer like me.' He sighed and went on. 'You've no idea how lonely I sometimes am. But no matter. Go to your dinner. But I must give you a present before you go. It's not every day that I see a little girl in my dingy old study; especially, if I may say so, such a very attractive young lady as yourself.'

Polly began to think he might not really be mad after all.

'Wouldn't you like a ring, my dear?' said Uncle Andrew to Polly.

'Do you mean one of those yellow or green ones?' said Polly.

'How lovely!'

'Not a green one,' said Uncle Andrew. 'I'm afraid I can't give the green ones away. But I'd be delighted to give you any of the yellow ones: with my love. Come and try one on.'

Polly had now quite got over her fright and felt sure that the old gentleman was not mad; and there was certainly something strangely attractive about those bright rings. She moved over to the tray.

'Why! I declare,' she said. 'That humming noise gets louder here. It's almost as if the rings were making it.'

'What a funny fancy, my dear,' said Uncle Andrew with a laugh. It sounded a very natural laugh, but Digory had seen an eager, almost a greedy, look on his face.

'Polly! Don't be a fool!' he shouted. 'Don't touch them.'

It was too late. Exactly as he spoke, Polly's hand went out to touch one of the rings. And immediately, without a flash or a noise or a warning of any sort, there was no Polly. Digory and his Uncle were alone in the room.

It was so sudden, and so horribly unlike anything that had ever happened to Digory even in a nightmare, that he let out a scream. Instantly Uncle Andrew's hand was over his mouth. 'None of that!' he hissed in Digory's ear. 'If you start making a noise your Mother'll hear it. And you know what a fright might do to her.'

As Digory said afterwards, the horrible meanness of getting at a chap in *that* way, almost made him sick. But of course he didn't scream again.

'That's better,' said Uncle Andrew. 'Perhaps you couldn't help it. It *is* a shock when you first see someone vanish. Why, it gave even me a turn when the guinea-pig did it the other night.'

'Was that when you yelled?' asked Digory.

'Oh, you heard *that*, did you? I hope you haven't been spying on me?'

'No, I haven't,' said Digory indignantly. 'But what's happened to Polly?'

'Congratulate me, my dear boy,' said Uncle Andrew, rubbing his hands. 'My experiment has succeeded. The little girl's gone – vanished – right out of the world.'

'What have you done to her?'

'Sent her to – well – to another place.'

'What *do* you mean?' asked Digory.

Uncle Andrew sat down and said, 'Well, I'll tell you all about it. Have you ever heard of old Mrs Lefay?'

'Wasn't she a great-aunt or something?' said Digory.

'Not exactly,' said Uncle Andrew. 'She was my godmother. That's her, there, on the wall.'

Digory looked and saw a faded photograph: it showed the face of an old woman in a bonnet. And he could now remember that he had once seen a photo of the same face in an old drawer, at home, in the country. He had asked his Mother who it was and Mother had not seemed to want to talk about the subject much. It was not at all a nice face, Digory thought, though of course with those early photographs one could never really tell.

'Was there – wasn't there – something wrong about her, Uncle Andrew?' he said.

'Well,' said Uncle Andrew with a chuckle, 'it depends what you call *wrong*. People are so narrow-minded. She certainly got very queer in later life. Did very unwise things. That was why they shut her up.'

'In an asylum, do you mean?'

'Oh no, no, no,' said Uncle Andrew in a shocked voice. 'Nothing of that sort. Only in prison.'

'I say!' said Digory. 'What had she done?'

'Ah, poor woman,' said Uncle Andrew. 'She had been very unwise. There were a good many different things. We needn't go into all that. She was always very kind to me.'

'But look here, what has all this got to do with Polly? I do wish you'd –'

'All in good time, my boy,' said Uncle Andrew. 'They let old Mrs Lefay out before she died and I was one of the very few people whom she would allow to see her in her last illness. She had got to dislike ordinary, ignorant people, you understand. I do myself. But she and I were interested in the same sort of things. It was only a few days before her death that she told me to go to an old bureau in her house and open a secret drawer and bring her a little box that I would find there. The moment I picked up that box I could tell by the pricking in my fingers that I held some great secret in my hands. She gave it me and made me promise that as soon as she was dead I would burn it, unopened, with certain ceremonies. That promise I did not keep.'

'Well, then, it was jolly rotten of you,' said Digory.

'Rotten?' said Uncle Andrew with a puzzled look. 'Oh, I see. You mean that little boys ought to keep their promises. Very true: most right and proper, I'm sure, and I'm very glad you have been taught to do it. But of course you must understand that rules of that sort, however excellent they may be for little boys – and servants – and women – and even people in general, can't possibly be expected to apply to profound students and great thinkers and sages. No, Digory. Men like me, who possess hidden wisdom, are freed from common rules just as we are cut off from common pleasures. Ours, my boy, is a high and lonely destiny.'

As he said this he sighed and looked so grave and noble and mysterious that for a second Digory really thought he was saying something rather fine. But then he remembered the ugly look he had seen on his Uncle's face the moment before Polly had vanished: and all at once he saw through Uncle Andrew's grand words. 'All it means,' he said to himself, 'is that he thinks he can do anything he likes to get anything he wants.'

'Of course,' said Uncle Andrew, 'I didn't dare to open the box for a long time, for I knew it might contain something highly dangerous. For my godmother was a *very* remarkable woman. The truth is, she was one of the last mortals in this country who had fairy blood in her. (She said there had been two others in her time. One was a duchess and the other was a charwoman.) In fact, Digory, you are now talking to the last man (possibly) who really had a fairy godmother. There! That'll be something for you to remember when you are an old man yourself.'

'I bet she was a bad fairy,' thought Digory; and added out loud. 'But what about Polly?'

'How you do harp on that!' said Uncle Andrew. 'As if that was what mattered! My first task was of course to study the box itself. It was very ancient. And I knew enough even then to know that it wasn't Greek, or Old Egyptian, or Babylonian, or Hittite, or Chinese. It was older than any of those nations. Ah – that was a great day when I at last found out the truth. The box was Atlantean; it came from the lost island of Atlantis. That meant it was centuries older than any of the stone-age things they dig up in Europe. And it wasn't a rough, crude thing like them either. For in the very dawn of time Atlantis was already a great city with palaces and temples and learned men.'

He paused for a moment as if he expected Digory to say something. But Digory was disliking his Uncle more every minute, so he said nothing.

'Meanwhile,' continued Uncle Andrew, 'I was learning a good deal in other ways (it wouldn't be proper to explain them to a child) about Magic in general. That meant that I came to have a fair idea what sort of things might be in the box. By various tests I narrowed down the possibilities. I had to get to know some – well, some devilish queer people, and go through some very disagreeable experiences. That was what turned my head grey. One doesn't become a magician for nothing. My health broke down in the end. But I got better. And at last I actually *knew*.'

Although there was not really the least chance of anyone overhearing them, he leaned forward and almost whispered as he said:

'The Atlantean box contained something that had been brought from another world when our world was only just beginning.'

'What?' asked Digory, who was now interested in spite of himself.

'Only dust,' said Uncle Andrew. 'Fine, dry dust. Nothing much to look at. Not much to show for a lifetime of toil, you might say. Ah, but when I looked at that dust (I took jolly good care not to touch it) and thought that every grain had once been in another world – I don't mean another planet, you know; they're part of our world and you could get to them if you went far enough – but a really Other World – another Nature – another universe – somewhere you would never reach even if you travelled through the space of this universe for ever and ever – a world that could be reached only by Magic – well!'

Here Uncle Andrew rubbed his hands till his knuckles crackled like fireworks.

'I knew,' he went on, 'that if only you could get it into the right form, that dust would draw you back to the place it had come from. But the difficulty was to get it into the right form. My earlier experiments were all failures. I tried them on guinea-pigs. Some of them only died. Some exploded like little bombs –'

'It was a jolly cruel thing to do,' said Digory who had once had a guinea-pig of his own.

'How you do keep on getting off the point!' said Uncle Andrew. 'That's what the creatures were there for. I'd bought them myself. Let me see – where was I? Ah yes. At last I succeeded in making the rings: the yellow rings. But now a new difficulty arose. I was pretty sure, now, that a yellow ring would send any creature that touched it into the Other Place. But what would be the good of that if I couldn't get them back to tell me what they had found there?'

'And what about *them*?' said Digory. 'A nice mess they'd be in if they couldn't get back!'

'You will keep on looking at everything from the wrong point of view,' said Uncle Andrew with a look of impatience. 'Can't you understand that the thing is a great experiment? The whole point of sending anyone into the Other Place is that I want to find out what it's like.'

'Well why didn't you go yourself then?'

Digory had hardly ever seen anyone look so surprised and offended as his Uncle did at this simple question. 'Me? Me?' he exclaimed. 'The boy must be mad! A man at my time of life, and in my state of health, to risk the shock and the dangers of being flung suddenly into a different universe? I never heard anything so preposterous in my life! Do you realize what you're saying? Think what Another World means – you might meet anything – anything.'

'And I suppose you've sent Polly into it then,' said Digory. His cheeks were flaming with anger now. 'And all I can say,' he added, 'even if you are my Uncle – is that you've behaved like a coward, sending a girl to a place you're afraid to go to yourself.'

'Silence, sir!' said Uncle Andrew, bringing his hand down on the table. 'I will not be talked to like that by a little, dirty, schoolboy. You don't understand. I am the great scholar, the magician, the adept, who is *doing* the experiment. Of course I need subjects to do it *on*. Bless my soul, you'll be telling me next that I ought to have asked the guinea-pigs' permission before I used *them*! No great wisdom can be reached without sacrifice. But the idea of my going myself is ridiculous. It's like asking a general to fight as a common soldier. Supposing I got killed, what would become of my life's work?'

'Oh, do stop jawing,' said Digory. 'Are you going to bring Polly back?'

'I was going to tell you, when you so rudely interrupted me,' said Uncle Andrew, 'that I did at last find out a way of doing the return journey. The green rings draw you back.'

'But Polly hasn't got a green ring.'

'No,' said Uncle Andrew with a cruel smile.

'Then she can't get back,' shouted Digory. 'And it's exactly the same as if you'd murdered her.'

'She can get back,' said Uncle Andrew, 'if someone else will go after her, wearing a yellow ring himself and taking two green rings, one to bring himself back and one to bring her back.'

And now of course Digory saw the trap in which he was caught: and he stared at Uncle Andrew, saying nothing, with his mouth wide open. His cheeks had gone very pale.

'I hope,' said Uncle Andrew presently in a very high and mighty voice, just as if he were a perfect Uncle who had given one a handsome tip and some good advice, 'I *hope*, Digory, you are not given to showing the white feather. I should be very sorry to think that anyone of our family had not enough honour and chivalry to go to the aid of – er – a lady in distress.'

'Oh shut up!' said Digory. 'If you had any honour and all that, you'd be going yourself. But I know you won't. Alright. I see I've got to go. But you *are* a beast. I suppose you planned the whole thing, so that she'd go without knowing it and then I'd have to go after her.'

'Of course,' said Uncle Andrew with his hateful smile.

'Very well. I'll go. But there's one thing I jolly well mean to say first. I didn't believe in Magic till today. I see now it's real. Well if it is, I suppose all the old fairy tales are more or less true. And you're simply a wicked, cruel magician like the ones in the stories. Well, I've never read a story in which people of that sort weren't paid out in the end, and I bet you will be. And serve you right.'

Of all the things Digory had said this was the first that really went home. Uncle Andrew started and there came over his face a look of such horror that, beast though he was, you could almost feel sorry for him. But a second later he smoothed it all away and said with a rather forced laugh, 'Well, well, I suppose that is a natural thing for a child to think – brought up among women, as you have been. Old wives' tales, eh? I don't think you need worry about *my* danger, Digory. Wouldn't it be better to worry about the danger of your little friend? She's been gone some time. If there are any dangers Over There – well, it would be a pity to arrive a moment too late.'

'A lot *you* care,' said Digory fiercely. 'But I'm sick of this jaw. What have I got to do?'

'You really must learn to control that temper of yours, my boy,' said Uncle Andrew coolly. 'Otherwise you'll grow up like your Aunt Letty. Now. Attend to me.'

He got up, put on a pair of gloves, and walked over to the tray that contained the rings.

'They only work,' he said, 'if they're actually touching your skin. Wearing gloves, I can pick them up – like this – and nothing happens. If you carried one in your pocket nothing would happen: but of course you'd have to be careful not to put your hand in your pocket and touch it by accident. The moment you touch a yellow ring, you vanish out of this world. When you are in the Other Place I expect – of course this hasn't been tested yet, but I *expect* – that the moment you touch a green ring you vanish out of that world and – I expect – re-appear in this. Now. I take these two greens and drop them into your right-hand pocket. Remember very carefully which pocket the greens are in. G for green and R for right. G.R. you see: which are the first two letters of green. One for you and one for the little girl. And now you pick up a yellow one for yourself. I should put it on – on your finger – if I were you. There'll be less chance of dropping it.'

Digory had almost picked up the yellow ring when he suddenly checked himself.

'Look here,' he said. 'What about Mother? Supposing she asks where I am?'

'The sooner you go, the sooner you'll be back,' said Uncle Andrew cheerfully.

'But you don't really know whether I can get back.'

Uncle Andrew shrugged his shoulders, walked across to the door, unlocked it, threw it open, and said:

'Oh very well then. Just as you please. Go down and have your dinner. Leave the little girl to be eaten by wild animals or drowned or starved in Otherworld or lost there for good, if that's what you prefer. It's all one to me. Perhaps before tea time you'd better drop in on Mrs Plummer and explain that she'll never see her daughter again; because you were afraid to put on a ring.'

'By gum,' said Digory, 'don't I just wish I was big enough to punch your head!'

Then he buttoned up his coat, took a deep breath, and picked up the ring. And he thought then, as he always thought afterwards too, that he could not decently have done anything else.

The Turbulent Term of Tyke Tiler

Gene Kemp

Tyke Tiler seems to get into trouble all the time at school but then looking after Danny Price is a trying task. Danny is rather helpless and not too bright and helping him out gives Tyke a lot of problems. This fast and funny story ends with a real surprise – here is the opening chapter to give a taste of the fun to come.

'What did the cross-eyed teacher say?'
'I can't control my pupils.'

We'd gone right through the school collecting the teachers' tea money and had got to the canteen door when Danny waved the ten-pound note at me. It took me a couple of minutes to realize what it was, 'cos it looked highly unlikely in Danny's grimy mitt. Then i pushed him into the canteen, sure to be empty on a Friday afternoon at five to three. The pandemonium of a wet school playtime died away, and we could hear the rain drumming on the roof instead.

'Where didja get that, you nutter?'

'Out of Bonfire's purse. She'd left it open. On the desk. So I took it. No one saw me, Tyke.'

Only he didn't say it like that, for my friend, Danny Price, speaks worse than anyone I know. Speech defect they call it. When he counts he goes, 'Don, Dwo, Dee, Dour, Dive, Dix, Devon,' and so on. And there he stood in the canteen that smelled of boiled swede and cabbage, enough to make you throw up, saying:

'Do di dood id. Do don daw dee,' and ringing all manner of alarms inside me.

I shook him. The tea money rattled in its tin, and at that moment a crowd of under-sized Chinamen streamed towards us, shouting, pushing, kicking, the second year doing *Aladdin* again, I suppose, unless it was everyday life in Red China for a change. I grabbed the ten-pound note and stuffed it up my sweater where it made a crunkly noise that I didn't like at all, and the boiled swede and cabbage smell stank so strong that I had to get out fast, so I pushed him into the corridor again.

'Don't you see? Don't you understand, you idiotic imbecile?' I shouted through the screeching din of 3H practising ten different tunes on recorders in the next classroom. Before he could reply the buzzer went for the end of play, so I headed for our classroom, 4M, with Danny running sideways trying to talk to me.

'Why you all mad, Tyke? Don't be mad at me, Tyke.'

I didn't answer.

'I got it for you. I want you to have half of it. You can buy anything you like, Tyke.'

I took no notice. He pulled at my arm. I shook him off.

'Get knotted.'

'Tyke. Tyke?'

We reached the classroom. Lorraine Fairchild and Linda Stoatway were dancing in a corner, all flying skirts and hair, showing off to the boys who couldn't have cared less. Ian Pitt, Pitthead, was having a scrap with Kevin Simms, and Martin Kneeshaw was standing on top of a cupboard shouting and giving orders as usual. I held tight to the front of my sweater in case the note fell out, and pushed Danny into the book corner.

'Listen, Danny. Don't you see? Don't you understand? You can't spend it, because they'll ask you where you got it from, and they won't believe what you say, and they'll want to ask your Mum, and then you'll be for it.'

His face went sad, like my dog at home when she's caught raiding the dustbins. She can't stop doing it, but she has terrible sorrow when anyone catches her. Danny's the same, though it's money with him, not dustbins. And when he's found out, he gets this mournful look, like my dog, and everyone feels sorry for him, because of his look. What a lovely face, say the old ladies in the street. All the people who come to see him at school to give him tests, the deaf lady, the talk lady, the shrinko chap, like him and take more trouble with him than anyone else.

'He looks bright,' I've heard people say. 'There must be a block.'

There is. I know that block. I've known it for years. It's his head. And something else I know, too. Even if he is as thick as two planks, he generally gets me to do the things he wants. But not this time. I wasn't getting mixed up in anything to do with this tenner. Not likely.

'It's no use, Danny boyo. You can't keep it.'

'I didn't think.'

'You never do, do you? Now, go and give it back to Bonfire.'

Red colour ran over his face, then flowed away, leaving it white. He began to tremble, like that dog of mine, called Crumble.

'I can't do that. You know the row I got in last time.'

'I'll take it back to her.'

'Oh, no. They'll know it was me what pinched it.'

'Just what are we going to do with it, then? Play Monopoly with it? Stick it up on the wall?'

'Hide it, and put it back later.'

'You must be joking!'

'Please, Tyke. You do it. You're clever. You can do anything.'

'Gee, t'anks!'

I felt sick. Boiled swede had followed me.

'Get stuffed, Danny Price ...' I would've said more, but Sir came in, and the noise died down. Sir is Mr William Merchant, and he's all right. I'll tell you more about him later. The end of Friday afternoon is ours to do what we like, make our own choice. For everybody but me, that is. As far as I could see I didn't have any choice. For any minute now, Bonfire would find out that she'd been robbed, and then along would come Chief Sir, the Headmaster, and we'd be searched. It's happened before. And so, before it happened again, I'd got to get this nasty bit of brown paper from under my sweater and stowed away somewhere safe, till I could put it back in Bonfire's bag. I went up to the desk.

'Can I take the tea money to the office, please, Sir?'

'Yes, Tyke.'

I suddenly felt sure the note was slipping. I held where I thought it was with one hand, the tea tin with the other.

'Anything the matter?'

'Nothing, Sir.'

'You look a bit green. Got a pain?'

I thought I heard voices outside.

'No, Sir.' I headed for the door as fast as possible to be out of the room before the searchers arrived. There was no one in the corridor, so I heaved a sigh of relief and ran to the office, by the quickest route, which is round the outside of the school. The rain was belting down as if someone was upending buckets up there. I splashed through a puddle the size of a mini-lake, when suddenly the note slithered out and on to the water. There it lay, on top, with the heavy raindrops bouncing it up and down. That's it. The answer, I thought. I'll just leave it there for someone to find. All solved.

And mincing round the corner, boots on feet, umbrella over her head, came Mrs Somers, my last year's teacher and my deadliest enemy. She skimmmed towards me over the shining tarmac. I scooped up the note faster than the speed of light.

'Oh, it's you, is it? What are you doing out here?'

'Taking tea money.'

'Don't mumble, child. And look up when a member of staff speaks to you.'

I looked up and got a mouthful of rain.

'Now, don't play about. Hurry along to the classroom.'

She used my real name, the one I hate, so I pulled my worst, most horrible face at her, the slit-eyed, yellow-tooth, ears-wiggling monster-from-the-centre-of-the-earth one. After she'd gone, of course. And I practised willing her to drop dead by my fabulous will-power. But it didn't work. It never does. She was still alive, and I'd still got a ten pound note under my sweater.

I was just about to let it fall in a puddle once more, when Sandra Hines from 4P, the parallel class to ours, joined me, jabbering all the way to the office. I didn't answer. What were all these slobs doing wandering about in the pouring rain? Where could I be alone to hide a soggy tenner in peace?

And the answer came to me, clear and strong. In the bogs, of course. So I web-footed along in that direction.

But I'll explain a bit.

Our school is one of the oldest in the country, state schools, that is. So old that it has beams in the roof, which leaks when it rains, and windows so high that you can't see out of them. And the bogs, well, you'd think they'd been built in Roman times except that Sir tells us that these Roman guys were fantastic plumbers, so it seems more likely that they date from the Dark Ages instead. Rusty, corrugated-iron roof, worm-eaten seats, flaking white-washed walls, wreathed in snaky pipes lagged in old sackcloth, and above all this a loft, high up and hard to get at, stuffed with books, chairs, scenery, costumes, papers, pictures. Old Buggsy, the caretaker, goes up about once a year on a ladder. I've been up there, as well. I think I'm the only kid in the school that has. You see, I like climbing. It feels good.

So, bearing in mind that at any moment somebody might find out about the missing money, I clambered on to a cistern, over the pipes, up to a gap, swung across quite a wide space, climbed a bit more, and was suddenly there among all the junk.. I didn't hang about. I pushed the tenner behind a picture of that sailor pointing out the

Atlantic, or some other sea, to Sir Walter Raleigh.

And in no time at all I was back in the classroom, leaning over Danny who was colouring a bird with a blue felt pen.

'What's that? A kingfisher?'

'No, a robin.'

'They're brown and red, twit.'

'I like it blue.'

I bent nearer and lowered my voice.

'It's O.K. I got rid of it.'

'What? What you got rid of, Tyke?'

I went to hit him, but then a look came over his face like Leonardo with a new invention, or Einstein solving a problem.

'Oh, yes. I know. The ten ...'

'Shut up, you halfwit!'

Sir looked up.

'Leave Danny alone. He was working well till you disturbed him. And Tyke ...'

'Yes, Sir.'

'Go and dry yourself. You're dripping everywhere.'

In the cloakroom I rubbed my hair and face with a scratchy paper towel and considered the unfairness of life. This is a very interesting subject, and one I spend some time on, especially at school, though there's a fair amount of injustice at home as well.

And when I got back to 4M, the Headmaster had arrived, with Miss Bonn, Bonfire, Buggsy, the caretaker, and Mrs Somers, yuck-yuck, she would have to push her nose in.

They all had faces as long as stretched elastic.

'Bonfire's bin crying,' hissed Linda Stoatway. I looked. She was right. Bonfire's eyes were as red as her hair.

'I want you all to listen to me,' said the Headmaster.

He told them about the missing money.

'Does anyone want to own up now, to save trouble and unpleasantness later?'

I looked around with interest to see if anyone would, and then remembered, with a horrible lurch in my stomach, that they weren't likely to, were they? After some moments of complete and beautiful hush, he turned to Sir.

'If the money has not been recovered by the time I've seen all the classes, then I'll send a message to you that all desks, bags, pockets and coats are to be searched. No one will be allowed home till everything has been checked.'

Uproar broke out when he and the others had gone.

'Don't see why we should stay in. 'Tisn't fair.'

370

'It wasn't me took it ...'

'Someone out of Bonfire's class ...'

'She looked ...'

'... as if she'd lost a tenner and found fivepence.'

'My Mum says it's a temptation to others to leave your money lying about.'

'Your Mum is an old boot.'

Sir told us to shut up at this point, and we sat quietly waiting to be searched. At least, the others were hoping they wouldn't have to be, but since I knew that the note was behind Sir Walter Raleigh and the sailor, I just waited. In due time the message came and Sir took us and our belongings to pieces. It took ages. Then Chanders, the music teacher, came in with Bonfire.

'As if wet Fridays weren't bad enough without this,' Sir complained, as he turned out three marbles, a packet of chewing gum, an Action Man battle-dress, two bus tickets, and a mini-bald koala bear out of Pitthead's pocket.

'I've sent mine home. It's after half past four,' Chanders said. He's known as Champers because of his teeth, enormous they are.

'Hang on. I've nearly finished. I haven't found it, but then, I didn't expect to. Is the Head sending for the police?'

The boiled swede and cabbage came up with ferocious force. I wanted to rush out of the room.

'No,' Bonfire replied. 'He's leaving it over the weekend. I don't want to get anyone into trouble, and it's all my fault, leaving that purse on the desk.'

She looked as if she was going to cry and Sir suddenly roared: 'All right. You can go home now.'

Out we went into the rain that seemed never-ending. Danny ran and caught up with me and we walked on without speaking. The rain dripped down the back of my neck. Danny sang:

> *Whistle while you work,*
> *Hitler is a twerp.*
> *He is barmy,*
> *So's his army,*
> *Whistle while you work.*

'I'll call for you if it stops raining,' he said.

'Don't bother. I don't care if you drop dead, Danny Price,' I shouted, and ran. He called after me but I didn't listen. I was a super being from the advanced planet Nerandia, and I could zoom at a million miles a minute. Zooming is faster than anything at all, even faster than the speed of light. Danny can never catch me when I zoom.

Dog Crumble waggled all over when I got in, so I chased her all over the house, and rolled with her on the floor till Mum stopped us. Then we sat by the fire and she licked me. Sometimes I think Crumble is better than anything, though I wish she looked fiercer, as she couldn't frighten anyone at all. She rolled on her back and I rubbed her tum, which is a bit fat 'cos she's so greedy. Like I told you, she steals out of dustbins. She rolls them over and knocks the tops off and then gets at the old tins and all the rubbish.

'When's Dad coming in?'
'Late. He's got a meeting. Why?'
'Want to ask him something.'
'Eat up your tea.'
'I'm not hungry.'
'Beefburgers are your favourite!'
'I'm not hungry.'
'I'll finish it if nobody else wants it.' My brother Spud is always hungry. He's two years older than me and at the Dawson Comprehensive where I go next term. My sister Beryl's at the Sixth Form college. She's bossy but better than Spud. He's horrible.

I mooched round, restless. There wasn't much on telly. I didn't want to read or play with anything. Beryl was playing records in her bedroom, so I went in and watched her sticking false eyelashes on with adhesive in a tiny tube.
'You look stupid.'
'So do you.'
'Foolish fool.'
'Wretched wretch.'
'Don't get your knickers in a twist.'
'Don't get your nappie in a niggle.'
I gave up. I couldn't get any go into it. All I could think of was the tenner lying behind the picture up in the loft, and Bonfire who'd been crying. Funny for teachers to cry. You don't think of them as being human like that. Perhaps you don't want them to be human. Mum called up the stairs.
'Tyke, take the dog for a walk.'
'Spud can do it.'
'He's got his homework, whereas you're messing about doing nothing. Off you go.'
'Errrrrgggggghhhhhugh. Yuck. Yuck.'
But I got out the lead and put it on her, while she jumped up and down, wriggling and waving all her fruffly bits on her legs and her chest. Outside a wind was blowing away a few last scuds of rain. We

ran along the road where it follows the river.

On one side of the road is a sheer rock-fall, and on the other the two weirs, Walter and Blackaller, about a hundred yards apart. You can hear their roar long before you reach them. The water was high, rolling along at tremendous speed, beer-brown with churned-up mud. It levelled almost with the banks, then threw itself over the weirs, taking logs and branches and strange rubbish with it. Below Blackaller a wave was held motionless in a curve of the bank, caught by the force of the current. I stood and watched for a long time, Crumble pulling at the lead from time to time. The river in flood is the most powerful thing I know. All the mucky feeling about the money washed away as I stood there. Nothing mattered very much except the noise of the water and the wetness in the air and the willows blowing in the wind on the other side of the bank.

Crumble whined. She wanted to be off the lead, but I didn't dare with the river so near, and her so stupid. She'd be over the weir with the rest.

We moved farther along into the big fields and I let her loose and we ran and ran and ran.

As Dad came in I jumped on him from behind the door.

'You crazy fool. Are you trying to flatten me?'

We wrestled in the hall.

'Submit,' he said. I submitted.

'Dad?'

'Tyke.'

'Would teachers miss ten pounds if they lost it?'

'Yes. Now bed. The day's long enough without you at the end of it, horrible.'

I pinched his ear, then moved fast as he pushed me up the stairs.

'Good night, Tyke.'

''Night, Dad.'

I knew quite clearly what I had to do as I fell asleep.

On Monday morning I got to school early. No one was in the bogs. I climbed up into the loft and looked round.

It had all been changed. The sailor and Sir Walter Raleigh had gone.

So had the ten-pound note.

Man-Eaters of Kumaon

Jim Corbett

In the Man-Eaters Of Kumaon *Colonel Jim Corbett describes his experiences when he is called in to rid certain areas of India of man-eating tigers. Although he shot man-eaters to protect human lives, Jim Corbett was in fact a distinguished naturalist who preferred to observe rather than destroy wild-life. This book gives us not only his thrilling accounts of many dangerous encounters with tigers, but also careful and loving descriptions of the wild-life and people of the jungle. This extract is from a chapter called 'The Mohan Man-Eater'. Jim Corbett and his men have travelled to a village called Kartkanoula and set up camp in a disused Foresters' Hut to begin their search for a man-eating tiger which is terrorising the district.*

THE Foresters' Hut was on a little knoll some twenty yards to the left of the road, and as the door was fastened only with a chain I opened it and walked inside. The room was about ten feet square and quite clean, but had a mouldy disused smell; I learnt later that the hut had not been occupied since the advent of the man-eater in that area eighteen months previously. On either side of the main room there were two narrow slips of rooms, one used as a kitchen, and the other as a fuel store. The hut would make a nice safe shelter for my men, and having opened the back door to let a current of air blow through the room, I went outside and selected a spot between the hut and the road for my 40-lb tent. There was no furniture of any kind in the hut, so I sat down on a rock near the road to await the arrival of my men.

The ridge at this point was about fifty yards wide, and as the hut was on the south edge of the ridge, and the village on the north face of the hill, the latter was not visible from the former. I had been sitting on the rock for about ten minutes when a head appeared over the crest from the direction of the village, followed by a second and a third. My friend the water-carrier had not been slow in informing the village of my arrival.

When strangers meet in India and wish to glean information from each other on any particular subject, it is customary to refrain from broaching the subject that has brought them together – whether accidentally or of set purpose – until the very last moment, and to fill up the interval by finding out everything concerning each other's domestic and private affairs; as, for instance, whether married and if so the number and sex of children and their ages; if not married, why not; occupation and amount of pay, and so on. Questions that would in any other part of the world earn one a thick ear are in India – and especially in our hills – asked so artlessly and universally that no one who has lived among the people dreams of taking offence at them.

In my conversation with the woman I had answered many of the set questions, and the ones of a domestic nature which it is not permissible for a woman to ask of a man were being put to me when my men arrived. They had filled a kettle at the little spring, and in an incredibly short time dry sticks were collected, a fire lit, the kettle boiled, and tea and biscuits produced. As I opened a tin of condensed milk I heard the men asking my servants why condensed milk was being used instead of fresh milk and receiving the answer that there was no fresh milk; and further that, as it had been apprehended that owing to some previous trouble in this area no fresh milk would be available, a large supply of tinned milk had been brought. The men appeared to be very distressed on hearing this and after a whispered conversation one of them, who I learnt later was the Headman of Kartkanoula, addressed me and said it was an insult to them to have brought tinned milk, when all the resources of the village were at my disposal. I admitted my mistake, which I said was due to my being a stranger to that locality, and told the Headman that if he had any milk to spare I would gladly purchase a small quantity for my daily requirements, but that beyond the milk, I wanted for nothing.

My loads had now been unstrapped, while more men had arrived from the village, and when I told my servants where I wanted them to pitch my tent there was a horrified exclamation from the assembled villagers. Live in a tent – indeed! Was I ignorant of the fact that there was a man-eating tiger in this area and that it used this road regularly every night? If I doubted their word, let me come and see the claw marks on the doors of the houses where the road ran through the upper end of the village. Moreover, if the tiger did not eat me in the tent it would certainly eat my men in the hut, if I was not there to protect them. This last statement made my men prick up their ears and add their entreaties to the advice of the villagers, so eventually I agreed to stay in the main room, while my two servants occupied the kitchen, and the six Garhwalis the fuel store.

The subject of the man-eater having been introduced, it was now possible for me to pursue it without admitting that it was the one subject I had wished to introduce from the moment the first man had put his head over the ridge. The path leading down to the tree where the tiger had claimed its last victim was pointed out to me, and the time of day, and the circumstances under which the woman had been killed, explained. The road along which the tiger came every night, I was informed, ran eastward to Baital Ghat with a branch down to Mohan, and westward to Chaknakl on the Ramganga River. The road going west, through the upper part of the village and through cultivated land for half a mile, turned south along the face of the hill, and on rejoining the ridge on which the hut was, followed the ridge right down to Chaknakl. This portion of the road between Kartkanoula and Chaknakl, some six miles long, was considered to be very dangerous, and had not been used since the advent of the man-eater; I subsequently found that after leaving the cultivated land the road entered dense tree and scrub jungle, which extended right down to the river.

The main cultivation of Kartkanoula village is on the north face of the hill, and beyond this cultivated land there are several small ridges with deep ravines between. On the nearest of these ridges, and distant about a thousand yards from the Foresters' Hut, there is a big pine tree. Near this tree, some ten days previously, the tiger had killed, partly eaten, and left a woman, and as the three sportsmen who were staying in a Forest Bungalow four miles away were unable to climb the pine tree, the villagers had put up three machans in three separate trees, at distances varying from one hundred to one hundred and fifty yards from the kill, and the machans had been occupied by the sportsmen and their servants a little before sunset. There was a young moon at the time, and after it had set the villagers heard a number of shots being fired, and when they questioned the servants next morning the servants said they did not know what had been fired at for they themselves had not seen anything. Two days later a cow had been killed over which the sportsmen had sat, and again, as on the previous occasion, shots had been fired after the moon had set. It is these admittedly sporting but unsuccessful attempts to bag man-eaters that makes them so wary, and the more difficult to shoot the longer they live.

The villagers gave me one very interesting item of news in connexion with the tiger. They said they always knew when it had come into the village by the low moaning sound it made. On questioning them closely I learnt that at times the sound was continuous as the tiger passed between the houses, while at other times the sound stopped for sometimes short and other times long periods.

From this information I concluded (a) that the tiger was suffering from a wound, (b) that the wound was of such a nature that the tiger only felt it when in motion, and that therefore (c) the wound was in one of its legs. I was assured that the tiger had not been wounded by any local shikari, or by any of the sportsmen from Ranikhet who had sat up for it; however, this was of little importance, for the tiger had been a man-eater for years, and the wound that I believed it was suffering from might have been the original cause of its becoming a man-eater. A very interesting point and one that could only be cleared up by examining the tiger – after it was dead.

The men were curious to know why I was so interested in the sound made by the tiger, and when I told them that it indicated the animal had a wound in one of its legs and that the wound had been caused either by a bullet, or by porcupine quills, they disagreed with my reasoning and said that on the occasions they had seen the tiger it appeared to be in sound condition, and further, that the ease with which it killed and carried off its victims was proof that it was not crippled in any way. However, what I told them was remembered and later earned me the reputation of being gifted with second sight.

—◦◅◉◅◉▻◉▻◦—

When passing through Ramnagar I had asked the Tahsildar to purchase two young male buffaloes for me and to send them to Mohan, where my men would take them over.

I told the villagers I intended tying up one of the buffaloes near the tree where three days previously the woman had been killed

378

and the other on the road to Chaknakl, and they said they could think of no better sites, but that they would talk the matter over among themselves and let me know in the morning if they had any other suggestions to make. Night was now drawing in, and, before leaving, the Headman promised to send word to all the adjoining villages in the morning to let them know of my arrival, the reason for my coming, and to impress on them the urgency of letting me know without loss of time of any kills or attacks by the tiger in their areas.

The musty smell in the room had much decreased, though it was still noticeable. However, I paid no attention to it, and after a bath and dinner put two stones against the doors – there being no other way of keeping them shut – and being bone-tired after my day's exertions went to bed and to sleep. I am a light sleeper, and two or three hours later I awoke on hearing an animal moving about in the jungle. It came right up to the back door. Getting hold of a rifle and a torch, I moved the stone aside with my foot and heard an animal moving off as I opened the door – it might from the sound it was making have been a tiger, but it might also have been a leopard or a porcupine. However, the jungle was too thick for me to see what it was. Back in the room and with the stone once more in position, I noticed I had developed a sore throat, which I attributed to having sat in the wind after the hot walk up from Mohan; but when my servant pushed the door open and brought in my early-morning

cup of tea, I found I was suffering from an attack of laryngitis, due possibly to my having slept in a long-disused hut, the roof of which was swarming with bats. My servant informed me that he and his companion had escaped infection, but that the six Garhwalis in the fuel store were all suffering from the same complaint as I was. My stock of medicine consisted of a two-ounce bottle of iodine and a few tabloids of quinine, and on rummaging in my gun-case I found a small paper packet of permanganate, which my sister had provided for me on a previous occasion. The packet was soaked through with gun oil, but the crystals were still soluble, and I put a liberal quantity of the crystals into a tin of hot water, together with some iodine. The resulting gargle was very potent, and while it blackened our teeth it did much to relieve the soreness in our throats.

After an early breakfast I sent four men down to Mohan to bring up the two buffaloes, and myself set off to prospect the ground where the woman had been killed. From the directions I had received overnight I had no difficulty in finding the spot where the tiger had attacked and killed the woman as she was tying the grass she had cut into a bundle. The grass and the rope she was using were lying just as they had been left, as were also two bundles of grass left by her companions when they had run off in fright to the village. The men had told me that the body of the woman had not been found, but from the fact that three perfectly good lengths of rope and the dead woman's sickle had been left in the jungle, I am inclined to think that no attempt had been made to find her.

The woman had been killed at the upper end of a small landslide, and the tiger had taken her down the slide and into a thick patch of undergrowth. Here the tiger had waited, possibly to give the two women time to get out of sight, and had then crossed the ridge visible from the hut, after which it had gone with its kill straight down the hill for a mile or more into dense tree and scrub jungle. The tracks were now four days old, and as there was nothing to be gained by following them farther, I turned back to the hut.

The climb back to the ridge was a very steep one, and when I reached the hut at about midday I found an array of pots and pans in various shapes and sizes on the verandah, all containing milk. In contrast to the famine of the day before there was now abundance, sufficient milk in fact for me to have bathed in. My servants informed me they had protested to no effect and that each man had said, as he deposited his vessel on the verandah, that he would take good care that I used no more condensed milk while I remained in their midst.

I did not expect the men to return from Mohan with the buffaloes before nightfall, so after lunch I set out to have a look at the road to Chaknakl.

From the hut the hill sloped gradually upwards to a height of about five hundred feet, and was roughly triangular in shape. The road, after running through cultivated land for half a mile, turned sharply to the left, went across a steep rocky hill until it regained the ridge, and then turned to the right and followed the ridge down to Chaknakl. The road was level for a short distance after coming out on the ridge, and then went steeply down, the gradient in places being eased by hairpin bends.

I had the whole afternoon before me, and examined about three miles of the road very carefully. When a tiger uses a road regularly it invariably leaves signs of its passage by making scratch marks on the side of the road. These scratch marks, made for the same purposes as similar marks made by domestic cats and all other members of the cat family, are of very great interest to sportsmen, for they provide him with the following very useful information: (1) whether the animal that has made the mark is a male or a female, (2) the direction in which he is travelling, (3) the length of time that has elapsed since it passed, (4) the direction and approximate distance of its headquarters, (5) the nature of its kills, and finally, (6) whether the animal has recently had a meal of human flesh. The value of this easily-acquired information to one who is hunting the man-eater on strange ground will be easily understood. Tigers also leave their pug marks on the roads they use and these pug marks can provide one with quite a lot of useful information, as for instance the direction and speed at which the animal was travelling, its sex and age, whether all four limbs are sound, and, if not sound, which particular limb is defective.

The road I was on had through long disuse got overgrown with short stiff grass and was therefore not, except in one or two damp places, a good medium on which to leave pug marks. One of these damp places was within a few yards of where the road came out on the ridge, and just below this spot there was a green and very stagnant pool of water; a regular drinking-place for sambur.

I found several scratch marks just round the corner where the road turned to the left after leaving the cultivated ground, the most recent of which was three days old. Two hundred yards from these scratch marks the road, for a third of its width, ran under an overhanging rock. This rock was ten feet high and at the top of it there was a flat piece of ground two or three yards wide, which was only visible from the road when approaching the rock from the village side. On the ridge I found more scratch marks, but I did not find any pug marks until I got to the first hairpin bend. Here, in cutting across the bend, the tiger had left its tracks where it had jumped down on to some soft earth. The tracks, which were a day old, were a little distorted, but even so it was possible to see that they had been made by a big, old, male tiger.

When one is moving in an area in which a man-eating tiger is operating, progress is of necessity very slow, for every obstruction in one's line of walk, be it a bush, a tree, a rock, or an inequality in the ground capable of concealing death, has to be cautiously approached, while at the same time, if a wind is not blowing – and there was no wind that evening – a careful and constant outlook has to be maintained behind and on either side. Further, there was much of interest to be looked at, for it was the month of May, when orchids at this elevation – 4,000 to 5,000 feet – are at their best, and I have never seen a greater variety or a greater wealth of bloom than the forests on that hill had to show. The beautiful white butterfly orchid was in greatest profusion, and every second tree of any size appeared to have decked itself out with them.

It was here that I first saw a bird that Prater, of the Bombay Natural History Society, later very kindly identified for me as the Mountain Crag Martin, a bird of a uniform ash colour, with a slight tinge of pink on its breast, and in size a little smaller than a Rosy Pastor. These birds had their broods with them, and while the young ones – four to a brood – sat in a row on a dry twig at the top of a high tree, the parent birds kept darting away – often to a distance of two or three hundred yards – to catch insects. The speed at which they flew was amazing, and I am quite sure there is nothing in feathers in North India, not excluding our winter visitor the great Tibetan Swallow, that these Martins could not make rings round. Another thing about these birds that was very interesting was their wonderful eyesight. On occasions they would fly in a dead straight line for several hundred yards before turning and coming back. It was not possible, at the speed they were going, that they were chasing insects on these long flights, and as after each flight the bird invariably thrust some minute object into one of the gaping mouths, I believe they were able to see insects at a range at which they would not have been visible to the human eye through the most powerful field-glasses.

Safeguarding my neck, looking out for tracks, enjoying nature generally, and listening to all the jungle sounds – a sambur a mile away down the hillside in the direction of Mohan was warning the jungle folk of the presence of a tiger, and a kakar and a langur (*Entellus* monkey) on the road to Chaknakl were warning other jungle folk of the presence of a leopard – time passed quickly, and I found myself back at the overhanging rock as the sun was setting. As I approached this rock I marked it as being quite the most dangerous spot in all the ground I had so far gone over. A tiger lying on the grass-covered bit of ground above the rock would only have to wait until anyone going either up or down the road was under or had passed it to have them at his mercy – a very dangerous spot indeed, and one that needed remembering.

When I got back to the hut I found the two buffaloes had arrived, but it was too late to do anything with them that evening.

My servants had kept a fire going most of the day in the hut, the air of which was now sweet and clean, but even so I was not going to risk sleeping in a closed room again; so I made them cut two thorn bushes and wedged them firmly into the doorways before going to bed. There was no movement in the jungle near the back door that night, and after a sound sleep I woke in the morning with my throat very much better.

I spent most of the morning talking to the village people and listening to the tales they had to tell of the man-eater and the attempts that had been made to shoot it, and after lunch I tied up one buffalo on the small ridge the tiger had crossed when carrying away the woman, and the other at the hairpin bend where I had seen the pug marks.

Next morning I found both buffaloes sleeping peacefully after having eaten most of the big feed of grass I had provided them with. I had tied bells round the necks of both animals, and the absence of any sound from these bells as I approached each buffalo gave me two disappointments for, as I have said, I found both of them asleep. That evening I changed the position of the second buffalo from the hairpin bend to where the road came out on the ridge, close to the pool of stagnant water.

The methods most generally employed in tiger shooting can briefly be described as (*a*) sitting up, and (*b*) beating, and young male buffaloes are used as bait in both cases. The procedure followed is to select the area most convenient for a sit-up, or for a beat, and to tie the bait out in the late evening, using a rope which the bait cannot, but which the tiger can, break; and when the bait is taken, either to sit up over the kill on a machan in a tree, or beat the cover into which the kill has been taken.

In the present case neither of these methods was feasible. My throat, though very much better, was still sore and it would not have been possible for me to have sat up for any length of time without coughing, and a beat over that vast area of heavily wooded and broken ground would have been hopeless even if I had been able to muster a thousand men; so I decided to stalk the tiger, and to this end carefully sited my two buffaloes and tied them to stout saplings with four one-inch-thick hemp ropes, and left them out in the jungle for the whole twenty-four hours.

I now stalked the buffaloes in turn each morning, as soon as there was sufficient light to shoot by, and again in the evening; for tigers, be they man-eaters or not, kill as readily in the day as they do at night in areas in which they are not disturbed; and during the day, while I waited for news from outlying villages, nursed my throat, and rested, my six Garhwalis fed and watered the buffaloes.

On the fourth evening when I was returning at sunset after visiting the buffalo on the ridge, as I came round a bend in the road thirty yards from the overhanging rock, I suddenly, and for the first time since my arrival at Kartkanoula, felt I was in danger, and that the danger that threatened me was on the rock in front of me. For five minutes I stood perfectly still with my eyes fixed on the upper edge of the rock, watching for movement. At that short range the flicker of an eyelid would have caught my eyes, but there was not even this small movement; and after going forward ten paces, I again stood watching for several minutes. The fact that I had seen no movement did not in any way reassure me – the man-eater was on the rock, of that I was sure; and the question was, what was I going to do about it? The hill, as I have already told you, was very steep, had great rocks jutting out of it, and was overgrown with long grass and tree and scrub jungle. Bad as the going was, had it been earlier in the day I would have gone back and worked round and above the tiger to try to get a shot at him; but with only half an hour of daylight left, and the best part of a mile still to go, it would have been madness to have left the road. So, slipping up the safety-catch and putting the rifle to my shoulder, I started to pass the rock.

The road here was about eight feet wide, and going to the extreme outer edge I started walking crab-fashion, feeling each step with my feet before putting my weight down to keep from stepping off into space. Progress was slow and difficult, but as I drew level with the overhanging rock and then began to pass it, hope rose high that the tiger would remain where he was until I reached that part of the road from which the flat bit of ground above the rock, on which he was lying, was visible. The tiger, however, having failed to catch me off my guard, was taking no chances, and I had just got clear of the rock when I heard a low muttered growl above me, and a little later first a kakar went off barking to the right, and then two hind sambur started belling near the crest of the triangular hill.

The tiger had got away with a sound skin, but, for the matter of that, so had I, so there was no occasion for regrets, and from the place on the hill where the sambur said he was, I felt sure he would hear the bell I had hung round the neck of the buffalo that was tied on the ridge near the stagnant pool.

When I reached the cultivated land I found a group of men waiting for me. They had heard the kakar and sambur and were very disappointed that I had not seen the tiger, but cheered up when I told them I had great hopes for the morrow.

During the night a dust-storm came on, followed by heavy rain, and I found to my discomfort that the roof of the hut was very porous. However, I eventually found a spot where it was leaking less than in others, dragged my camp bed to it, and continued my sleep. It was a brilliantly clear morning when I awoke; the rain had washed the heat haze and dust out of the atmosphere, and every leaf and blade of grass was glistening in the newly risen sun.

Hitherto I had visited the nearer buffalo first, but this morning I had an urge to reverse the daily procedure, and after instructing my men to wait until the sun was well up and then go to feed and water the nearer buffalo, I set off with high hopes down the Chaknakl road, having first cleaned and oiled my 450/400 rifle – a very efficient weapon, and a good and faithful friend of many years' standing.

The overhanging rock that I had passed with such trouble the previous evening did not give me a moment's uneasiness now, and after passing it I started looking for tracks, for the rain had softened the surface of the road. I saw nothing, however, until I came to the damp place on the road, which, as I have said, was on the near side of the ridge and close to the pool where the buffalo was tied. Here in the soft earth I found the pug marks of the tiger, made before the storm had come on, and going in the direction of the ridge. Close to this spot there is a rock about three feet high, on the Khud side of the road. On the previous occasions that I had stalked down the road I had found that by standing on this rock I could look over a hump in the road and see the buffalo where it was tied forty yards away. When I now climbed on to the rock and slowly raised my head, I found that the buffalo had gone. This discovery was as disconcerting as it was inexplicable. To prevent the tiger from carrying the buffalo away to some distant part of the jungle, where the only method of getting a shot would have been by sitting up on the ground or in a tree – a hopeless proceeding with my throat in the condition it was in – I had used four thicknesses of strong one-inch-thick hemp rope, and even so the tiger had got away with the kill.

I was wearing the thinnest of rubber-soled shoes, and very silently I approached the sapling to which the buffalo had been tied and examined the ground. The buffalo had been killed before the storm, but had been carried away after the rain had stopped, without any portion of it having been eaten. Three of the ropes I had twisted together had been gnawed through, and the fourth had been broken. Tigers do not usually gnaw through ropes; however, this one had done so, and had carried off the kill down the hill facing Mohan. My plans had been badly upset, but very fortunately the rain had come to my assistance. The thick carpet of dead leaves which the day before had been as dry as tinder were now wet and pliable, and, provided I made no mistakes, the pains the tiger had been to in getting away with the kill might yet prove his undoing.

When entering a jungle in which rapid shooting might at any moment become necessary, I never feel happy until I have reassured myself that my rifle is loaded. To pull a trigger in an emergency and wake up in the Happy Hunting Grounds – or elsewhere – because one had omitted to load a weapon, would be one of those acts of carelessness for which no excuse could be found; so though I knew I had loaded my rifle before I came to the overhanging rock, I now opened it and extracted the cartridges. I changed one that was discoloured and dented, and after moving the safety-catch up and down several times to make sure it was working smoothly – I have never carried a cocked weapon – I set off to follow the drag.

This word 'drag', when it is used to describe the mark left on the ground by a tiger when it is moving its kill from one place to another, is misleading, for a tiger when taking its kill any distance (I have seen a tiger carry a full-grown cow for four miles) does not drag it, it carries it; and if the kill is too heavy to be carried, it is left. The drag is distinct or faint according to the size of the animal that is being carried, and the manner in which it is being held. For instance, assuming the kill is a sambur and the tiger is holding it by the neck, the hind quarters will trail on the ground leaving a distinct drag mark. On the other hand, if the sambur is being held by the middle of the back, there may be a faint drag mark, or there may be none at all.

In the present case the tiger was carrying the buffalo by the neck, and the hind quarters trailing on the ground were leaving a drag mark it was easy to follow. For a hundred yards the tiger went diagonally across the face of the hill until he came to a steep clay bank. In attempting to cross this bank he had slipped and relinquished his hold of the kill, which had rolled down the hill for thirty or forty yards until it had fetched up against a tree. On recovering the kill the tiger picked it up by the back, and from now on only one leg occasionally touched the ground, leaving a faint drag mark, which nevertheless, owing to the hillside's being carpeted with bracken, was not very difficult to follow. In his fall the tiger had lost direction, and now appeared to be undecided where to take the kill. First he went a couple of hundred yards to the right, then a hundred yards straight down the hill through a dense patch of ringals (stunted bamboo). After forcing his way with considerable difficulty through the ringals he turned to the left and went diagonally across the hill for a few hundred yards until he came to a great rock, to the right of which he skirted. This rock was flush with the ground on the approach side, and, rising gently for twenty feet, appeared to project out over a hollow or dell of considerable extent. If there was a cave or recess under the projection, it would be a very likely place for the tiger to have taken his kill to, so leaving the drag I stepped on to the rock and moved forward very slowly, examining every yard of ground below and on either side of me, as it came into view. On reaching the end of the projection and looking over I was disappointed to find that the hill came up steeply to meet the rock, and that there was no cave or recess under it as I had expected there would be.

As the point of the rock offered a good view of the dell and of the surrounding jungle – and was comparatively safe from an attack from the man-eater – I sat down; and as I did so, I caught sight of a red and white object in a dense patch of short undergrowth, forty or fifty yards directly below me. When one is looking for a tiger in heavy jungle everything red that catches the eye is immediately taken for the tiger, and here, not only could I see the red of the tiger, but I could also see his stripes. For a long minute I watched the object intently, and then, as the face you are told to look for in a freak picture suddenly resolves itself, I saw that the object I was looking at was the kill, and not the tiger; the red was blood where he had recently been eating, and the stripes were the ribs from which he had torn away the skin. I was thankful for having held my fire for that long minute, for in a somewhat similar case a friend of mine ruined his chance of bagging a very fine tiger by putting two bullets into a kill over which he had intended sitting; fortunately he was a good shot, and the two men whom he had sent out in advance to find the kill and put up a machan over it, and who were, at the time he fired, standing near the kill screened by a bush, escaped injury.

When a tiger that has not been disturbed leaves his kill out in the open, it can be assumed that he is lying up close at hand to guard the kill from vultures and other scavengers, and the fact that I could not see the tiger did not mean that he was not lying somewhere close by in the dense undergrowth.

Tigers are troubled by flies and do not lie long in one position, so I decided to remain where I was and watch for movement; but hardly had I come to this decision, when I felt an irritation in my throat. I had not quite recovered from my attack of laryngitis and the irritation grew rapidly worse until it became imperative for me to cough. The usual methods one employs on these occasions, whether in church or the jungle, such as holding the breath and swallowing hard, gave no relief until it became a case of cough, or burst; and in desperation I tried to relieve my throat by giving the alarm-call of the langur. Sounds are difficult to translate into words and for those of you who are not acquainted with our jungles I would try to describe this alarm-call, which can be heard for half a mile, as *khok, khok, khok*, repeated again and again at short intervals, and ending up with *khokorror*. All langurs do not call at tigers, but the ones in our hills certainly do, and as this tiger had probably heard the call every day of his life it was the one sound I could make to which he would not pay the slightest attention. My rendering of the call in this emergency did not sound very convincing, but it had the desired effect of removing the irritation from my throat.

For half an hour thereafter I continued to sit on the rock, watching for movement and listening for news from the jungle folk, and when I had satisfied myself that the tiger was not anywhere within my range of vision, I got off the rock, and, moving with the utmost caution, went down to the kill.

I regret I am not able to tell you what weight of flesh a full-grown tiger can consume at a meal, but you will have some idea of his capacity when I tell you he can eat a sambur in two days, and a buffalo in three, leaving possibly a small snack for the fourth day.

The buffalo I had tied up was not full-grown but he was by no means a small animal, and the tiger had eaten approximately half of him. With a meal of that dimension inside of him I felt sure he had not gone far, and as the ground was still wet, and would remain so for another hour or two, I decided to find out in what direction he had gone, and if possible, stalk him.

There were a confusion of tracks near the kill but by going round in widening circles I found the track the tiger had made when leaving. Soft-footed animals are a little more difficult to track than hard-footed ones, yet after long years of experience tracking needs as little effort as a gun dog exerts when following a scent. As silently and as slowly as a shadow I took up the track, knowing that the tiger would be close at hand. When I had gone a hundred yards I came on a flat bit of ground, twenty feet square, and carpeted with that variety of short soft grass that has highly scented roots; on this grass the tiger had lain, the imprint of his body being clearly visible.

As I was looking at the imprint and guessing at the size of the animal that had made it, I saw some of the blades of grass that had been crushed down spring erect. This indicated that the tiger had been gone only a minute or so.

You will have some idea of the lay-out when I tell you that the tiger had brought the kill down from the north, and on leaving it had gone west, and that the rock on which I had sat, the kill, and the spot where I was now standing formed the points of a triangle, one side of which was forty yards, and the other two sides a hundred yards long.

My first thought on seeing the grass spring erect was that the tiger had seen me and moved off, but this I soon found was not likely, for neither the rock nor the kill was visible from the grass plot, and that he had not seen me and moved after I had taken up his track I was quite certain. Why then had he left his comfortable bed and gone away? The sun shining on the back of my neck provided the answer. It was now nine o'clock of an unpleasantly hot May morning, and a glance at the sun and the tree-tops over which it had come showed that it had been shining on the grass for ten minutes. The tiger had evidently found it too hot, and gone away a few minutes before my arrival to look for a shady spot.

I have told you that the grass plot was twenty feet square. On the far side to that from which I had approached there was a fallen tree, lying north and south. This tree was about four feet in diameter, and as it was lying along the edge of the grass plot in the middle of which I was standing, it was ten feet away from me. The root end of the tree was resting on the hillside, which here went up steeply and was overgrown with brushwood, and the branch end (which had been snapped off when the tree had fallen) was projecting out over the hillside. Beyond the tree the hill appeared to be more or less perpendicular, and running across the face of it was a narrow ledge of rock, which disappeared into dense jungle thirty yards farther on.

If my surmise, that the sun had been the cause of the tiger's changing his position, was correct, there was no more suitable place than the lee of the tree for him to have taken shelter in, and the only way of satisfying myself on this point was to walk up to the tree – and look over. Here a picture seen long years ago in *Punch* flashed into memory. The picture was of a lone sportsman who had gone out to hunt lions and who, on glancing up on to the rock he was passing, looking straight into the grinning face of the most enormous lion in Africa. Underneath the picture was written, 'When you go out looking for a lion, be quite sure that you want to see him.' True, there would be this small difference, that whereas my friend in Africa looked up – into the lion's face, I would look down – into the tiger's; otherwise the two cases – assuming that the tiger *was* on the far side of the tree – would be very similar.

Slipping my feet forward an inch at a time on the soft grass, I now started to approach the tree, and had covered about half the distance that separated me from it when I caught sight of a black-and-yellow object about three inches long on the rocky edge, which I now saw was a well-used game path. For a long minute I stared at this motionless object, until I was convinced that it was the tip of the tiger's tail. If the tail was pointing away from me the head must obviously be towards me, and as the ledge was only some two feet wide, the tiger could only be crouching down and waiting to spring the moment my head appeared over the bole of the tree. The tip of the tail was twenty feet from me, and allowing eight feet for the tiger's length while crouching, his head would be twelve feet away. But I should have to approach much nearer before I should be able to see enough of his body to get in a crippling shot, and a crippling shot it would have to be if I wanted to leave on my feet. And now, for the first time in my life, I regretted my habit of carrying an uncocked rifle. The safety-catch of my 450/400 makes a very distinct click when thrown off, and to make any sound now would either bring the tiger right on top of me, or send him straight down the steep hillside without any possibility of my getting a shot.

Inch by inch I again started to creep forward, until the whole of the tail, and after it the hind quarters, came into view. When I saw the hind quarters I could have shouted with delight, for they showed that the tiger was not crouching and ready to spring, but was lying down. As there was only room for his body on the two-foot-wide ledge, he had stretched his hind legs out and was resting them on the upper branches of an oak sapling growing up the face of the almost perpendicular hillside. Another foot forward and his belly came into view, and from the regular way in which it was heaving up and down I knew that he was asleep. Less slowly now I moved forward, until his shoulder, and then his whole length, was exposed to my view. The back of his head was resting on the edge of the grass plot, which extended for three or four feet beyond the fallen tree; his eyes were fast shut, and his nose was pointing to heaven.

Aligning the sights of the rifle on his forehead I pressed the trigger and, while maintaining a steady pressure on it, pushed up the safety-catch. I had no idea how this reversal of the usual method of discharging a rifle would work, but it did work; and when the heavy bullet at that short range crashed into his forehead not so much as a quiver went through his body. His tail remained stretched straight out; his hind legs continued to rest on the upper branches of the sapling; and his nose still pointed to heaven. Nor did his position change in the slightest when I sent a second, and quite unnecessary, bullet to follow the first. The only change noticeable was that his stomach had stopped heaving up and down, and that blood was trickling down his forehead from two surprisingly small holes.

I do not know how the close proximity of a tiger reacts on others, but me it always leaves with a breathless feeling – due possibly as much to fear as to excitement – and a desire for a little rest. I sat down on the fallen tree and lit the cigarette I had denied myself from the day my throat had got bad, and allowed my thoughts to wander. Any task well accomplished gives satisfaction, and the one just completed was no exception. The reason for my presence at that spot was the destruction of the man-eater, and from the time I had left the road two hours previously right up to the moment I pushed up the safety-catch, everything – including the langur call – had worked smoothly and without a single fault. In this there was great satisfaction, the kind of satisfaction I imagine an author must feel when he writes *Finis* to the plot that, stage by stage, has unfolded itself just as he desired it to. In this case, however, the finish had not been satisfactory, for I had killed the animal that was lying five feet from me, in his sleep.

My personal feelings in the matter are I know of little interest to others, but it occurs to me that possibly you also might think it was not cricket, and in that case I should like to put the arguments before you that I used on myself, in the hope that you will find them more satisfactory than I did. These arguments were (*a*) the tiger was a man-eater that was better dead than alive, (*b*) therefore it made no difference whether he was awake or asleep when killed, and *c*) that had I walked away when I saw his belly heaving up and down I should have been morally responsible for the deaths of all human beings he killed thereafter. All good and sound arguments, you will admit, for my having acted as I did; but the regret remains that through fear of the consequences to myself, or fear of losing the only chance I might ever get, or possibly a combination of the two, I did not awaken the sleeping animal and give him a sporting chance.

The tiger was dead, and if my trophy was to be saved from falling into the valley below and ruined, it was advisable to get him off the ledge with as little delay as possible. Leaning the rifle, for which I had no further use, against the fallen tree, I climbed up to the road and, once round the corner near the cultivated land, I cupped my hands and sent a cooee echoing over the hills and valleys. I had no occasion to repeat the call, for my men had heard my two shots when returning from attending to the first buffalo and had run back to the hut to collect as many villagers as were within calling distance. Now, on hearing my cooee, the whole crowd came helter-skelter down the road to meet me.

When stout ropes and an axe had been procured I took the crowd back with me, and after I had secured the ropes round the tiger, willing hands half carried and half dragged him off the ledge and over the fallen tree, on to the plot of grass. Here I would have skinned him, but the villagers of Kartkanoula and the adjoining villages would be very disappointed if they were not given an opportunity of seeing the tiger with their own eyes and satisfying themselves that the man-eater, in fear of whom they had lived for so many years, and who had established a reign of terror over the whole district, was really and truly dead.

While a couple of saplings to assist in carrying the tiger back to the hut were being felled, I saw some of the men passing their hands over the tiger's limbs, and knew they were satisfying themselves that their assertion that the tiger had not been suffering from any old, or crippling, wounds was correct. At the hut the tiger was placed in the shade of a wide-spreading tree and the villagers were informed that it was at their disposal up to two o'clock – longer I could not give them, for it was a very hot day and there was fear of the hair slipping, and the skin being ruined.

I myself had not looked closely at the tiger, but at 2 p.m., when I laid him on his back to start the skinning, I noticed that most of the hair from the inner side of his left foreleg was missing, and that there were a number of small punctures in the skin, from which yellow fluid was exuding. I did not draw attention to these punctures, and left the skinning of the leg, which was considerably thinner than the right leg, to the last. When the skin had been removed from the rest of the animal, I made a long cut from the chest to the pad of the festering leg, and as I removed the skin, drew out of the flesh, one after another, porcupine quills which the men standing around eagerly seized as souvenirs; the longest of these quills was about five inches, and their total number was between twenty-five and thirty. The flesh under the skin, from the tiger's chest to the pad of his foot, was soapy, and of a dark yellow colour; cause enough to have made the poor beast moan when he walked, and quite sufficient reason for his having become – and having remained – a man-eater, for porcupine quills do not dissolve no matter how long they are embedded in flesh.

I have extracted, possibly, a couple of hundred porcupine quills from the man-eating tigers I have shot. Many of these quills have been over nine inches in length and as thick as pencils. The majority were embedded in hard muscles, a few were wedged firmly between bones, and all were broken off short under the skin.

Unquestionably the tigers acquired the quills when killing porcupines for food, but the question arises – to which I regret I am unable to give any satisfactory answer – why animals with the intelligence, and the agility, of tigers should have been so careless as to drive quills deep into themselves, or be so slow in their movements as to permit porcupines – whose only method of defending themselves is by walking backwards – to do so; and further, why the quills should have been broken off short, for porcupine quills are not brittle.

Leopards are just as partial to porcupines as our hill tigers are, but they do not get quills stuck in them, for they kill porcupines – as I have seen – by catching them by the head; and why tigers do not employ the same safe and obvious method of killing as leopards employ, and so avoid injury to themselves, is a mystery to me.

And now I have done telling you the story of the second of the three man-eating tigers mentioned at that District Conference of long ago and, when opportunity offers, I will tell you how the third tiger, the Kanda man-eater, died.

The Silver Sword

Ian Serraillier

In war terrible things can happen to families. During the Second World War in Poland, the Balicki parents, Joseph and Margrit are taken prisoner and their three children – Ruth, Edek and Bronia – are left to fend for themselves. Seeking their parents, the children and their friend Jan eventually travel right across Europe in great danger and hardship. In this excerpt from the beginning of Ian Serraillier's fine story (which is based on fact), we see the children's mother being taken away and Ruth, Edek and Bronia trying to survive hidden in a cellar.

WHAT had happened to Joseph's family that night over a year ago when the Nazi storm troopers called at the schoolhouse? Was what Mrs Krause said true? Had they taken his wife away? Had they returned and blown up the house with the children in it?

This is what happened.

That night there was an inch of snow on the roofs of Warsaw. Ruth and Bronia were asleep in the bedroom next to their mother's. Edek's room was on the top floor, below the attic. He was asleep when the Nazi soldiers broke into the house, but he woke up when he heard a noise outside his door. He jumped out of bed and turned the handle. The door was locked. He shouted and banged on it with his fists, but it was no use. Then he lay down with his ear to the floor and listened. In his mother's room the men were rapping out orders, but he could not catch a word that was said.

In the ceiling was a small trapdoor that led into the attic. A ladder lay between his bed and the wall. Quietly he removed it, hooked it under the trap, and climbed up.

Hidden between the water tank and the felt jacket round it was his rifle. He was a member of the Boys' Rifle Brigade and had used it in the siege of Warsaw. It was loaded. He took it out and quickly climbed down to his room.

The noise in the room below had stopped. Looking out of the window into the street, he saw a Nazi van waiting outside the front door. Two storm troopers were taking his mother down the steps, and she was struggling.

Quietly Edek lifted the window sash till it was half open. He dared not shoot in case he hit his mother. He had to wait till she was in the van and the doors were being closed.

His first shot hit a soldier in the arm. Yelling, he jumped in beside the driver. With the next two shots Edek aimed at the tyres. One punctured the rear wheel, but the van got away, skidding and roaring up the street. His other shots went wide.

With the butt of his rifle he broke down the door and ran down to his sisters. They were locked in, too. He burst open the door.

Bronia was sitting up in bed and Ruth was trying to calm her. She was almost as distraught herself. Only the effort to comfort Bronia kept her from losing control.

'I hit one of the swine,' said Edek.

'That was very silly of you,' said Ruth. 'They'll come back for us now.'

'I couldn't let them take Mother away like that,' said Edek. 'Oh, be quiet, Bronia! Howling won't help.'

'We must get away from here before they come back,' said Ruth.

With some difficulty she dressed Bronia, while Edek went into the hall to fetch overcoats and boots and fur caps.

There was no time for Ruth to dress properly. She put on a coat over her nightdress and wound a woollen scarf round Bronia.

'We can't get out the front way,' said Edek. 'There's another van coming. I heard the whistle.'

'What about the back?' said Ruth.

'The wall's too high. We'd never get Bronia over. Besides, there are Nazis billeted in that street. There's only one way – over the roof.'

'We'll never manage that,' said Ruth.

'It's the only way,' said Edek. 'I'll carry Bronia. Be quick – I can hear them coming.'

He picked up the sobbing Bronia and led the way upstairs. He was wearing his father's thick overcoat over his pyjamas, a pair of stout boots on his bare feet, and his rifle slung on his back.

When they were all up in the attic, he smashed the skylight.

'Now listen, Bronia,' said Edek. 'If you make a sound, we shall never see Mother again. We shall all be killed.'

'Of course we shall see her again,' Ruth added. 'But only if you do as Edek says.'

He climbed through the skylight on to the slippery roof. Ruth handed Bronia up to him, then followed herself. The bitterly cold air made her gasp.

'I can't carry you yet, Bronia,' said Edek. 'You must walk behind me and hold on to the rifle. It doesn't matter if you slip, if you hold on to the rifle. And don't look down.'

The first few steps – as far as the V between the chimney and the roof ridge – were ghastly. Edek made a dash for it, grabbed the telephone bracket and hauled himself up, with Bronia clinging on behind. She was speechless with terror. He reached back and hauled Ruth up after him.

After a few moments' rest, they slid down a few feet on to a flat part that jutted out, a sort of parapet.

The roof ridge lay between them and the street, so they could not see what was happening down there. But they could hear shouting, the whine of cars, the screech of brakes.

Luckily for them, all the houses on this side of the school were joined together in one long terrace, otherwise they could not have got away. Even so, it was a miracle that none of their slips and tumbles ended in disaster.

They must have gone fully a hundred yards when the first explosion shook the air. A sheet of fire leapt up from their home into the frosty night sky. They fell flat in the snow and lay there. The roof shook, the whole city seemed to tremble. Another explosion. Smoke and flames poured from the windows. Sparks showered into the darkness.

'Come along,' said Edek. 'We shan't let them have us now.'

With growing confidence they hurried along the rooftops. At last, by descending a twisted fire escape, they reached street level. On and on they hurried, not knowing or caring where they went so long as they left those roaring flames behind them.

They did not stop till the fire was far away and the pale winter dawn was breaking.

They took shelter in the cellar of a bombed house. Exhausted, huddled together for warmth, they slept till long after midday, when cold and hunger woke them.

They made their new home in a cellar at the other end of the city. They had tunnelled their way into it. From the street it looked like a rabbit's burrow in a mound of rubble, with part of a wall rising behind. On the far side there was a hole in the lower part of the wall, and this let in light and air as well as rain.

When they asked the Polish Council of Protection about their mother, they were told she had been taken off to Germany to work on the land. Nobody could say which part of Germany. Though they went many times to ask, they never found out any more. 'The war will end soon,' they were told. 'Be patient, and your mother will come back.'

But the war dragged on, and their patience was to be sorely tried.

They quickly made their new home as comfortable as they could.

Edek, who could climb like a monkey, scaled three storeys of a bombed building to fetch a mattress and some curtains. The mattress he gave to Ruth and Bronia. The curtains made good sheets. On wet days they could be used over the hole in the wall to keep the rain out. With floorboards he made two beds, chairs and a table. With bricks from the rubble he built a wall to divide the cellar into two rooms, one to live in and one to sleep in. He stole blankets from a Nazi supply dump, one for each of them.

Here they lived for the rest of that winter and the following spring.

Food was not easy to find. Ruth and Bronia had green Polish ration cards and were allowed to draw the small rations that the Nazis allowed. But, except when Edek found casual work, they had no money to buy food. Edek had no ration card. He had not dared to apply for one, as that would have meant disclosing his age. Everyone over twelve had to register, and he would almost certainly have been carried off to Germany as a slave worker.

Whenever possible they ate at the soup kitchens which Polish Welfare had set up. Sometimes they begged at a nearby convent. Sometimes they stole from the Nazis or scrounged from their garbage bins. They saw nothing wrong in stealing from their enemies, but they were careful never to steal from their own people.

War had made Edek sharp and self-reliant for his years. Ruth was slower to adapt herself to the new life. At first, during that long-drawn-out winter and the biting winds of early spring, it seemed as if she were too young to take on responsibility. But she learned gradually. She saw that Edek was always cheerful – because he was always busy. She knew she must get out of the habit of leaving all the practical details to him. One thing she could do was to make Bronia less miserable. She remembered that Bronia had always loved drawing. Ever since her little fist had been able to hold a pencil, she had delighted her father with her scribbles. So Ruth encouraged her to go on drawing now. They had no pencils or paper, but they had the cellar walls and plenty of charred wood from which to make charcoal. Bronia drew what she saw. Soon the walls were covered with pictures of people queueing outside the soup kitchen and of children playing hide and seek among the ruins.

Then Ruth started a school. She invited other lost children, of Bronia's age and a little older. While Edek was out at work or finding food, she told them stories in the cellar. When she ran out of stories, the others took their turn. She made them speak out clearly, without mumbling. One day at the soup kitchen she talked about her school. Next time she went she was given slates and chalk and a pocket Bible. News of these presents spread like a heath fire, and soon she had a mob of urchins outside the cellar window begging to be allowed to join the school. But there was only room for twelve, and very reluctantly she had to turn them away.

Ruth was a born teacher. She could hold the children spellbound for as long as she liked. She varied the work as much as possible, giving the mornings to lessons and the afternoons to play. The day started with a Bible story. She read it herself, with the children round her – three to a blanket if it was cold. Next came reading and writing, followed by a break in the open air. Up they shot from their rabbits' warren into the sunlight. They ran down the street to the wooden fence which they called 'the Riviera'. Here they would sit in a long line, pressing their backs to the sun-drenched wood, soaking up the warmth till their bodies were glowing all over. On sunless days they played a brisk game before returning to the cellar for another story.

They liked the stories from the Old Testament best. Their favourite was always Daniel in the lions' den. They enjoyed it just as a story, but for Ruth it had a deeper meaning. She thought of it as the story of their own troubles. The lions were the cold and the hunger and the hardships of their life. If only they were patient and trustful like Daniel, they would be delivered from them. She remembered a picture of Daniel that her mother had once given her. He was standing in the dungeon, with his hands chained behind him and his face lifted towards a small barred window high above his head. He was smiling and did not notice the lions that prowled about his feet, powerless to touch him. At night she liked to fall asleep with this picture in her mind. She could not always see it clearly. Sometimes Daniel's face was clouded and the light from the window fell upon the lions. They were scowling and snarling, and they filled her dreams with terror.

In the early summer they left the city and went to live in the woods outside. It was cold at night out in the open. They slept huddled together in their blankets under an oak tree which Edek had chosen for the shelter of its branches. There was not much rain that summer, though they had one or two drenchings in May. After that Edek cut down some branches, lashed them together and made a lean-to. This was thick enough to keep out all but the heaviest rain.

Life was much healthier here than in the city. The sun browned their limbs. There were plenty of other families to play with, some of them Jews who had escaped from the Warsaw ghetto. They could run about freely and hold their classes under the trees, without having to keep a look-out for police patrols. Sometimes Ruth had as many as twenty-five in her school. She would have taken more, but they had no paper, very few slates, and no books at all. Occasionally they received a smuggled copy of a secret journal specially published for children by the Polish Underground press. It was called *Biedronka*, 'The Ladybird', and was full of the kind of stories and pictures and jokes that children enjoy. The grubby finger marks showed that other families had seen it before them. When Ruth's children had finished with it, there was nothing left but a few tattered strips.

Because of the kindness of the peasants, food was more plentiful. Though they were forbidden to store food or to sell it to anyone but the Nazis, they gave the children whatever they could spare. They hid it, too, in cellars, in haystacks, in holes in the ground. With the help of the older children they smuggled it to the towns and sold it to the Poles on the black market.

Edek was one of the chief smugglers. In return for his services, he was given all the food he needed for the family. One of his dodges was to go off to town with pats of butter sewn into the lining of his coat. But he could only do this on cool days or at night. On hot days the butter melted. So he preferred to work at night if he could. In time the Germans became wary and posted patrols on all the main roads into the city. After that he cut across country, using paths and rough tracks. He was well aware of the penalties if he was caught. A younger child might get away with a beating. But boys as strong as he was would be carried off to Germany, for the Nazis were getting short of labour at home.

Another of Edek's dodges was the cartload of logs which he drove into the suburbs.

412

Some of the logs were split, their centres scraped out and packed with butter and eggs, then glued together again. Once he drove his cartload into a police patrol, which was searching everything on the road. They emptied the logs on to the pavement. Edek didn't stay to see if the glue would stand up to that treatment. He dived into the crowd and made off. Police whistles were blowing and the chase had started, when some kind friend lifted him up and pitched him head first into a garbage cart. Here he lay hidden, under cinders and dust and rotting vegetables.

After that, Edek did all his smuggling at night.

There came a morning, towards the end of August, when he failed to return. Ruth questioned other families in the forest, but no one had seen him. After some days of searching, she traced him to a village ten miles away. Edek had called at a house there while the secret police were searching for hidden stores. They had found cheese sewn into the lining of his coat. After setting fire to the house, they had taken him away in the van, with the house owner as well.

Ruth returned to the forest with a heavy heart, dreading to break the news to Bronia.

Edek had been their life-line. Food, clothes, money – they depended on him for all these. In the city he had made a home out of a ruin. In the woods no tree gave better shelter than the oak he had chosen. And after dark, when the wind blew cold and the damp oozed out of the ground, none knew better than he how to keep the fire in untended till dawn, so that the glow from the embers should warm them all night as they slept.

Now Ruth and Bronia must fend for themselves. It was an ordeal before which the bravest spirit might quail.

Acknowledgements

Grateful acknowledgement is made to the following publishers, authors, and other copyright holders, for permission to reprint copyrighted material.

From *Smith* by Leon Garfield
Chapters 1 and 2 (Longman Young Books, 1967, pages 7–21). Copyright © 1967 by Leon Garfield. Reprinted by permission of Penguin Books Ltd and Pantheon Books, a division of Random House, Inc.

From *The Kon-Tiki Expedition* by Thor Heyerdahl
Copyright © 1950, 1978, 1984 by Thor Heyerdahl. Reprinted by permission of George Allen & Unwin Ltd and Rand McNally & Co.

From *The Haunting* by Margaret Mahy
Chapters 1 and 2. Reprinted by permission of J.M. Dent & Sons Ltd and Atheneum Publishers.

From *Carrie's War* by Nina Bawden
Chapter 4 and the beginning of Chapter 5. Copyright © 1973 by Nina Bawden. Reprinted by permission of Victor Gollancz Ltd and J.B. Lippincott Company, Publishers.

From *The Wool-Pack* by Cynthia Harnett
Chapter 1 (Along the Skyline) and Chapter 2 (Shepherd's Cot). Reprinted by permission of Metheun Children's Books Ltd. Published in the USA under the title *The Merchant's Mark* and reprinted there by permission of Lerner Publications Company.

From *The White Mountains* by John Christopher
Chapter 1 (Capping Day). Copyright © 1967 by John Christopher. Reprinted by permission of C.S. Youd and Macmillan Publishing Company.

From *The Eighteenth Emergency* by Betsy Byars
Copyright © 1973 by Betsy Byars. Reprinted by permission of The Bodley Head and Viking Penguin Inc.

From *Charlie and the Chocolate Factory* by Roald Dahl
Chapter 13 (The Big Day Arrives), Chapter 14 (Mr Willy Wonka), Chapter 15 (The Chocolate Room). Copyright © 1964 by Roald Dahl. Reprinted by permission of George Allen & Unwin and Alfred A. Knopf, Inc.

From *Born Free, The Story of Elsa* by Joy Adamson
Chapter 5 (Elsa and the Wild Lions) and the beginning of Chapter 6 (The First Release). Copyright © 1960 by Joy Adamson. Reprinted by permission of Collins Publishers and Random House, Inc.

From *The Owl Service* by Alan Garner
Chapter 1, 2 and 3. Copyright © 1967 by Alan Garner. Reprinted by permission of Collins Publishers and Philomel Books.

From *Mrs Frisby and the Rats of Nimh* by Robert C. O'Brien
Chapters 11, 12 and 13. Copyright © 1971 by Robert C. O'Brien. Reprinted by permission of Victor Gollancz Ltd and Atheneum Publishers.

From *Man-Eaters of Kumaon* by Jim Corbett (1944)
An extract from the episode 'The Mohan Man-Eater'. Reprinted by
permission of Oxford University Press.

From *The Silver Sword* by Ian Serraillier
Chapter 6 (The Night of the Storm Troopers) and Chapter 7 (Winter and
Summer Homes). Reprinted by permission of the author and the publishers –
Jonathan Cape Ltd.